INVENTORY CONTROL

McGraw-Hill Series in Industrial Engineering and Management Science

Consulting Editor

James L. Riggs, *Department of Industrial Engineering, Oregon State University*

Barish and Kaplan: *Economic Analysis: For Engineering and Managerial Decision Making*
Gillett: *Introduction to Operations Research: A Computer-oriented Algorithmic Approach*
Hicks: *Introduction to Industrial Engineering and Management Science*
Love: *Inventory Control*
Riggs: *Engineering Economics*
Riggs and Inoue: *Introduction to Operations Research and Management Science: A General Systems Approach*

INVENTORY CONTROL

Stephen F. Love, Ph.D.
Industrial Engineering Manager
Tektronix, Inc.

McGraw-Hill Book Company

New York St. Louis San Francisco Auckland Bogotá Düsseldorf
Johannesburg London Madrid Mexico Montreal New Delhi
Panama Paris São Paulo Singapore Sydney Tokyo Toronto

INVENTORY CONTROL

Copyright © 1979 by McGraw-Hill, Inc. All rights reserved. Printed in the United States of America. No part of this publication may be reproduced, stored in a retrieval system, or transmitted, in any form or by any means, electronic, mechanical, photocopying, recording, or otherwise, without the prior written permission of the publisher.

1234567890 DODO 7832109

This book was set in Times Roman.
The editors were Julienne V. Brown and Frances A. Neal;
the production supervisor was Donna Piligra.
The drawings were done by Santype Limited.
R. R. Donnelley & Sons Company was printer and binder.

Library of Congress Cataloging in Publication Data

Love, Stephen F.
    Inventory control.

    (McGraw-Hill series in industrial engineering and management science)
        Bibliography: p.
        Includes index.
        1. Inventory control—Mathematical models.
I. Title.
HD55.L68   658.7'87   78-18546
ISBN 0-07-038782-6

CONTENTS

Preface ix

Part 1 Orientation

1 INVENTORY CONTROL CONCEPTS 3
1-1 Functions of Inventories 4
1-2 Inventory-related Costs and Revenues 6
1-3 Controlling Inventories 7
1-4 Text Overview 9
1-5 Summary 10

Part 2 Inventory Control Models

2 ORDERING DECISION MODELING 13
2-1 Modeling Supply and Demand Behavior 14
   Supply Behavior / Demand Behavior / Inventory-Time Plots
2-2 Single-Item Ordering Policies 20
2-3 Decision Effectiveness Criteria 21
2-4 Cost Modeling 24
2-5 Decision Making Using an Ordering Decision Model 28
2-6 Decision Model Classification 34
2-7 Summary 36

3 CONTINUOUS-REVIEW ORDERING DECISION MODELS   40

3-1   Continuous Ordering Policies   40
3-2   Deterministic Models   41
       Formulation of Demands and Costs / Models Recognizing an Ordering Cost / Models Recognizing No Ordering Cost / Discounted Price Models
3-3   Stochastic Models   56
       A General Continuous-Review Stochastic Model Framework / Models Not Recognizing an Ordering Cost / Models Recognizing an Ordering Cost
3-4   Summary   65

4 PERIODIC-REVIEW ORDERING DECISION MODELS   69

4-1   Periodic Ordering Policies   70
4-2   Deterministic Models   71
       Notation and Mathematical Background / Models Recognizing Concave Costs / Models Recognizing Convex Costs
4-3   Stochastic Models   89
       A General Periodic Stochastic Model Framework / Models Not Recognizing an Ordering Cost / Models Recognizing an Ordering Cost
4-4   Model Comparison   100
4-5   Summary   106

5 COORDINATED REPLENISHMENT OF MULTIPLE ITEMS   111

5-1   Models Recognizing Cost Interaction   112
       Ordering Cost Interaction / Material Cost Interaction
5-2   Models Recognizing Resource Interaction   125
5-3   Models Recognizing Demand Interaction   134
5-4   Summary   138

6 CONTROLLING MULTIECHELON INVENTORIES   142

6-1   The Behavior of Multiechelon Inventories   145
6-2   Material Requirements Planning (MRP)   150
6-3   Applicability of MRP   161
6-4   Multiechelon Lot Sizing   165
6-5   Summary   173

Part 3 Inventory Control Data

7 DEMAND FORECASTING — 179
- 7-1 The Forecasting Problem — 179
- 7-2 Modeling Demand as a Time Series — 181
  Observation of Time Series Characteristics / Model Construction / Coefficient Estimation / Calculation of Forecast Values / Monitoring Forecast Quality
- 7-3 Analysis of Stationary Models — 190
- 7-4 Analysis of Linear Trend Models — 194
- 7-5 Analysis of Cyclic Models — 198
  Base Series Models / Fourier Series Models
- 7-6 Models Recognizing Demand Series Autocorrelation — 202
- 7-7 Extrinsic Forecasting — 208
- 7-8 Comparison of Forecasting Approaches — 210
- 7-9 Forecasting in the Inventory Control Context — 213
- 7-10 Summary — 217

8 COST ESTIMATION — 221
- 8-1 Material Costs — 222
- 8-2 Holding Costs — 229
- 8-3 Shortage Costs — 233
- 8-4 Ordering Costs — 235
- 8-5 Summary — 239

Part 4 Inventory Control Systems

9 THE INVENTORY CONTROL SYSTEM — 243
- 9-1 Inventory Control System Procedures — 244
  Planning Procedures / Execution Procedures / System Maintenance Procedures / External Reporting Procedures / Computerization of Procedures
- 9-2 Inventory Control System Data — 250
- 9-3 Inventory Control System Integrity — 256
  Data Integrity / Procedural Integrity
- 9-4 Summary — 261

Appendix A Cumulative Distribution Function of the Standard Normal Probability Density — 263
Appendix B Unit Normal-Loss Integrals — 264

Index — 265

PREFACE

This text addresses problems associated with the quantity control of inventories. Collectively, the approaches covered here apply to both single-item and many-item control. The types of stock involved may reside in wholesale/retail or manufacturing organizations; they may be controlled manually or by computer.

The emphasis is on those techniques which are most readily applicable. Exotic or computationally intractable procedures are avoided. This is evidenced by the fact that while the techniques lend themselves to computerization, they can all be exercised without it. Computer solutions are recommended not because of the heavy calculations per item, but because of the typically large number of items being controlled.

Some of the features to be noted about the text are:

1. The book is quantitative, but not abstract. Models are selected to be as simple as possible without undue violation of reality.
2. Although procedures are justified, rigorous proofs are not included. References to the source literature enable the user to obtain such information.
3. Heuristic or approximate approaches are used where they are effective.
4. In the case of probabilistic situations, the methods are largely distribution-free. Thus, although for purposes of illustration and definiteness specific probability distributions are employed, most algorithms are not restricted to any particular distribution.
5. Coordinated control models for multiple items are given more than the customary exposure. Cost savings accruing from recognizing multi-item interdependencies in the models are quantified.

The book treats its central theme of inventory control very broadly. Not only are the usual modeling techniques covered, but also the concepts needed to put the models to work: model comparison, cost and demand data development, and systems implementation.

Programs in industrial engineering, operations analysis, management science, or production generally include the subject of inventory control. This text is designed to complement either junior-senior or first-year-graduate programs, depending on program emphasis. The presumed mathematical background is commensurate with the preparation commonly being expected in engineering and graduate business schools. It includes some exposure to basic calculus and probability concepts. Although a student who happens to be familiar with common operations research models will occasionally be able to relate them to material in this text, knowledge of such models is not required.

The material is adequate for a one-semester stand-alone course and can be easily tailored to one of shorter duration. Some other possible formats include:

1. One-half of a two-term offering in production planning and inventory control.
2. A sequel to a first course in purchasing and materials management.
3. A more theoretical course in inventory modeling, with the inclusion of supplementary advanced material, some of which is contained in the end-of-chapter references

A recommended chapter progression is as follows:

Chapter	Immediate Predecessors
1	—
2	1
3	2
4	2
5	3, 4
6	4
7	1
8	1
9	5, 6, 7, 8

The author gratefully acknowledges Arthur Veinott of Stanford University who planted the seed; the many students who provided enrichment; and his wife Marla who, in her own way, pushed the plow through soil thick and thin.

Stephen F. Love

INVENTORY CONTROL

PART ONE

ORIENTATION

CHAPTER
ONE

INVENTORY CONTROL CONCEPTS

This chapter introduces a study of the control of inventories. In an effort to define just what kinds of inventories are involved in this study, the following is offered:

> *Inventory* (n): A quantity of goods or materials in the control of an enterprise and held for a time in a relatively idle or unproductive state, awaiting its intended use or sale.

This definition suggests that the existence of an inventory reflects a temporary lull between two activities which will be termed the *supply and demand processes*. Customarily the supply process precedes and contributes goods to the inventory, while the demand process succeeds and depletes the same inventory. Returned goods constitute a natural exception to this. "Process" is used in the singular here although frequently a composite of supply and demand mechanisms is at work.

At the outset it should be made clear that pipeline inventories are excluded from the above definition. These inventories include oil in a pipeline, goods being transported, and goods being aged. They are excluded in the sense that they are unavailable to satisfy demand while they are in the pipeline. They become inventory when they are truly idle, which pipeline inventories are not.

The inventory exists because the supply and demand processes differ in the rates at which they respectively provide or require stock. Let $x(t)$ and $d(t)$ represent the supply and demand rates at time t affecting a given inventory, and let the resulting inventory level at time t be denoted by $y(t)$. Then one

Table 1-1 A classification of inventories

Class	Inventory $y(t)$	Supply process $x(t)$	Demand process $d(t)$	Percent by dollar value
I	Raw materials	Supplier	Production	25
II	Work in process	Production	Production	25
III	Finished goods	Production	Wholesaler	19
IV	Wholesale	Manufacturer	Retailer	12
V	Retail	Wholesaler	Consumer	19

way of expressing the relationship between these quantities is

$$y(t) = y(0) + \int_0^t [x(\tau) - d(\tau)] \, d\tau \qquad (1\text{-}1)$$

Five classes of inventories are distinguished in table 1-1 according to their supply and demand processes. This classification will provide a framework for discussion of inventory costs and control concepts. Each class is controlled differently, according to different objectives. The approximate distribution by dollar value of aggregate (national) inventories by class is included in table 1-1 as a matter of interest.

1-1 FUNCTIONS OF INVENTORIES

Since inventories exist because of differences in supply and demand process rates, any meaningful purpose for their existence will be rooted in either the desirability or the necessity that these two rates differ. Within this general framework, perhaps five functions of inventory can be identified.

Market exploitation Often the vagaries of the market create an economic advantage for maintaining an inventory. Price fluctuations of supply may dictate premature acquisition. Anticipation of a future increase in selling price suggests a delay in disposing of stock on hand. Conversely, declining market prices are a motivation for creating a negative inventory (such as "selling short" in the securities market). Such market advantages are certainly not confined to material prices. A pending increase in labor costs may make it advantageous to stock finished goods. Market exploitation is often associated with speculation, but many market conditions are sufficiently determinable to render this connotation unfounded.

Protection against stockouts To the extent that the supply or demand process fluctuates unpredictably, there is the risk of running out of stock and suffering the associated customer strife, disruption of operations, expediting costs, etc. Insurance against such stockouts is provided by so-called *buffer stocks*. The need for such stocks increases as the time between the occurrence of the random fluctuation and the compensation for it (by obtaining the necessary replacement stock) increases and also, of course, as the fluctuations increase.

Operations smoothing Demand processes are typically subject to foreseeable (but not entirely controllable) rate change. This fluctuation is usually synchronous with the season of the year or with the phenomenon of the business cycle. Although such fluctuation can be accommodated in other ways, such as changing production rates, there is usually the alternative of producing and storing in anticipation of peak demands. Just as with buffer stocks, smoothing stocks may also accommodate known fluctuations in supply (as with food processing).

Lot-size economy Even if it were possible to maintain supply and demand processes which were equal and time-invariant, usually it would not be desirable to do so. This is because supply of goods at a constant rate implies a large number of deliveries with a small number of items per delivery. This would disregard the economies associated with a smaller number of deliveries and a larger number of items per delivery. If the supply process involves shipment and receipt of goods from an outside supplier, the economy basically arises from lower shipping and delivery costs. In some cases, this may consist of a supplier's offer of a quantity discount on large orders. If the supply process is internal production, the economy accrues from fewer machine setups. In either case, there will likely be less materials handling effort and paperwork if there are fewer replenishments of stock.

Control system economy An often-overlooked purpose for carrying larger inventories is that less control effort is required. For example, it may be cheaper to carry larger stocks and review stock levels less frequently. The person who keeps an extra $1000 in a bank account does not have to exercise as much control over the balance, since he or she knows that the chance of overdrawing the account is more remote. Inventory control systems are costly to design, implement, and maintain. A lower-cost, "looser" mode of control, with attendant larger stocks, may be justified.

An often-cited sixth "function" of inventories is that of supporting a process which requires the presence of the inventory. "Pipeline" stocks, or goods in transit, are examples. As pointed out earlier, these are not considered a controllable inventory in this book, inasmuch as this stock is functional, not idle. Moreover, the decision making needed regarding the levels of such stocks involves production as well as inventory decisions.

A thorough and provocative discussion of the functions of stocks in business enterprises is contained in [1].

1-2 INVENTORY-RELATED COSTS AND REVENUES

The functions of inventory introduced above can be unified into a single, overall function. The purpose of maintaining inventories is to avoid the costs associated with not doing so. However, inventory maintenance is itself a costly activity. Therefore the justification for holding stocks must be that the costs avoided exceed the holding costs. The first item examined below is the holding costs, after which the types of costs avoided by holding inventories are categorized and discussed.

Holding costs The costs of carrying inventory begin with the investment. Money tied up in the acquisition of stock is prevented from earning a return elsewhere. This results in an opportunity cost, which is normally expressed as a percentage of the investment. There is considerable lack of agreement regarding the appropriate value of this percentage, but capital costs turn out to be one of the most significant holding costs. (Chapter 8 addresses the problems of estimating costs.) The inventory investment must be physically accommodated. To the extent that storage costs are dependent on the quantity of goods to be stored, such costs should be recognized. Higher inventory levels may create additional warehouse ownership or rental costs. Materials handling efforts are likely to increase, either because more shuffling is necessary or because goods must be stored at a greater distance from their points of use. Higher stock levels usually increase either the risks of deterioration (unless the stock is cheese or wine), obsolesence, and pilferage or the costs of reducing these risks. Property taxes are frequently levied on inventories on hand on a given date or on the average over a time period.

Shortage costs When a stockout occurs, demands cannot be satisfied out of inventory. This has a number of consequences. First, the demand (sales) may be lost. The cost of this eventuality includes the lost revenue contribution of the sales, as well as a likely loss of future sales revenue from customers whose allegiance disappears. Second, the unsatisfied demand may be backlogged, with resulting costs of excess paperwork required to process the backorder and possibly a penalty for late delivery. If the demand process is in-house production, the cost of the interruption or shutdown of this activity is likely to be severe. The third possibility is that the demand can be satisfied from an alternate source. This involves the extra cost of rush-order purchasing or purchasing from a higher-cost supplier; or, if the supply process is in-house production, it involves the cost of expediting and use of overtime or extra shifts. No matter which of the three outcomes occurs, a certain amount of ill will (with an intangible cost) is generated. Shortage (or "penalty") costs are frequently the most significant inventory-related costs. To compound the problem, they are also the most difficult to measure (see chapter 8).

Ordering costs "Ordering costs" are those costs which increase when a given total amount desired over a period of time is procured with many small orders rather than fewer, larger ones. For purchase orders, these costs may take the form of higher total freight charges or the failure to qualify for quantity discounts. For shop (production) orders, the costs are of additional machine setups and possibly some material startup costs for rejects early in the run. Whether purchased or produced, additional orders create additional paperwork, inspection, and materials handling costs.

Material costs For the most part, materials costs are not affected by the decision to maintain inventories. The exceptions are quantity discounts (which are accounted for in the ordering cost category) and price fluctuations. Most inventory control procedures do not recognize price fluctuations, and they are treated only casually in this book (see chapter 3).

Systems costs The term "systems costs" refers to costs which depend on the quantity and quality of effort expended in controlling inventories. "Quantity" refers to frequency of execution of control procedures and directly affects costs of inventory review (physical counts), forecasting, updating of records, and other clerical costs. "Quality" refers loosely to the level of sophistication of control procedures. High-powered techniques for forecasting, determining reorder points, and the like may reduce the level of inventory investment required to meet demands reliably. It would be naive to suppose that the design and maintenance of such systems cost nothing.

1-3 CONTROLLING INVENTORIES

In this book inventory control is interpreted as effort to achieve and maintain an economic balance between the costs incurred and the costs saved by holding material in stock. This is not always the connotation given to the phrase "inventory control." To a warehouse manager, controlling inventory means controlling its physical storage location; age; security from theft, fire, moisture, and the like; and maintaining information which provides traceability and accurate quantity records. To a quality assurance manager, controlling inventory is related to preserving its fitness for use, which involves similar security measures and record-keeping requirements. To an accountant or auditor, inventory is controlled through the use of cost and quantity information which enhances proper asset valuation, determination of net income, and other financial indicators. Sometimes the predominant concern is control of accessibility to the inventory, especially if the item is unsafe in the wrong hands (e.g., pharmaceuticals, explosives, or corrosives).

Thus control of inventory can be viewed as control of one or more of its *attributes*. In this book, the attribute of most importance is *availability for use*. Of course, physical control must be exerted over the inventory, but this book stresses control over the inventory *level*, or quantity on hand and/or on order. Even in this context, the term "inventory control" is somewhat of a misnomer. It is not actually the inventory (level) which is controlled, but the supply and demand processes. The level $y(t)$ is a resultant of the supply and demand processes $x(t)$ and $d(t)$. For a particular type of inventory, control effort may rest with the supply process, the demand process, or both. For example, for a retailer, $x(t)$ is fairly completely controllable while $d(t)$ is only partially so, via marketing efforts. On the other hand, an inventory of unprocessed agricultural products at a cannery is controlled by the demand process (canning or freezing, say), the supply being predetermined by contact with the grower/farmer. However, in general, the usual control mechanism involves regulation of the supply process. Accordingly, the predominant concern in this book will be the effectiveness of decisions regarding *when* and *how much* to order or produce *to supply* an inventory.

The effectiveness of supply decisions is measured differently by different people, depending on their role in the organization. Purchasing personnel seek to provide stocks adequate to ensure satisfactory service levels in the face of supply, demand, and quality uncertainties. At the same time, they are concerned about economies associated with order quantities (e.g., discounts) and vendor price/quality considerations. Production people place the highest priority on having the right part at the right time so that capacity-sensitive production schedules are met and in-process inventories are held down. Moreover, they feel that finished goods inventory supply rates should be governed to some extent by production batch sizes which avoid excessive machine changeover or setup costs. Marketing people desire instant availability, or at least a short quoted finished goods delivery lag time. They are natural adherents to the "complete library" syndrome, which expresses the sentiment that when a patron visits the library, she or he should be able to obtain every publication desired.

This diversity of effectiveness goals demands resolution or compromise. A common denominator is needed to unify thought and promote communication among people with varying organizational responsibilities. This book uses costs as the common denominator.

Accordingly, in this book the emphasis is on designing cost-sensitive, cost-effective, and cost-minimizing inventory supply systems.

1-4 TEXT OVERVIEW

A perusal of the Contents reveals that the body of this text is divided into four parts. The first part, chapter 1, presents the orientation needed for this text. The second part, consisting of five chapters and the bulk of the book, is concerned with the development of inventory control models, assuming that adequate data are available. The third part consists of two chapters which address the problems of obtaining the data needed to drive the models developed in part two. The final chapter constitutes part four, which treats the integration of data and procedures into a control system.

Chapter 2 introduces the modeling section with an exposition of the modeling process. An inventory control model is seen to be a composite of three submodels—one for supply and demand, one for the ordering policy used, and one for the costs or other criteria of effectiveness. This modeling process is illustrated with a classic inventory control model. The model's usefulness as an aid to decision making is illustrated. The chapter concludes with a classification of models, which provides a structure for the ensuing chapters.

Chapters 3 and 4 represent parallel developments of single-item control models. Chapter 3 considers the continuous-review situation in which orders may be placed at any time, while chapter 4 treats models in which orders may be placed only periodically. This distinction is a fundamental one in that the choice between controlling an inventory (or an item) continuously or periodically is usually one of the first decisions made. Within each chapter, models are segregated primarily into deterministic and stochastic models and secondarily on the basis of cost assumptions.

Chapters 5 and 6 treat multiple-item models, i.e., models which recognize interactions among the items being controlled. Chapter 5 considers multiple items at a single stocking point. Three types of interaction are recognized among such items: cost interactions, demand interactions, and interactions resulting from the fact that the items share common resources such as capital and storage space. In chapter 6, the interactions modeled are supply-demand relationships among the items under common control. These are termed "multiechelon models": Items at one echelon supply the inventory at the next echelon, as in product assembly or distribution.

Chapters 7 and 8 treat the two predominant types of data needed to use the models developed earlier—demand data and cost data. In chapter 7, a host of demand forecasting approaches are exposed and compared. Chapter 8 treats the problems associated with the estimation of inventory-related costs.

Chapter 9 considers issues related to the design of a functional inventory control system. These issues involve the synthesis of inventory control procedures and the required data in a computer environment. The problems of system integrity are considered a major concern and receive attention accordingly.

1-5 SUMMARY

Inventories are held for a variety of reasons. The cost of holding inventories is justified by the benefits obtained, which may include cheaper purchase prices, avoidance of stockouts, smoothing of operations, and lower control costs. Thus holding costs are incurred to achieve reduction in costs of material, ordering, and control systems.

This text stresses controlling inventories in such a way that the total of all these costs is held to a minimum. The inventories are usually controlled by regulating the supply process. Accordingly, the emphasis in this book is on determining cost-effective answers to these questions: When should an order be placed? How much should be ordered?

These questions are answered through the use of inventory cost models, which are developed in chapters 2 through 6. Ways of obtaining the data needed to use these models and of integrating the resulting models into a usable system are discussed in chapters 7 through 9 of the book.

REFERENCES

1. Barrett, D. A.: "Automatic Inventory Control Techniques," Business Books, London, 1969, 156 pp.
2. Mack, Ruth P.: "Information, Expectations, and Inventory Fluctuations," National Bureau of Economic Research, Columbia University Press, New York, 1967. See chapter 2.

PART TWO

INVENTORY CONTROL MODELS

CHAPTER
TWO
ORDERING DECISION MODELING

A model is an imitation of reality. A model is valuable to the extent that its use enables effective decisions to be made and made efficiently. To attain this value, a model must capture the essence of reality sufficiently well without undue effort and expense. One measure of this value is the sum of costs associated with the use of the model. These costs fall naturally into two categories. The *controllable* costs are those costs which are incurred in developing, using, and maintaining the model. These costs are related to analysts' time, data gathering, data processing, and the like. The *resultant* costs are those which occur as a consequence of using the model, and they include inventory-related costs such as holding, shortage, and ordering costs. The general relationship between these costs is shown in figure 2-1. The cost curves appearing there are designed to depict general relationships only. Such curves would be difficult to construct accurately in any particular situation, since the component costs are generally not readily measured. This is a major reason why an ideal level of model reality is difficult to achieve. In the ensuing chapters, some effort is made to compare alternative models in terms of their associated resultant costs (or at least to show how such a comparison might be made in a particular application). This will provide a partial answer to the question, How refined should a model be? The controllable costs mentioned above are not going to be explicitly measured. However, from figure 2-1, the answer to this question evidently is "as simple as possible—so long as the resultant costs do not get out of hand." That is the theme of the modeling approaches in this book.

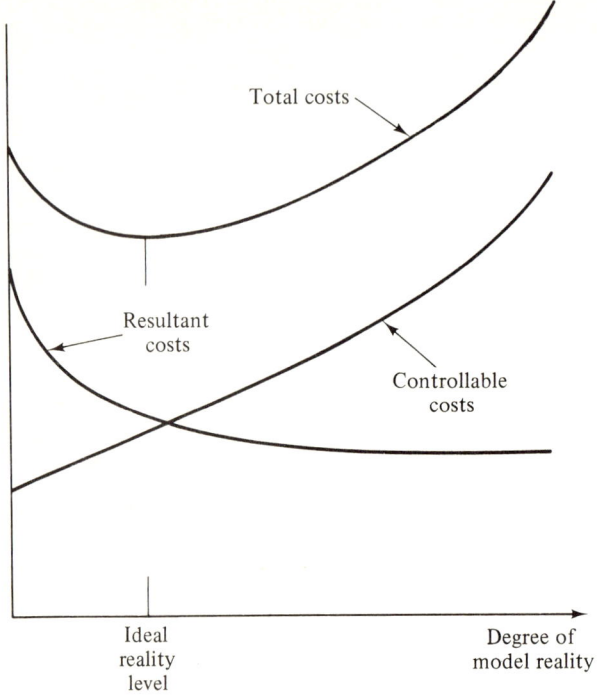

Figure 2-1 General cost relationships to model reality.

2-1 MODELING SUPPLY AND DEMAND BEHAVIOR

The most fundamental task required to develop an adequate inventory control model is to describe the physical consequences of making a control decision. Since in this book the primary control over inventory is taken to involve a supply activity, the terms "control" and "supply" are closely related. The distinction is that supply occurs as a *result* of a control decision. In this book, a more proper synonym for "control decision" is "ordering decision." Ordering decisions are considered next.

Supply Behavior

Modeling of supply behavior involves relating an actual supply to an ordering decision. The two quantities may differ in quantity or timing or both. Most inventory models in use today assume that the quantity supplied will be equal to that ordered. The reader should pause to think of situations in which this might not be so. A common one occurs when quality problems prevent some supplied items from being used to satisfy demand.

The timing of supply will generally lag behind the placement of an order for two reasons. An order for purchase is supplied only after the necessary paperwork, materials handling, and transportation activities are completed. These delays are lumped together to form a delivery lag or *lead time L*. In the model, L may be treated either as constant or as a random variable. Sometimes the lead time is ignored altogether in the model. In this case, if in fact there is an appreciable lead time, the timing of an ordering decision may be thought of as a decision regarding when an ordered supply should *arrive*, rather than when the order should be placed. Although this is an expedient convention, it is not entirely satisfactory, especially if there is a high random variation in demand. This problem is discussed further below.

The other reason why supply is not coincident in time with an ordering decision is that the supply *rate* may be finite. This is the case when the order is a shop (production) order rather than a purchase order. For simplicity, most models treat the supply rate as a constant in this case. Also, lead times (between shop order placement and the start of production) are usually ignored in this case, although they could be included in the model.

Demand Behavior

While supply quantities are usually realistically modeled as known (i.e., predictable, based on their respective order quantities), future demand quantities frequently cannot be. If demands are predictable, it should be reasonable to treat them as known. For example, raw materials which support in-house manufacturing activities have future demands which are known to the extent that production schedules are known. (Even here, careful account must be taken of unforeseen variations resulting from such events as quality problems, scrap allowances, and engineering changes.) It is the degree of predictability which governs the modeling decision to treat future demands as known or unknown. Degree of predictability is not intended to be a precisely defined quantity. In cases where demand forecasts are used and monitored, a high degree of predictability corresponds to a low forecast error, and vice versa. The subject of forecasts and forecast errors is treated in chapter 7. The important distinction to be made here is that unpredictability is not to be confused as being synonymous with variability. Demands can be highly variable but nonetheless predictable (e.g., monthly demand for license plate renewal stickers). It is the *random* variation in demands which causes future demands to be unpredictable.

Thus demands for future time periods are considered to be either known quantities or random variables. Since demand is usually the only quantity (other than possibly lead times) treated as a random variable in an ordering decision model, such models will be called *deterministic* if demands are treated as known. If demand is modeled as a random variable, the model is called *probabilistic* or *stochastic*.

When a deterministic model is used, demand is further described as being constant or variable. If variable, demand can be thought of as either continuously variable (i.e., having a demand rate which can change at any point in time) or periodically variable. In the latter case, time is broken into segments, called "periods," of equal length, and demand quantities are specified for each period. If demand is considered constant, the distinction between demand rate and demand per period reduces to a difference between the time units involved. Obviously there is no real difference between a constant demand rate of 10 units per week and a constant demand of 20 units per two-week period.

In the case of stochastic models, the periodic approach to expressing demand is preferred here to the continuous (demand rate) approach. This is because it is conceptually much more straightforward to treat demand per fixed time interval (period) as a random variable, rather than the demand rate. A random, continuously varying demand rate would render calculations of inventory levels prohibitively complex. Thus in the stochastic models considered in this text, demand per period is assigned a probability distribution. When this is done, a commonly known probability distribution, such as normal or uniform, is usually assumed. This is done because of the availability of tabulated values for such distributions. In practice, any probability distribution can be used.

A prevalent problem exists whenever a stochastic model is used. It involves the assumptions to be made regarding multiperiod demands. The problem is that multiperiod demands should be modeled consistently with single-period demands and at the same time consistently with reality. An example will illustrate the difficulty associated with this dual requirement. Suppose that demand D_1 for an item for the next period has been modeled stochastically, as in table 2-1(a). Then how does one model demand $(D_1 + D_2)$ for the next two periods? One way is the approach used most commonly in stochastic models. This method assumes that the demands in two adjacent periods are independent, identically distributed random variables. If this is the case, then demand in the second period (D_2) obeys the same probability distribution as D_1. Therefore, the two-period demand is obtained by using the relationship

$$P[D_1 + D_2 = d'] = \sum \{P[D_1 = d]P[D_2 = d' - d]\} \qquad (2\text{-}1)$$

where $P[E]$ is the probability that the event E occurs and the summation ($\sum$) is over all possible values of d. Thus, for example,

$$P[D_1 + D_2 = 7] = P[D_1 = 3]P[D_2 = 4] + P[D_1 = 4]P[D_2 = 3]$$
$$= (0.5)(0.2) + (0.2)(0.5)$$
$$= 0.2$$

The complete probability distribution for the two-period demand, $D_1 + D_2$,

Table 2-1 Modeling of two-period stochastic demand

(a) Single-period demand D_1

Quantity d	2	3	4		
Prob $[D_1 = d]$	0.30	0.50	0.20		

(b) Two-period demand $D_1 + D_2$, assuming D_1 and D_2 are independent

Quantity d'	4	5	6	7	8
Prob $[D_1 + D_2 = d']$	0.09	0.30	0.37	0.20	0.04

(c) Two-period demand $D_1 + D_2$, assuming D_1 and D_2 are positively correlated

Quantity d'	4	5	6	7	8
Prob $[D_1 + D_2 = d']$	0.28	0.03	0.48	0.03	0.18

(d) Two-period demand $D_1 + D_2$, assuming D_1 and D_2 are negatively correlated

Quantity d'	4	5	6	7	8
Prob $[D_1 + D_2 = d']$	0.03	0.09	0.72	0.11	0.05

assuming independence of demands in adjacent periods, is shown in table 2-1(b). The reader should become confident that he or she can obtain the probabilities in table 2-1(b) by using equation (2-1). Note that the five probabilities sum to 1, as they must in any valid probability distribution.

The tacit assumption of independence of adjacent-period demands should not go unchallenged. Often, demand in a given period will have an effect on demand in adjacent periods. In this case, we would say that the two demands D_1 and D_2 are *correlated*. If a high (low) value of D_1 tends to cause a high (low) value of D_2, then D_1 and D_2 are said to be *positively* correlated. For example, the higher the demand for newspapers on a given street corner on Tuesday, the higher the demands are likely to be on Wednesday. Thus, if table 2-1(a) represents such demand, the two-period demand might appear as in table 2-1(c). The high probabilities of obtaining a two-period demand $D_1 + D_2$ of 4, 6, or 8 reflect the tendency for the corresponding one-period demand D_1 of 2, 3, or 4 to repeat itself. These probabilities were not derived, but were contrived for illustrative purposes only.

If, on the other hand, a high (low) value of D_1 tends to cause a low (high) value of D_2, then D_1 and D_2 are said to be *negatively* correlated. An example of this would be weekly demand for haircuts at a barber shop. If a higher than average number of haircuts are demanded in one week, this will tend to be followed by a week of lower than average demands, since some of the barber's regular customers have merely chosen to come in during the first week, rather than during the second. Table 2-1(*d*) represents what the distribution of two-period demand might look like if D_1 and D_2 are negatively correlated. The extremely high probability that $D_1 + D_2 = 6$ reflects the fact that the two-week demand is likely to be fairly near twice the average weekly demand, any deviation from the average in period one being offset by a deviation in the opposite direction in period two. Again, these probabilities were not calculated from table 2-1(*a*).

The choice of a multiperiod demand model has a marked effect on the behavior of the inventory system. For example, suppose it is desired to have enough inventory on hand to keep the probability of running out of stock during the next two periods below 0.05. If the "$D_1 + D_2$ independent" model is chosen to reflect reality, the appropriate on-hand stock level is 7 units. If D_1 and D_2 are in fact strongly positively correlated, so that table 2-1(*c*) applies, these 7 units will fail to satisfy two-period demands 18 percent of the time. The modeler must consider this sort of phenomenon in deciding whether to go along with the common assumption that demands in adjacent periods are independent.

Another important consideration is the way in which a shortage affects demand. Demands which cannot be satisfied when they occur are usually either backlogged or lost or a combination of both. (Occasionally, unsatisfied demand may generate more demand than would have normally occurred! For example, demand for needed maintenance materials, if not provided, may cause additional events to occur which require more maintenance. A stitch in time saves nine, if the thread is available.) Backlogged demand is assumed to be satisfied as soon as supply is available. Unsatisfied demands may also affect subsequent demands, as when dissatisfied customers take their business elsewhere or persuade their acquaintances to do likewise.

Inventory-Time Plots

At a number of places in this book it will be convenient to depict supply and demand behavior graphically. This will be accomplished by plotting inventory levels over time. To simplify these plots as much as possible, a number of conventions are consistently employed. The reader may refer to figure 2-2 and to the discussion below to become familiar with these conventions:

1. Depletion of inventory is usually shown as if it occurs continually. Thus

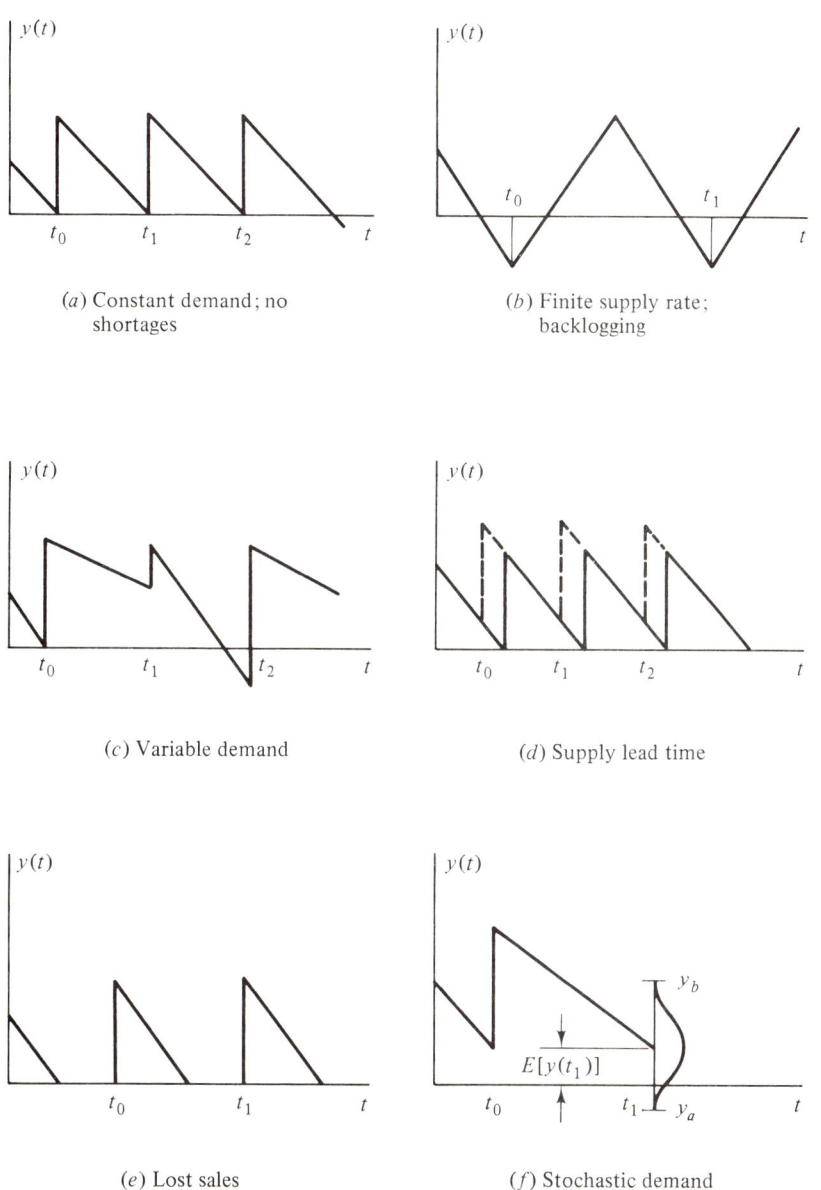

Figure 2-2 Plots of inventory levels $y(t)$ as a function of time. The times t_0, t_1, and t_2 are order release times.

lump withdrawals are smoothed (i.e., converted to a withdrawal rate) and individual units of stock are considered infinitely divisible.
2. Inventory on hand is represented by a solid line; inventory on order is shown as a dashed line. The quantity on order is the vertical distance between the solid line and the dashed line, as in figure 2-2(d).
3. Stochastic demand is shown as if it occurs at its average (expected) rate. Random deviations from the average rate appear in the form of a probability distribution along the vertical (inventory level) axis, if at all.

Thus in figure 2-2(f) the order placed at time t_0 will result in an expected inventory level at time t_1 of $E[y(t_1)]$. Moreover, there is a high probability that the actual inventory level $y(t_1)$ will fall between y_a and y_b. The probability distribution shown reflects the distribution of demand during the time interval $t_1 - t_0$.

2-2 SINGLE-ITEM ORDERING POLICIES

In this section, several ordering decision rules or policies are introduced. An ordering policy is not to be confused with an ordering decision. An *ordering decision* is made by applying an ordering policy to an actual situation at some point in time. For example, an ordering policy may specify that, say, 20 units of stock are to be ordered when the inventory level falls to 5 units. Then, if at some point in time the inventory level is observed to be 10 units, the appropriate decision is not to order. Once such a policy is established, it can remain invariant over time, while the actual ordering decisions change as the inventory level changes. This is not to say that the policy cannot be changed, but it does imply that policy changes are higher-level (planning) decisions and are changed less frequently than ordering decisions.

One way that an ordering policy may be modified is by changing one of its parameters. For example, the above policy might be revised to say that 25 (rather than 20) units of stock will be ordered when the inventory level falls to 5 units. This change does not alter the *form* of the policy. Both these policies have the same form: Order Q units when the inventory level falls to s units. This policy has two parameters: Q and s. Only the parameter Q differs between the two policies.

Generally when an ordering decision model is formulated, the form of the ordering policy is specified, but the parameter values are not. After the formulation is complete, the model is "solved" to determine the values of the parameters.

Solving models cannot be meaningfully discussed until the formulation process is complete. Model solutions are introduced below in section 2-6. At this point, it is sufficient to reemphasize that formulation of a model includes the specification of the form of ordering policy to be considered.

An ordering policy can be classified as continuous or periodic. The distinction involves the frequency with which the inventory level must be observed (reviewed) in order to implement the policy. A continuous-review policy requires knowledge of the inventory level at all times. The policy involving Q and s in the example above is in the continuous-review class. A periodic-review policy is one in which the inventory level is observed only at equally spaced points in time. The time interval between two such points is called a "period." An example of a periodic policy is: "Every week, place an order which brings the stock level up to 30 units."

The choice between a periodic-review and a continuous-review ordering policy is one of the most fundamental decisions to be made in designing an inventory control system. For this reason, single-item ordering decision models have been segregated in this book into those employing continuous-review policies (chapter 3) and those assuming periodic review (chapter 4). The use of a periodic-review (rather than a continuous-review) policy will result in higher holding and shortage costs, lower ordering costs, and lower control (data processing) costs. Specific forms of single-item policies in each class are discussed in sections 3-1 and 4-1.

Sometimes ordering policies must be consistent with certain external requirements. For example, limits may be desired on the quantity of an order placed or on the level of inventory held in stock. These limits may be constant or may vary with time. In any case, such limits may be incorporated into the model as constraints. The most common constraint types are lower bounds of zero on either quantities ordered or inventory levels. The first lower bound would preclude return of stock to the owner of the inventory, while the second would prohibit planned shortages.

2-3 DECISION EFFECTIVENESS CRITERIA

Management has a healthy habit of measuring (or attempting to measure) the effectiveness of the activities being managed. Inventory control activities are no exception. Inventory control procedures and decisions can be compared, monitored over time, and hopefully improved through the use of such measures. Thus it is only natural to associate with a given control procedure certain criteria such as cost, profit, or level of customer service. The particular criteria used should, of course, reflect management's concerns. This book assumes that in evaluating inventory control effectiveness, a predominant concern of management is costs. This certainly is not meant to imply that costs are the only concern, but that they are an important one, worthy of attention.

If costs are to be deemed the primary yardstick of effectiveness, they must be measurable and be built into the model. Cost estimation is discussed in some detail in chapter 8; cost modeling is treated in the next section. This section is devoted to an examination of the relationships between costs and other effectiveness criteria.

Costs are considered either directly or via a cost *surrogate*. The use of surrogates is prevalent when for some reason it is felt to be more practical to measure the surrogate than the costs themselves. For example, in the field of quality control, sampling procedures may be designed to achieve specified producer and consumer risks. These risks are stated as probabilities and are surrogates for costs. In inventory control, examples of cost surrogates are percentage of orders not filled on time; number of square feet of work-in-process inventory space required; and number of minutes of CPU time required per week to process inventory control programs. Perhaps in a limited analysis, meaningful comparisons can be made using cost surrogates. However, in the interest of consolidating many effectiveness criteria into one, the use of cost surrogates is minimized in this book. Direct estimation of costs prior to model solution is encouraged.

A commonly used effectiveness criterion is the so-called *customer service level*, which is defined here as the percentage of demand filled directly, without delay, from stock. One reason for the popularity of this criterion is that it can be measured. In reality, the service level is a surrogate for shortage cost, which is relatively difficult to measure precisely. The following example is designed to show that the difficulty of measuring shortage costs does not imply that management must resort to the use of a cost surrogate.

Example 2-1 Suppose demand is known to occur at the constant rate of 400 units per week. An order is placed at the beginning of each week for 400 units. There is no delivery lead time. Management has specified a 75 percent service level. Thus only 300 units of demand per week are satisfied on time. The inventory-time plot of this situation appears in figure 2-3. Management's policy may be stated more formally as follows. When the stock level falls to s, order the Q which brings the inventory level up to S. The values of s, Q, and S are -100, 400, and 300, respectively, for this example.

For the purpose of illustration, suppose that it costs h dollars per week per unit of stock held and p dollars per week per unit of demand not satisfied. Then the total cost per week TC is (refer to figure 2-3) $h \cdot$ (area of triangle VWX) $+ p \cdot$ (area of triangle XYZ). That is, for any values of S and s,

$$TC = h \left(\frac{1}{2}\right)\left(\frac{S}{S-s}\right)(S) + p\left(\frac{1}{2}\right)\left(\frac{-s}{S-s}\right)(-s) \qquad (2\text{-}2)$$

The demand of 400 units per week implies that $S - s = 400$; so the cost

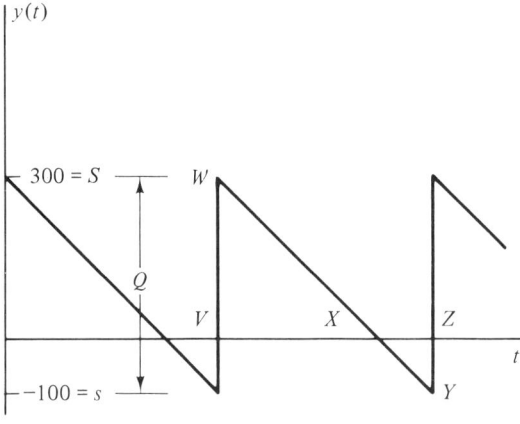

Figure 2-3 An inventory time plot for the situation described in example 2-1.

in equation (2-2) can be rewritten as

$$TC = \frac{hS^2 + p(S - 400)^2}{2(400)} \quad (2\text{-}3)$$

Now if the values for h and p were known, it would be easy for management to determine the *best* (i.e., least-cost) value of S by differentiating equation (2-3) with respect to S:

$$\frac{\partial TC}{\partial S} = 0 = \frac{2hS + 2p(S - 400)}{2(400)} \quad (2\text{-}4)$$

which yields

$$S = \frac{400p}{p + h} \quad (2\text{-}5)$$

The reader should verify that equation (2-5) is reasonable by observing what the best value of S is for various values of p between $p = 0$ and $p = \infty$. It is of particular interest here to observe that if $p = 3h$, then the best value of S is 300, which was the value of S specified above by management. Thus if h (which is easy to estimate, compared to p) is found to be, say, \$0.25 per week per unit of stock held, then management, by choosing $S = 300$, is behaving as if they knew that $p = 3(0.25) = \$0.75$ per week per unit of unsatisfied demand. That is, management saying "We want to have a service level of 75 percent" leads to the same ordering policy as management saying "We know that $h = 0.25$ and $p = 3h = 0.75$, and we want to choose an ordering policy which will minimize the cost per week." In either case, the result is $S = 300$. Moreover, while the value of h was *estimated* to be 0.25, the

24 PART II: INVENTORY CONTROL MODELS

value of 0.75 for *p* was *not* estimated, but was *im*plicitly com*puted*, or *imputed*, from management's prechosen value, 300, of *S*.

This book follows the philosophy that to obtain some kind of estimate of costs (such as p) and to use such estimates to derive an ordering policy (such as $S = 300$) is preferable to arbitrarily stating a service level. After all, in the above example, it might turn out that p could be estimated to be about $1 which, via equation (2-5), suggests that a more appropriate policy is $S = 320$. This implies that $s = -80$ and that an 80 percent service level would minimize costs per week. In general, then, the approach in this book is to develop a cost model, such as equation (2-2) or (2-3), and derive an ordering policy, using the cost model as a criterion. The next section focuses on cost modeling.

2-4 COST MODELING

In section 1-1, a general discussion of inventory-related costs identified five cost categories: holding costs, shortage costs, ordering costs, material costs, and systems costs. The reader may want to review that section. In this section it will be seen how such costs are formalized into cost models. The concepts in cost modeling are more easily understood if one keeps clearly in mind that costs are accounted for by using the cost categories mentioned above.

A cost model is a part of an ordering decision model and is inseparable from it. This is because costs cannot be meaningfully written down without reference to an ordering policy. The general steps followed in cost-based ordering decision modeling are

1. Specify an ordering policy.
2. Write a cost model in terms of the parameters of the ordering policy.
3. Use the cost model to determine the best (i.e., least-cost) values of the policy parameters.

If more than one policy is to be considered, steps 1 to 3 are repeated for each policy. In this case, the systems costs (fifth category in section 1-2) can be included, since they vary when more than one policy is considered. Otherwise, the systems costs are usually ignored. Step 2 is the subject of this section.

Throughout this book consistent symbols are used to represent each cost category in a given model. It is felt that this uniformity of notation greatly enhances one's ability to absorb new concepts as they are encountered. Table 2-2 introduces these symbols. There is no symbol for the

Table 2-2 Model symbols for costs by cost category

Cost category	Symbol	Major cost ingredients
Holding costs	h	Capital, storage, insurance, taxes, obsolescence
Shortage costs	p, π	Penalties, lost sales, expediting, lost goodwill
Ordering costs	k	Paperwork, freight, setups
Material costs	c	Price changes, quantity discounts
Total costs	TC	The sum of all the above

systems cost category since such costs are normally considered only when comparing two or more policies. The exact interpretation of the cost symbols depends on the situation being modeled. Preliminary modeling approaches for each cost category are now introduced.

Holding costs will typically be assessed on the *average* inventory held during a certain period of time or on the inventory level at one or more *points* in time during that same interval, or on both. For example, suppose that at the beginning of a given month the inventory level of an item is brought up to a level S. Each unit of the item costs $1.50. During the month, 400 units are demanded at a uniform rate, leaving $S - 400$ units at the end of the month. It costs $0.10 per unit of storage capacity needed to store this item. Property taxes of $0.06 per unit are payable on the inventory at the end of the month. Money is worth 2 percent per month to the company who manages this inventory. What is an appropriate holding cost model for this situation? The three ingredients of the holding cost are storage cost $h_1(S)$, taxes $h_2(S)$, and capital costs $h_3(S)$. The given data imply that

$$h_1(S) = 0.10S \tag{2-6}$$

$$h_2(S) = 0.06(S - 400) \tag{2-7}$$

$$h_3(S) = 0.02(1.50)\left[\frac{S + (S - 400)}{2}\right] \tag{2-8}$$

Note that $h_1(S)$ is assessed on inventory at the beginning of the month, $h_2(S)$ on end-of-month inventory, and $h_3(S)$ on average inventory. The holding cost HC then becomes

$$HC(S) = h_1(S) + h_2(S) + h_3(S) = 0.19S - 30 \tag{2-9}$$

Now suppose that the value of S is not fixed but is to be chosen by an ordering decision maker. From the point of view of the ordering decision maker, the important segment of the holding cost in equation (2-9) is $0.19S$, not the 30. This is because the decision maker will choose a value for S based on the knowledge that holding costs increase by $0.19 per month for each unit increase in S. The $30 is not affected by the choice of S; so it may be ignored by the decision maker and deleted from the cost model. Thus equation (2-9) may be simplified to

$$HC(S) = 0.19S \qquad (2\text{-}10)$$

A controversy sometimes arises over the timing of the assessment of holding costs. For example, storage costs may be assessed on maximum inventory (as they were above) or, say, on average inventory. The latter choice might be made when storage capacity is shared between the item in question and many other items, in which case storage capacity is provided for the average amount of each item stored. In this case, the storage cost expressed in equation (2-6) would be replaced by

$$h_1(S) = 0.10 \, \frac{S + (S - 400)}{2} = 0.10S - 20 \qquad (2\text{-}11)$$

Then equation (2-9) would be modified to read

$$HC(S) = 0.19S - 50 \qquad (2\text{-}12)$$

But we have already seen that the $50 may be ignored in determining a value for S. Thus equation (2-10) still reflects the relevant holding cost. As may be readily verified by the reader, this would remain true if the storage cost were assessed on the minimum inventory, $S - 400$. In fact, equation (2-10) is still sufficient if the timing of the assessment of taxes and capital costs is similarly changed. The incremental holding cost remains $0.19S$. In general, if the holding costs are a linear function of the parameters, then the time at which the holding costs are assessed is immaterial, provided that demand occurs at a constant, known rate and that no shortages occur.

Shortage costs are modeled in a variety of ways. To illustrate, suppose in the example above that S is chosen to be 300. Then every month there is a shortage of 100 units. The inventory-time plot for this situation appears in figure 2-3. A realistic shortage cost model depends on the implication of the shortage. The cost of a shortage usually depends on the quantity of unsatisfied demand, the duration of the shortage, both, or neither. This gives rise to the four cases shown below. These cases are typical but by no means the only possibilities.

The shortage cost may depend on the quantity of demand unsatisfied, but not the duration. This would occur, for example, if unsatisfied demand were lost. Letting SC represent the shortage cost per month in the example above, this could be modeled as

$$SC = p(100) \qquad (2\text{-}13)$$

Here, p would be the contribution (i.e., the unit selling price less the variable cost) per unit.

The second case would be one in which the shortage cost depends on the duration of the shortage:

$$SC = p(\tfrac{1}{4} \text{ month}) \tag{2-14}$$

In this case, p might represent a penalty cost per month resulting from disruption of the activities of the demander of the material because of a lack of material. Idle labor and idle equipment are two such costs.

An example in which the cost of shortage depends on both the quantity and the duration of shortage would be one in which each unit of the item being supplied provides productive capacity. The cost then depends on the number of unit-periods short. In applying this to the example, an appropriate model would be

$$SC = p(12.5) \tag{2-15}$$

where p is the cost per unit short per month and 12.5 is the number of unit-months of shortage each month. (The 12.5 figure is the area of triangle XYZ in figure 2-3.)

The last case to be considered here is one in which the shortage cost depends not on the quantity or duration of the shortage, but merely on the fact that a shortage exists at all. The model might take the form

$$SC = p \tag{2-16}$$

where the cost p is incurred whenever there is a shortage (once a month in the example). This model would apply if a special shipment had to be ordered to fill the shortage and the ordering cost (freight, say) was p.

The ordering cost OC reflects the cost of placing and receiving orders exclusive of the cost of the material being ordered. In its simplest form, this cost is independent of the quantity ordered and depends only on the ordering frequency:

$$OC = k(\text{ordering frequency}) \tag{2-17}$$

The cost per order k may include freight, paperwork, materials handling, and other fixed costs of ordering. If orders are for production (i.e., shop orders) rather than outside purchase, then k includes machine setup costs.

The material cost per unit time MC is a function of the unit cost c and the demand rate:

$$MC = c(\text{demand rate}) \tag{2-18}$$

If the unit cost is the same for all units ordered and if demands are always met, then the material cost can be deleted from the ordering decision model. The reasoning behind ignoring MC in this case is that it is not affected by the values of the parameters of the model; i.e., it is a constant cost regardless of what ordering decision is made. Eliminating such a constant cost from the model is an example of the principle of parsimony. This principle says that a model should be kept as simple as possible, so long as the reality of the model does not suffer to the extent of rendering the model ineffective as an aid to decision making.

Deleting the material cost from the model is not appropriate if the unit cost can vary, as it can if quantity discounts or cost price changes over time exist. Nor can MC be ignored if demands are affected by ordering decisions, as they would be, for example, if unsatisfied demands resulted in lost sales.

The complete cost model is obtained by adding the four cost components:

$$TC = HC + SC + OC + MC \qquad (2\text{-}19)$$

Here, TC is the total cost *per unit time*. In the next section we will see how to use this model as an aid to making good ordering decisions. Equation (2-19) is the generic form of cost model. It serves to reemphasize that throughout this book cost models will reflect the fact that costs related to an ordering decision generally fall into four categories.

2-5 DECISION MAKING USING AN ORDERING DECISION MODEL

The previous four sections of this chapter have addressed the ingredients to be considered in formulating an ordering decision model. It was seen that it is necessary to perform the following steps.

Step 1 Model supply and demand behavior.
Step 2 Choose the form of ordering policy.
Step 3 Agree on a decision effectiveness criterion.
Step 4 Model the criteria chosen in step 3 by relating it to the supply and demand behavior and to the chosen parameters of the ordering policy.

In this section two more steps will complete the modeling process. The first is

Step 5 Use the model developed in steps 1 through 4 to determine desirable values of the parameters of the ordering policy.

In other words, step 5 applies the model to provide answers to the basic ordering concerns—when to order and how much to order. The stepwise procedure is now illustrated by assuming a situation which is kept as simple as possible for exposition purposes.

Step 1 Demand for an item occurs at a constant rate of d units per time period. Orders are received immediately after they are placed. Unsatisfied demand is backlogged until it can be satisfied.

Step 2 The ordering policy is to place an order for Q units of stock whenever the stock level falls to s. The receipt of the order brings the stock level up to S; that is, $S = s + Q$.

Step 3 The decision effectiveness criterion is chosen to be cost per time period. It costs h dollars per period for each unit of stock held and p dollars per period for each unit of demand not satisfied. It costs k dollars to place an order for stock. Material costs c dollars per unit.

The inventory-time plot for this situation is shown in figure 2-4. Notice that s has a negative value in the plot. It will be seen below that this is appropriate.

Step 4 The information supplied by steps 1 through 3 above is now used to develop a cost model. Consider first HC, the holding cost per period. HC is simply h times the average inventory. The average inventory y can be determined for one cycle, where a cycle is the period of time between successive orders. In referring to figure 2-4, one cycle is a length of time represented by line VZ.

During the time represented by line segment VX, the average inventory is $S/2$, and during the time represented by line segment XZ the average inventory is zero. Therefore the average inventory over the cycle is

$$\bar{y} = \frac{S}{2} \left(\frac{\text{length of line segment } VX}{\text{length of line segment } VZ} \right) \tag{2-20}$$

By using plane geometry, this equation can be replaced by

$$\bar{y} = \frac{S}{2} \frac{S}{S - s} \tag{2-21}$$

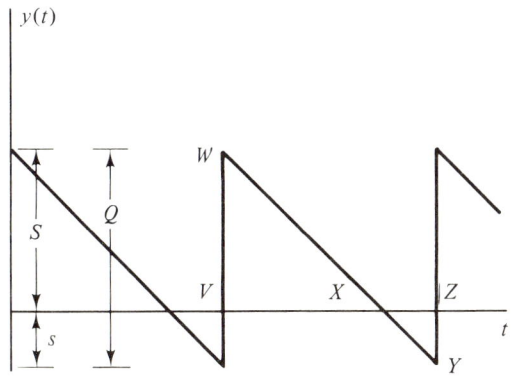

Figure 2-4 An inventory-time plot for the situation described in section 2-5.

Thus the holding cost per period is

$$HC = \frac{hS^2}{2(S-s)} \quad (2\text{-}22)$$

The shortage cost per period SC is determined by employing the same reasoning used for HC. In other words, by symmetry,

$$SC = p(\text{average shortage}) = p\left(\frac{s}{2}\frac{s}{S-s}\right) = \frac{ps^2}{2(S-s)} \quad (2\text{-}23)$$

The ordering cost per period OC is simply the ordering cost per cycle times the number of cycles per period:

$$OC = k\frac{d}{Q} = k\frac{d}{S-s} \quad (2\text{-}24)$$

The material cost per period MC is the product of the unit cost of the material and the usage rate:

$$MC = cd \quad (2\text{-}25)$$

The total cost TC can now be expressed in the form of equation (2-19) using the relationships derived in equations (2-22) through (2-25):

$$TC = \frac{hS^2}{2(S-s)} + \frac{ps^2}{2(S-s)} + \frac{kd}{S-s} + cd \quad (2\text{-}26)$$

Step 5 The least-cost values for S and s (and consequently for Q) are easily determined by differentiating equation (2-26) with respect to S and s, equating the derivatives to zero, and solving:

$$\frac{\partial TC}{\partial S} = 0 = \frac{2(S-s)2hS - 2(hS^2 + ps^2 + 2kd)}{4(S-s)^2} \quad (2\text{-}27)$$

$$\frac{\partial TC}{\partial s} = 0 = \frac{2(S-s)2ps + 2(hS^2 + ps^2 + 2kd)}{4(S-s)^2} \quad (2\text{-}28)$$

From the symmetry of equations (2-27) and (2-28) it is seen that

$$-ps = hS \quad (2\text{-}29)$$

Thus substituting $s = -hS/p$ into equation (2-27) yields, after simplification,

$$S^2 = \frac{2kd}{h}\frac{p}{p+h} \quad (2\text{-}30)$$

or

$$S = \sqrt{\frac{2kd}{h}}\sqrt{\frac{p}{p+h}} \quad (2\text{-}31)$$

Then, again substituting $s = -hS/p$ into equation (2-31) yields

$$s = -\sqrt{\frac{2kd}{h}}\sqrt{\frac{h^2}{p(p+h)}} \qquad (2\text{-}32)$$

Finally, the least-cost order quantity Q is

$$Q = S - s = \sqrt{\frac{2kd}{h}}\sqrt{\frac{p+h}{p}} \qquad (2\text{-}33)$$

This completes the fifth step of the modeling process.

Example 2-2 As an example of the application of the model developed up to this point, the situation described in the earlier sections of this chapter is extracted and analyzed. Suppose $h = \$0.25$, $p = \$0.75$, $k = \$2$, and $c = \$1.50$. Also suppose that the demand rate is $d = 400$ units per time period. Then according to equations (2-31) to (2-33), $S = 69.3$, $s = -23.1$, and $Q = 92.4$.

The acid test of effectiveness of the model is the total cost per unit time. By using equation (2-26), the value of TC for the solution just obtained is

$$TC = \$6.50 + \$2.17 + \$8.66 + \$600 = \$617.33$$

Recall earlier a situation in which "management" had chosen $S = 300$, $s = -100$, and $Q = 400$ to control an inventory for which $h = 0.25$ and $p = 3h = 0.75$. (The value for p had been imputed from management's 75 percent service level.) At that time, no value for k was specified. Thus, although the ratio $S/-s = 300/(100) = p/h$ was correct for these values of p and h, they turn out to be inappropriate when the ordering cost $k = \$2$ is taken into account. By using equation (2-26) again, the cost of management's policy is

$$TC = \$28.13 + \$9.37 + \$2 + \$600 = \$639.50$$

This represents an unnecessary cost of $\$639.50 - \$617.33 = \$22.17$ per time period, which is $\$22.17/\$17.33 = 128$ percent above the costs (exclusive of material costs) which are affected by the choice of an inventory control policy.

Several properties of the model are worth noting at this point. First, the model is seen to be independent of the material cost c. This should not be surprising since the demand is backlogged and must be met regardless of the timing of orders or the quantity ordered. Another property of interest is the way in which the values of S, s, and Q depend on the costs h and p. If $p = \infty$, then $s = 0$; that is, no shortages are allowed to occur. Moreover,

$$Q = S = \sqrt{\frac{2kd}{h}} \qquad (2\text{-}34)$$

Equation (2-34) is the classic *economic order quantity (EOQ)* reputed to have been developed by Harris [1], but it is also known as the Wilson economic lot size.

Carrying the special case further, the time T between orders is given by

$$T = \frac{Q}{d} = \sqrt{\frac{2k}{dh}} \qquad (2\text{-}35)$$

Finally, the total cost TC per unit time becomes [from equation (2-26)]

$$TC = \frac{hQ}{2} + \frac{kd}{Q} = 2\sqrt{\frac{k\,dh}{2}} = \sqrt{2k\,dh} \qquad (2\text{-}36)$$

exclusive of the material cost. Equations (2-34) through (2-36) play a central role in inventory modeling and will be brought into play several times in more complex models in this book.

Other values of p or h, when used in equations (2-31) through (2-33), lead to sensible values for S, s, and Q. If $p = h$, then $S = -s$. If $h = 0$, then $Q = \infty$. These results should appeal to one's intuition.

The development of the cost model above has borne fruit. Values of the parameters of an ordering policy have been determined as the result of a cost minimization procedure. However, the parameter values so specified represent only *one* solution to the ordering decision problem. To treat this as the only solution is to deny the ordering decision maker his or her full prerogative. Ordering decision models are used to *suggest* solutions, not dictate them. A model solution may be optimal in the sense that it minimizes modeled costs; this does not imply that this solution is the best one to implement.

Suppose in example 2-2 that the decision maker prefers to order in quantities of $Q = 400$ rather than $Q = 92.4$. Perhaps this is because the supplier insists on full carloads of 400 units. What is the economic effect of this constraint? It has already been seen that the total costs will increase to $639.50. This was $22.17 more than the minimum cost, according to the model. This cost difference might become the basis for negotiating a lower material cost from the supplier who insists on full carload shipments. Figure 2-5 illustrates the *sensitivity* of costs to changes in the chosen value of the decision variable Q. In a similar manner, the sensitivity of costs to changes in other decision variables can be investigated (see problem 2-7).

A different type of sensitivity analysis involves determining the cost effect of changing the value of a parameter, rather than a decision variable, in the model. The motivation for this is that costs or demand or supply characteristics may not be precisely known. For example, suppose that the cost of placing an order is falsely assumed to be $2.50 rather than $2 as in example 2-2. Then the assumed ordering cost is 25 percent above its true value. This then constitutes a modeling error. The cost effect of this error can

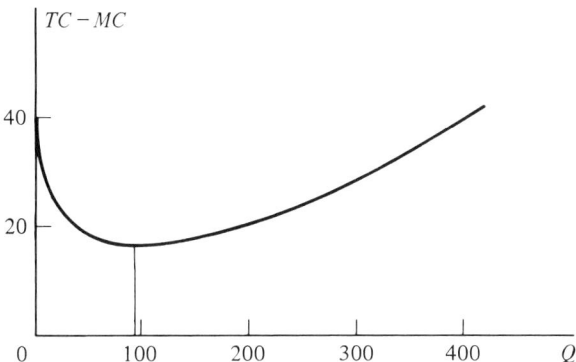

Figure 2-5 Sensitivity of total cost (exclusive of material cost) to the chosen value of Q in example 2-2.

be determined as follows. If k is taken to be $2.50, then the values of the decision variables become $S = 77.5$, $s = -25.8$, and $Q = 103.3$, by using equations (2-31), (2-32), and (2-33), respectively. Substituting these three values into equation (2-26) yields a true total cost (using $k = 2$, of course) of $TC = \$617.44$. This cost is illustrated in figure 2-6 which shows the sensitivity of total cost to the assumed value of k. The sensitivity of costs to other parameter estimation errors can be similarly analyzed (see problem 2-8). Thus a potentially valuable and often overlooked step in the modeling process is the following:

Step 6 Examine the sensitivity of costs either to chosen changes in values of decision variables or to errors in the estimated values of parameters.

The sixth step completes the ordering decision modeling sequence. Although the steps will not be explicitly mentioned when models are

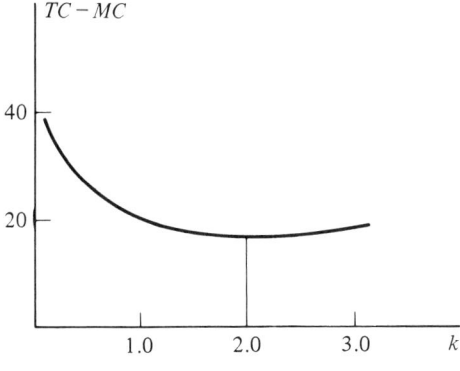

Figure 2-6 Sensitivity of total cost (exclusive of material cost) to the assumed value of k when the true value of k is 2.0 in example 2-2.

developed in future chapters, they are nonetheless being followed in every model developed. The first five steps are mandatory; the last one is optional.

2-6 DECISION MODEL CLASSIFICATION

In the next four chapters, a variety of ordering decision models will be investigated. These models have in common the fact that each of them, without exception, has been developed using the modeling process introduced in the first five sections of this chapter. The value of this thread of commonality among models will become more apparent as the reader progresses through the coming chapters. The models to be encountered are so widely disparate that, without a unifying structure, they would appear to be a hodgepodge of miscellaneous derivations. The classification of models presented in this section provides a preview of this disparity.

The source of the model disparity problem lies in the modeling process itself. During the modeling process many (presumably valid) assumptions must be made. It has been seen that these assumptions refer to the nature of the supply and demand processes, to the type of ordering policy, and to the effect of these two things on the chosen effectiveness criterion. Each assumption that has to be made adds to the number of possible resulting models which can be constructed. One way of keeping track of what thus becomes a very large number of alternatives is to classify the models. The classifications are over alternatives, or bases.

The following bases for model classification are well recognized:

Number of items If the model pertains to one item, it is called a *single-item* model. Otherwise, it is a *multi-item* model. An item here may be one stockkeeping unit, or it may be an entire product line. In any event, a single-item model recognizes only one stock level and only one demand rate.

Material flow structure In the multi-item case, the resulting material flow structure may assume a variety of forms. The simplest is a *parallel* structure in which each item is subject only to external supply and demand. This contrasts with a *series* structure in which material flows through a unique sequence of stock locations. In this structure, only the first location is supplied externally, while only the last location is subject to external demand. Such a structure is called a *multiechelon* structure (see chapter 6).

Review frequency It has already been mentioned that review of the stock level is designated as *periodic* if it takes place at *discrete* points in time. Placement of orders is assumed to be restricted to these times. If review and order placement can occur at any time, review is said to be *continuous*.

Order quantity variability The quantity ordered may be restricted to be the same amount every time an order is placed. If so, the model has a *fixed* order quantity; otherwise, the order quantity is *variable*. Most continuous-review models assume a fixed order quantity.

Planning horizon The planning horizon is the period of time over which demands are recognized. The horizon is assumed to be either *finite* or *infinite*. A finite horizon is likely to consist of an exact number of time periods if review is periodic.

Demand certainty If demands are assumed to be known over the entire planning horizon, the model is said to be *deterministic*. Otherwise, it is said to be *stochastic*, or *probabilistic*. Even if demands are known, they may or may not occur at a constant rate. If they do, the model is termed *static*. Otherwise it is said to be *dynamic*. If demands are recognized as stochastic, then a demand may or may not be assumed to have a known probability distribution. If the distribution is assumed known (unknown), the ordering decision model is said to be a model of decision making under *risk* (*uncertainty*).

Supply rate The rate of supply may be assumed to be infinite, as in the receipt of a purchased order, or finite, as in production to a shop order.

Delivery lag The delivery lag—time between placement and receipt of an order—may be recognized to be nonzero or assumed to be zero. The nonzero delivery lag may itself be assumed to be constant or a (random) variable.

Satisfaction of demand It may be assumed that demands must be satisfied or that shortages are allowed to occur. In the latter case, demands not satisfied when they occur may be assumed to be backlogged, or lost, or partially backlogged and partially lost.

Cost assumptions There are virtually hundreds of ways of modeling costs related to ordering decisions. The more common functional forms are linear; linear plus fixed charge; concave; convex; subadditive; monotone; and unimodal. These functional forms have technical definitions which will not be discussed until they are encountered in later chapters.

Special situations A wide variety of special conditions may be included in an ordering decision model. Some of the more common are price changes; seasonal supply; bounds on order quantities; bounds on inventory levels; and perishability or obsolescence of stock.

In the context of the above classification, the model developed in section 2-5 is classified as a single-item continuous review, infinite horizon, constant known demand rate model with backlogging of demands, zero delivery lag, and linear costs. It should be easy to see that thousands of unique models can be derived, each one being classified differently from every other model for at least one of the above bases.

The next four chapters, as well as sections within chapters, are organized with the above classifications in mind. Chapters 3 and 4 discuss single-item models; chapter 5 treats multi-item, single-echelon models; and multi-echelon situations are covered in chapter 6. Once a single-item approach has been chosen, one of the most important and fundamental considerations is ordering or review frequency. For this reason, each type of review is treated separately in chapters 3 and 4.

Within each chapter it will be seen that sections are formed according to the classification scheme above. Thus, sections separate deterministic and stochastic models, with subsections identifying different cost structures.

This completes the groundwork in preparation for the full discussion of models in the chapters to come.

2-7 SUMMARY

The control of inventories can be strengthened through the use of appropriate models. These models are developed using a process which systematically considers all of the characteristics of the inventories being controlled. The behavior of the supply and demand processes should be examined first. Supply may occur at a finite or infinite rate, and possibly after a lead time. Demands may be modeled as certain (deterministic) or uncertain (probabilistic). A valuable way of graphically portraying some of the supply/demand attributes is the inventory-time plot.

The next phase of the modeling process is the specification of ordering policy itself. A primary distinction is made between periodic-review and continuous-review policies. In the former, orders can be placed only once per time period, while in the latter, orders may be placed at any time. The policy is usually specified in terms of parameters, such as the parameter S in the policy "order up to level S every period."

In order to determine appropriate values for the policy parameters, criteria for judging the effectiveness of the resulting control decisions are established. In this book the predominant criterion is total cost per unit time. This total cost is made up of four components: holding costs, shortage costs, ordering costs, and material costs. Occasionally a cost surrogate, such as percentage of demand satisfied on time, is used.

After the cost model is formulated, values of the policy parameters are sought which minimize the total cost per unit time. In this chapter calculus was sometimes used to accomplish this by setting the derivatives of the total cost equation with respect to each policy parameter equal to zero and solving. The cost model can also be used to test the sensitivity of the total cost to changes in the values of the policy parameters or to the cost data themselves.

The above modeling process can result in a wide variety of models, which may be classified on the bases of supply and demand characteristics, ordering policy, planning horizon, cost assumptions, and the number of items modeled. Such classification serves to clarify model assumptions, to increase understanding, and to facilitate comparison of results for various models.

REFERENCE

1. Harris, F.: "Operations and Cost," Factory Management Series, Shaw, Chicago, 1915, pp. 48–52.

EXERCISES

2-1 Demands for a certain product occur steadily at the rate of 5 units per month. It costs $8 to place an order for stock. Storage space costs $2 per year per unit of stock. Capital costs amount to $1 per year for each unit of stock on hand. It costs $1 per unit of demand which cannot be satisfied on time in a given month. Material costs $0.80 per unit.
    (*a*) What is the most economical quantity to order?
    (*b*) What should the stock level be just before an order is placed?
    (*c*) What is the total cost per month of the policy indicated in (*a*) and (*b*)?
    (*d*) Repeat (*a*), (*b*), and (*c*) if shortages are prohibited.

2-2 For the conditions stated in problem 2-1, suppose that a second supplier offers to sell you material at $0.70 per unit, but insists that you order in lots of size 30. Perform cost calculations that determine whether to switch to the new supplier.

2-3 In step 3 of section 2-5, suppose that the holding and shortage costs are changed as follows. The holding and shortage costs per time period are proportional to the square of the average inventory or shortage, respectively. That is, $HC(y) = ay^2$ and $PC(z) = az^2$ where a is a constant, y is the average inventory level, and z is the average shortage. Find the minimum cost values of S, Q, and s in this case. That is, repeat steps 4 and 5 of the modeling process.

2-4 A company is engaged in a dragline rock mining operation which is composed of the following steps: (1) drill holes; (2) place dynamite in holes; (3) detonate; (4) remove rock with a dragline. The first three steps are carried on intermittently by an outside firm, while the fourth step is done continuously on a regular 40-hour-per-week schedule. Each time the blasting work is contracted, there is a charge of f dollars to cover the cost of getting the necessary equipment and workers to the work site. The cost of performing steps 1, 2, and 3 comes to v dollars per hole, including the cost of the dynamite.

Currently the company is borrowing money to finance its operations at a rate of i dollars per dollar borrowed per year. At the rate at which rock is being mined, w holes must be drilled per year.

How many times per year should the blasting work be contracted?

Note: Problem 2-5 should be assigned and class time provided to ensure student mastery. It gives the student a chance to go through the process of model formulation, and it forms the basis of discussion of a portion of section 5-2.

2-5 The stepwise procedure in section 2-5 was illustrated using an example in which it was assumed that whenever an order was placed, it was immediately received in total. Suppose, instead, that the order will be received at the rate of R units per time period, where $R > d$, the demand rate. This would be the case if the item were produced in-house, rather than ordered from a supplier's inventory. Thus step 1 is revised to reflect this change. Steps 2 and 3 remain unchanged. Steps 4 and 5 are to be repeated for this new finite production rate. It is helpful first to redraw figure 2-4 to reflect this situation.

(*a*) Repeat step 4; i.e., derive an expression for the total cost TC per unit time.

(*b*) Repeat step 5; i.e., find values of S, Q, and s which minimize TC.

(*c*) Show that the values of S, Q, and s reduce to those in equations (2-31), (2-32), and (2-33) when $R = \infty$.

2-6 A finished goods inventory of an item is being held by a company until enough is ready to warrant a delivery run of the goods to customers in a city across the state. It costs $275 to make the delivery. This cost is insensitive to the quantity delivered. Items are produced at a uniform rate of 300 units per week. These items cost $650 each to produce, and they sell for $800 each. The customers do not mind waiting until the company decides to make a delivery. Money is worth 0.5 percent per week to the company. The company is paid on delivery of the goods.

(*a*) How often should deliveries be made?

(*b*) Draw an inventory-time plot for this situation.

2-7 Plot a graph similar to figure 2-5 which shows the sensitivity of total cost to the value of s in example 2-2. Give the points on the graphed curve for $s = -30$ and $s = 0$.

2-8 Plot a graph similar to figure 2-6 which shows the sensitivity of total cost to the assumed value of p if the true value of p is $0.75 in example 2-2. Give the points on the graphed curve for assumed p values of $0.50 and $1.

2-9 A certain item is demanded at the rate of 350 units per month. Since the items are highly perishable, no inventory of the item is held. All units are "made to order." Orders are satisfied on a first-come–first-served basis. It costs $150 to set up the equipment to produce a batch of these items. The agreed-upon price of the units is $20 minus a contractual late-delivery charge of $1 per day late per unit. Assume a 30-day month.

    (*a*) Draw an inventory-time plot to reflect this situation.

    (*b*) Determine the batch size which will maximize profits to the firm.

2-10 Demand per week D_1 for an item obeys the probability distribution

Quantity d	0	1	2	3
Prob $[D_1 = d]$	0.4	0.2	0.3	0.1

    (*a*) Derive the probability distribution for demand $D_1 + D_2$ in two weeks, assuming that demand each week is independent of demand in any other week.

    (*b*) Repeat (*a*) assuming that demand in two adjacent weeks is positively correlated, as follows:

Value v	-1	0	1
$P[D_2 - D_1 = v]$	0.3	0.5	0.2

However, if v would cause D_2 to equal -1, then $D_2 = 0$; and if v would cause D_2 to equal 4, then $D_2 = 3$.

CHAPTER
THREE
CONTINUOUS-REVIEW ORDERING DECISION MODELS

This chapter is concerned with effective ways of making decisions affecting inventory levels of a single item when decisions can be made at any time. It is presumed that the knowledge needed to make such control decisions is continually available. This includes information with respect to both present inventory status (amount on hand and on order) and prospective demands. In a practical sense, this assumption is considered valid if the time lag between the occurrence of any transaction and knowledge of its occurrence is negligibly small compared with the typical interval between successive demands.

Chapter 4 will treat situations in which ordering decisions are made periodically rather than continuously. This is one of the primary distinctions to be made in modeling ordering decisions. Both this chapter and the next are divided into sections based on another important distinction: whether future demands are considered known with certainty. After some common types of continuous-review ordering policies are treated in the first section, the remaining two sections consider deterministic and stochastic models, respectively.

3-1 CONTINUOUS ORDERING POLICIES

Continuous ordering policies assume that information regarding the inventory level is instantaneously available following any transaction. It is therefore logical that such ordering policies will specify that an order is triggered whenever the stock level falls to a given level. In this chapter, that level will usually be called s and referred to as the *reorder point*. The quantity to be ordered when an order is placed can be either fixed or variable.

Suppose t is the time at which an order is placed. Let $y(t)$ be the inventory level (on hand plus on order) at time t, and let $x(t)$ be the amount ordered at that time. Then one policy which dictates that the quantity ordered is always a fixed quantity Q is given by

$$x(t) = \begin{cases} Q & \text{when } y(t) \leq s \\ 0 & \text{when } y(t) > s \end{cases}$$

This policy is known as a *lot-size reorder-point policy*, or (s, Q) *policy*. It is also referred to as a "two-bin policy." More properly, a *two-bin policy* is an (s, Q) policy in which $s = Q$. The interpretation is that when one bin of capacity s is depleted, a second bin, also of capacity s, is used to satisfy demands while an order of size s is placed to refill the first bin.

A policy involving variable-order quantities usually specifies that the inventory level (on hand plus on order) be brought up to a level S whenever an order is placed. This policy, called an (s, S) *policy* in this text, states that

$$x(t) = \begin{cases} S - y(t) & \text{when } y(t) \leq s \\ 0 & \text{when } y(t) > s \end{cases}$$

A special type of ordering policy, called a *base stock policy*, or (S) policy, requires that an order be placed whenever any demand occurs:

$$x(t) = \begin{cases} S - y(t) & \text{when } y(t) < S \\ 0 & \text{when } y(t) \geq S \end{cases}$$

Of course, an (S) policy is a special case of an (s, S) policy with $s = S - 1$.

Policies of all the types mentioned above will be encountered in the sections which follow.

3-2 DETERMINISTIC MODELS

The models in this section are based on the assumption that the demand rate is known for a period ranging from the present ($t = 0$) to a future point in time ($t = T$). The period of time $(0, T)$ is referred to as the *planning horizon*. Although demands are not always known exactly for the entire planning horizon, the uncertainty in demands may be sufficiently small to assume that the estimated demand rate is the actual rate.

Formulation of Demands and Costs

In this subsection the notation and conventions to be followed in this chapter are developed. Unless otherwise specified, these formulations will be assumed to hold.

The distinguishing feature of continuous-review models is that demands must first be expressed as rates. Thus $d(t)$ will be the demand rate (units demanded per unit time) at time t. In all the models in this chapter, a planning horizon of length T, beginning at present ($t = 0$) and extending T time units into the future, will be the time over which the inventory level is to be controlled. The cumulative demand $D(t)$, at time t, then, will be

$$D(t) = \int_0^t d(\tau)\, d\tau \qquad \text{for } 0 \leq t \leq T \tag{3-1}$$

Now $x(t)$ will be the quantity ordered at time t, and $X(t)$ will be the cumulative amount ordered up to time t. Thus, suppose that k orders have been placed at times $t_1, t_2, \ldots, t_k$. Then

$$X(t_k) = \sum_{i=1}^{k} x(t_i) \tag{3-2}$$

The inventory level $y(t)$ at time t can now be expressed in terms of demands and orders:

$$y(t) = y(0) + X(t) - D(t) \qquad 0 \leq t \leq T \tag{3-3}$$

where $y(0)$ is the initial inventory. A negative value of $y(t)$ indicates a shortage condition. Unsatisfied demand is assumed to be backlogged unless another assumption is stated.

Unless otherwise specified, the following straightforward cost conditions will be assumed to be in effect. An ordering cost of k dollars is incurred whenever an order is placed. Material costs c dollars per unit ordered. The holding and shortage costs are both expressed as rates; it costs h dollars per unit time per unit held in stock and p dollars per unit time per unit of unsatisfied demand. Thus a general way of expressing the holding costs $HC(t_1, t_2)$ between two points of time t_1 and t_2 is

$$HC(t_1, t_2) = \int_{t_1}^{t_2} hy(t)\, dt \tag{3-4}$$

Thus $HC(t_1, t_2)$ is h times the average inventory level during the interval (t_1, t_2). This assumes that $y(t) \geq 0$ for $t_1 \leq t \leq t_2$. It also requires that it be possible to perform the integration between t_1 and t_2; i.e., there are no discontinuities in the function $y(t)$ between $t = t_1$ and $t = t_2$. For example, if an order is received at time t_3, where $t_1 \leq t_3 \leq t_2$, then the holding cost is expressed as

$$HC(t_1, t_2) = \int_{t_1}^{t_3} hy(t)\, dt + \int_{t_3}^{t_2} hy(t)\, dt$$

Similarly, the penalty cost $PC(t_1, t_2)$ between t_1 and t_2 is [assuming $y(t) \leq 0$ for $t_1 \leq t \leq t_2$]

$$PC(t_1, t_2) = \int_{t_1}^{t_2} -py(t)\, dt \qquad (3\text{-}5)$$

The following example will illustrate the calculation of holding and shortage costs for a continuous-review situation. The example will also be used in later developments.

Example 3-1 Suppose $T = 10$, $y(0) = 6$, $x(8) = 19$, $d(t) = 2$ for $0 \leq t \leq 5$, and $d(t) = 3$ for $5 < t \leq 10$. These conditions are depicted in figure 3-1. A shortage condition exists between $t = 3$ and $t = 8$. Suppose $h = \$1.30$ and $p = \$9.70$. Then the total holding and shortage costs over the planning horizon are $HC(0, 3) + PC(3, 5) + PC(5, 8) + HC(8, 10)$, which is calculated as

$$\int_0^3 1.30(6 - 2t)\, dt + \int_3^5 9.70(2t - 6)\, dt$$
$$+ \int_5^8 9.70(3t - 11)\, dt + \int_8^{10} 1.30(30 - 3t)\, dt = \$305.65$$

This is seen to be based on the area of the shaded region of figure 3-1. The portion of the area which represents a shortage condition is multiplied by $9.70, and the remaining area is multiplied by $1.30; the two products are added to obtain the total holding and shortage costs.

Models Recognizing an Ordering Cost

The first model to be considered will assume that demand during the planning horizon $[0, T]$ is to be exactly satisfied $[y(T) = 0]$ with no shortages $[y(t) \geq 0, 0 \leq t \leq T]$. This situation occurs, for example, for inventories supplying parts for a manufacturing process. Shortages may cause severe production delays and hence are to be avoided.

The following solution to this problem is iterative in nature:

1. Assume that some number n of orders will be placed.
2. For the n chosen in step 1, determine the best times $(t_1, t_2, \ldots, t_n)$ at which to order.
3. Calculate total costs for the solution obtained in step 2.
4. Repeat steps 1 to 3 for other values of n until a minimal cost solution is obtained.

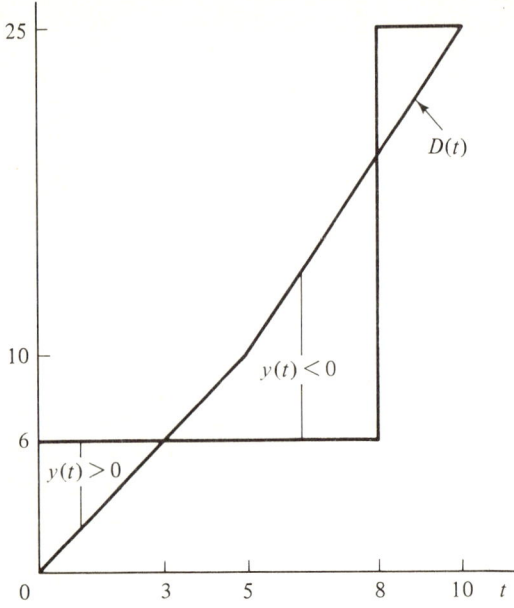

Figure 3-1 A cumulative inventory-time plot for the situation of example 3-1.

For step 2 it should be noted that if the times at which orders are placed are specified, then the order quantities are automatically determined since the quantity ordered at time t_j will be just sufficient to last until time t_{j+1}. That is, the inventory level should be zero when an order is placed. In fact, if there is an initial inventory $[y(0) > 0]$, then the first order should be placed when the initial inventory is depleted. Thus t_1 is the time at which

$$D(t_1) = y(0) \tag{3-6}$$

To determine the remaining times in step 2, only the holding cost need be considered. This is because the ordering cost is fixed as long as n is fixed. In order to minimize holding costs, the relationship shown in equation (3-7) must hold. The rationale behind this relationship will be developed now. Suppose the value of t_k is being decided upon (t_{k-1} and t_{k+1} have already been chosen). Consider the effect of the choice of t_k on the holding cost H between times t_{k-1} and t_{k+1}. This cost is

$$H = h \left[\int_{t_{k-1}}^{t_k} D(t_k) - D(t)\, dt + \int_{t_k}^{t_{k+1}} D(t_{k+1}) - D(t)\, dt \right]$$

$$= h \left[D(t_k)(t_k - t_{k-1}) + D(t_{k+1})(t_{k+1} - t_k) - \int_{t_{k-1}}^{t_{k+1}} D(t)\, dt \right]$$

The minimum cost choice of t_k is found by differentiation:

$$\frac{\partial H}{\partial t_k} = 0 = h[d(t_k)(t_k - t_{k-1}) + D(t_k) - D(t_{k+1})]$$

Thus t_k should have values which solve

$$D(t_{k+1}) = D(t_k) + (t_k - t_{k-1})d(t_k) \qquad k = 2, 3, \ldots, n \qquad (3\text{-}7)$$

Equation (3-7) is used to determine the values of $t_2, t_3, \ldots, t_n$ in a trial-and-error fashion as follows. Assume a value for t_2. Solve equation (3-7) for t_3, $t_4, \ldots, t_n$. Then check to see if equation (3-7) holds for t_{n+1}; that is, determine whether $t_{n+1} = T$. If t_{n+1} is not equal to T, assume another value for t_2 and repeat the process.

Before an example is attempted, a labor-saving device will be described. The procedure described above can be tedious and time-consuming. Computer solution is difficult, especially since continuous functions are involved. The device involves an easily obtained approximate solution which makes a good starting point for using the optimum-seeking procedure. It can also be used as a solution without further refinement if an optimal solution is not deemed necessary.

The approximate solution is obtained by first assuming that the number of orders to be placed is equal to the number which would be placed if the demand occurred at a constant rate equal to the average demand rate over the interval $[t_1, T]$. That is, assume that

$$d(t) = \bar{d} \equiv \frac{D(T) - D(t_1)}{T - t_1}$$

From equation (2-35) the average time between orders is $\sqrt{2k/(\bar{d}h)}$. Therefore the number n of orders to be placed in the interval $[t_1, T]$ is approximately

$$n = \frac{T - t_1}{\sqrt{2k/(\bar{d}h)}} \qquad (3\text{-}8)$$

Once the number of orders to be placed is determined, a rule of thumb for determining the order times is to choose the time t_2 as if the total demand in the interval $[t_1, T]$ were going to be shared equally by all orders placed. That is, t_2 is selected to satisfy

$$D(t_2) = D(t_1) + \frac{D(T) - D(t_1)}{n} \qquad (3\text{-}9)$$

Then equation (3-7) can be used to obtain $t_3, \ldots, t_n$. An example will illustrate the procedures developed in this section.

Example 3-2 Assume the conditions of example 3-1 are in effect. That is, $T = 10$, $y(0) = 6$, $d(t) = 2$ for $0 \leq t \leq 5$, $d(t) = 3$ for $5 \leq t \leq 10$, and $h = \$1.30$. Add to this the assumption that the ordering cost $k = \$10$. Determine the number and timing of order placement to minimize costs over the planning horizon. Also specify the order quantities which follow from this.

The first order will be placed when existing stock runs out at time $t_1 = 3$.

The approximate solution employs equations (3-8) and (3-9) with $\bar{d} = 19/7$:

$$n = \frac{10 - 3}{\sqrt{(2 \cdot 10)/(19/7)1.3}} \doteq 3$$

$$D(t_2) = 6 + \frac{25 - 6}{3} = 12.33$$

from which $t_2 = 5.78$. Then t_3 is obtained from equation (3-7):

$$D(t_3) = 12.33 + (5.78 - 3)3 = 20.67$$

from which $t_3 = 8.9$.

The cost of the approximate solution is the sum of the holding cost and the ordering cost. The holding cost is expressed in equation (3-4), but is most easily found here by referring to figure 3-2(a). The area between the two curves $X(t)$ and $D(t)$ represents the number of unit-periods of stock held during the interval $[0, T]$. Multiplying this area by h yields HC, the total holding cost. For the approximate solution, $HC = \$1.30(33.29) = \$43.28$. The ordering cost OC is $nk = 3(\$10) = \$30$. Thus the total cost is $\$73.28$.

Using the approximate solution as a starting point for the exact solution, equation (3-7) (with $k = 3$) is used to check the optimality of the choice of t_2. From equation (3-7)

$$D(t_4) = 20.67 + (8.9 - 5.78)3 = 29$$

Since $D(t_4) > D(T) = 25$, another choice of t_2 is called for. By trying $t_2 = 5.33$, equation (3-7) yields $D(t_3) = 18$, for which $t_3 = 7.67$. Then equation (3-7) with $k = 3$ yields $D(t_4) = 25 = D(T)$. Thus $t_2 = 5.33$ and $t_3 = 7.67$ are optimal for $n = 3$. This solution is illustrated in figure 3-2(b). The procedure above is repeated for $n = 2$ and $n = 4$, resulting in the solutions shown in figure 3-2(c) and (d). The solutions and costs are shown in table 3-1.

It is seen that the optimal solution is to order 5 at time 3.00, 7 at time 5.33, and 7 at time 7.67. Notice that the approximate solution yielded a nearly optimal result.

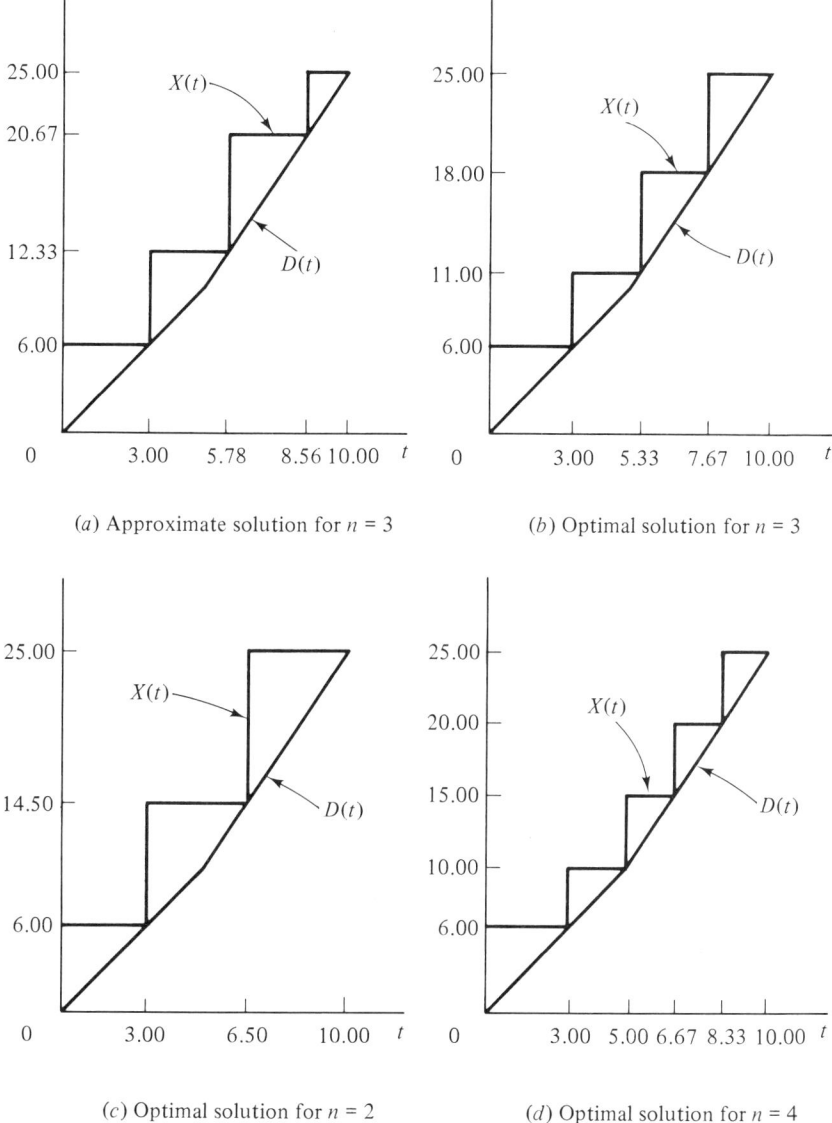

Figure 3-2 Solutions to example 3-2. Order points and quantities are labeled on the axes.

total cost per unit time $TC_j(Q)$ is expressed as a function of both the quantity discount j in effect and the quantity ordered Q. Thus $TC_2(10)$ would be the total cost per unit time if $c = c_2$ and $Q = 10$. Now this cost is only attainable (*physically realizable*) if $m_2 \leq 10$ (and $m_3 > 10$). However, the function $TC_2(Q)$ is defined for all $Q \geq 0$, including values of $Q < m_2$ or $Q > m_3$. In general, if $Q < m_j$ or $Q > m_{j+1}$, the cost is *unattainable*. Thus if, say, $m_2 = 14$, then $TC_2(10)$ is unattainable but still mathematically defined. This will be quite helpful in executing the procedure for finding the minimum-cost order quantity.

The total cost per unit time consists of the material cost, ordering cost, and holding cost:

$$TC_j(Q) = c_j d + \frac{kd}{Q} + \frac{(h_s + ic_j)Q}{2} \qquad j = 0, 1, \ldots, J \qquad (3\text{-}11)$$

This total cost is shown graphically in figure 3-3. The attainable costs are shown as a solid line, while the unattainable costs are depicted as dashed lines.

The first thing to recognize from equation (3-11) is that for any given value of Q

$$TC_0(Q) > TC_1(Q) > \cdots > TC_J(Q) \qquad (3\text{-}12)$$

This relationship is illustrated in figure 3-3. The minimum-cost point on the curve $TC_j(Q)$ will be called Q_j^*. By equation (2-34), this point is

$$Q_j^* = \sqrt{\frac{2kd}{h_s + ic_j}} \qquad j = 0, 1, \ldots, J \qquad (3\text{-}13)$$

Since $c_0 > c_1 > \cdots > c_j$, it follows that

$$Q_0^* < Q_1^* < \cdots < Q_J^* \qquad (3\text{-}14)$$

This is also illustrated in figure 3-3.

Equations (3-12) through (3-14) provide the rationale for the procedure to determine the order quantity Q^* which minimizes total cost per unit time. The procedure is as follows:

Step 1 Evaluate Q_j^* successively for $j = J, J - 1, J - 2, \ldots$ until the first j is reached for which $Q_j^* \geq m_j$. The cost $TC_j(Q_j^*)$ is thus attainable.

Step 2 For the value of j reached in step 1 compare the costs $TC_j(Q_j^*)$, $TC_{j+1}(m_{j+1}), \ldots, TC_J(m_J)$ and choose as Q^* the value from the set $\{Q_j^*, m_{j+1}, \ldots, m_J\}$ which gives the least total cost.

By equations (3-12) and (3-13), $TC_j(Q_j^*) \leq TC_j(Q) < TC_{j-1}(Q) < \cdots < TC_0(Q)$ for any Q, so that it is impossible to find a $Q < Q_j^*$ which results in total costs lower than those if $Q = Q^*$.

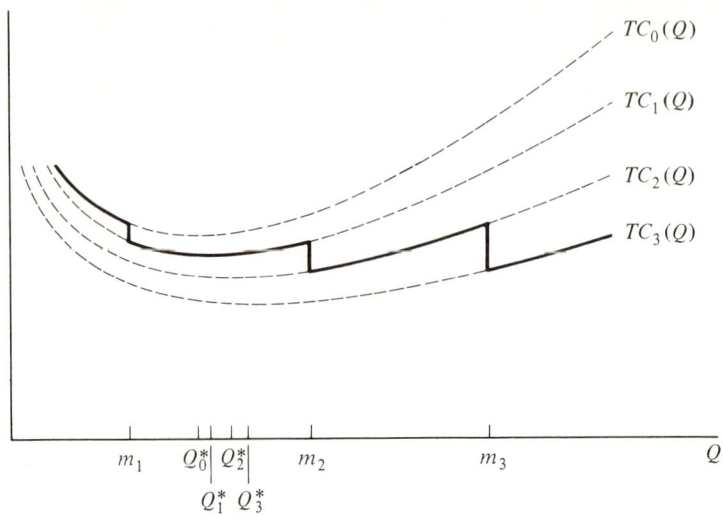

Figure 3-3 Total cost curves for an all-units quantity discount model with three price break points. The solid line is the actual (attainable) cost curve.

For the situation illustrated in figure 3-3, the values of Q which are candidates for yielding the minimum cost are $Q = Q_1^*$, $Q = m_2$, and $Q = m_3$. The two-step procedure above will now be illustrated by an example.

Example 3-3 Demands for an item occur at a uniform rate of 9 units per month. It costs $4 to place an order for more stock and $0.50 per month per unit stored. A supplier offers the following quantity discount: $c = \$10$ per unit for $Q \leq 9$, $9.50 per unit for $10 \leq Q \leq 39$, and $9 per unit for $Q \geq 40$. Find Q^* and the minimal cost per month (a) if a capital cost of 1 percent per month is assumed and (b) ignoring the capital cost.

Notationally, the problem translates to $d = 9$, $k = 4$, $h_s = 0.50$, $c_0 = 10$, $c_1 = 9.5$, $c_2 = 9$, $m_1 = 10$, and $m_2 = 40$. For part (a), $i = 0.01$. From equation (3-13)

$$Q_2^* = \sqrt{\frac{2 \cdot 4 \cdot 9}{0.5 + (0.01)(9)}} = 11.04 < m_2 = 40$$

Similarly, $Q_1^* = 11 > m_1 = 10$. Therefore it suffices to calculate $TC_1(11)$ and $TC_2(40)$. By using equation (3-11), the first of these is evaluated as

$$TC_1(11) = \frac{(4)(9)}{11} + \frac{[0.5 + (0.01)(9)](11)}{2} + (9.5)(9) = 92$$

Similarly, $TC_2(40) = 93.7$. Thus the minimal cost per month is $92, which is achieved for $Q^* = 11$.

For solution (b) the procedure is slightly simpler since Q_1^* has the same value for all j. From equation (3-13), $Q_1^* = 12$. Then since $m_1 = 10 < 12 < 40 = m_2$, the procedure again calls for the evaluation of $TC_1(12)$ and $TC_2(40)$. These values are $91.50 per month and $91.90 per month, respectively. Therefore $Q^* = 12$.

The second form of price discount to be considered is called an *incremental quantity discount*. The unit material cost in this case has this form: For each order placed, the cost per unit is

$$c = \begin{cases} c_0 & \text{for each of the first } m_1 - 1 \text{ units} \\ c_1 & \text{for each of the next } m_2 - m_1 \text{ units} \\ c_J & \text{for each unit in excess of } m_J - 1 \end{cases} \quad (3\text{-}15)$$

As before, $c_0 > c_1 > \cdots > c_J$. $TC_j(Q)$ is defined as it was for the all-units discount, but it is calculated differently. Define $MC(Q)$ as the material cost if Q units are ordered. This cost can be calculated recursively as

$$MC(Q) = MC(m_j - 1) + c_j[Q - (m_j - 1)] \quad (3\text{-}16)$$

where $m_j \leq Q < m_{j+1}$. Thus the total cost per unit time can be expressed as

$$TC_j(Q) = \frac{MC(Q)d}{Q} + \frac{kd}{Q} + \frac{(h_s + ic_j)Q}{2} \quad (3\text{-}17)$$

Substitution of equation (3-16) into equation (3-17) yields, after rearranging,

$$TC_j(Q) = dc_j + \frac{d}{Q}[k + MC(m_j - 1) - c_j(m_j - 1)]$$

$$+ \frac{(h_s + ic_j)Q}{2} \qquad j = 0, 1, \ldots, J \quad (3\text{-}18)$$

Equation (3-18) has a meaningful physical interpretation. The quantity $MC(m_j - 1) - c_j(m_j - 1)$ is the excess material cost resulting from the fact that, when $m_j \leq Q < m_{j+1}$, not all the Q units ordered are obtained at the unit cost c_j. Since this excess cost is incurred every time an order is placed, it can be treated as part of the ordering cost. Thus the ordering cost terms in equation (3-18) are all terms which multiply d/Q. With this interpretation, the minimum cost Q_j^* is obtained by using equation (2-34) as ($m_0 = 1$):

$$Q_j^* = \sqrt{\frac{2[k + MC(m_j - 1) - c_j(m_j - 1)]d}{h_s + ic_j}} \qquad j = 0, 1, \ldots, J \quad (3\text{-}19)$$

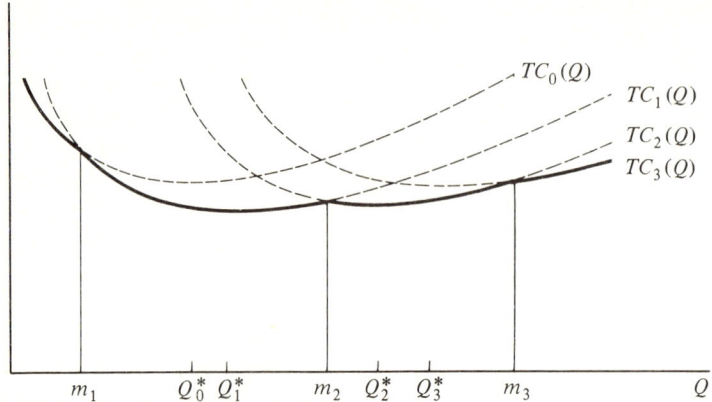

Figure 3-4 Total cost curves for an incremental quantity discount model with three price break points. The solid line is the actual (attainable) cost curve.

Figure 3-4 illustrates typical total cost curves of equation (3-18) and minimum-cost points of equation (3-19). Note that in the illustrated case, the costs $TC_j(Q_j^*)$ are attainable for $j = 1$ and 2 but not attainable for $j = 0$ or 3.

The solution procedure for minimizing the total cost per unit time for an incremental quantity discount is now stated. It simply chooses from among the attainable values of Q_j^* that value which minimizes cost per unit time.

Step 1 Calculate $MC(m_j - 1)$ recursively for $j = 0, 1, \ldots, J$, using equation (3-16).
Step 2 Compute Q_j^* for $j = 0, 1, \ldots, J$, using equation (3-19).
Step 3 For those Q^* which represent attainable costs (i.e., those for which $m_j \leq Q_j^* < m_{j+1}$), calculate $TC_j(Q_j^*)$.
Step 4 The Q_j^* corresponding to the smallest $TC_j(Q_j^*)$ in step 3 is the minimum-cost value Q^*.

Example 3-4 Suppose that the conditions of example 3-3 are in effect and a second supplier offers the following quantity discount: c is $10 per unit for the first 10 units, $9.50 per unit for the next 20 units, and $9 per unit for each additional unit.

For this supplier, find Q^* and the minimal cost per month, ignoring the capital cost.

Evidently $m_0 = 0$, $m_1 = 11$, and $m_2 = 31$. By using equation (3-16), $MC(10) = \$100$ and $MC(30) = \$290$. Then from equation (3-19), $Q_0^* = 12$, $Q_1^* = 18$, and $Q_2^* = 29.4$. Thus $Q_0^* > m_1 = 11$ and $Q_2^* < m_2 = 31$. Thus neither $TC_0(Q_0^*)$ nor $TC_2(Q_2^*)$ is an attainable cost.

This leaves Q_1^* as the optimal solution. From equation (3-18), the cost per month for $Q^* = 18$ is

$$TC_1(18) = 9(9.5) + \frac{9}{18}(4 + 100 - 95) + \frac{0.5(18)}{2}$$

$$= \$94.50 \text{ per month}$$

It is interesting to note that in the all-units discount case, the value of Q^* is frequently at a breakpoint m_j, for some j, while for the incremental discount, Q^* is never at such a breakpoint.

The third price discount model to be considered is one in which the price depends on the time at which the order is placed. Specifically, the material cost is assumed to be c_0 per unit for orders placed up until ($\leq$) time t_1 and $c_1 > c_0$ per unit after ($>$) time t_1. Two decisions need to be made: (1) Should a special order for Q^* units be placed at some time t^* to take advantage of the lower unit cost? (2) If so, what should be the values of Q^* and t^*?

Let t_0 be the time at which the last *regular* order (before the price increase) would ordinarily be placed. It would not be economic to place a special order for Q^* prior to time t_0 since it would only result in excess holding costs. Thus $t_0 \leq t^* \leq t_1$. Figure 3-5 illustrates this situation. The times t_2 and t_3 in this figure are defined as the first stockout point after t_0 if a special order of size Q^* is not, or is, respectively, placed. It is easy to see from the geometry of figure 3-5 that $t_2 = t^* + y(t^*)/d$ and $t_3 = t_2 + Q^*/d$.

Determination of whether to place a special order at time t^* depends on the magnitude of the total savings TS. This savings is defined to be the sum of a material cost savings and the routine ordering and holding costs

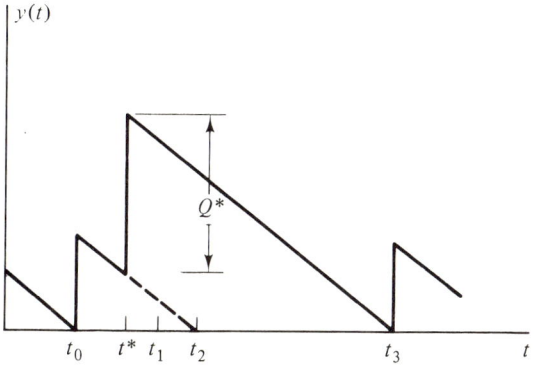

Figure 3-5 An inventory-time plot depicting the placement of a special order for Q^* units in advance of a price increase.

avoided because the special order is placed, less the holding cost associated with the special order. The routine costs avoided would be the average cost of ordering and holding material between times t_2 and t_3. From equation (2-36) this would be $\sqrt{2kd(h_s + ic_1)}$. The resulting total savings (which deliberately ignores the ordering cost of the special order) is

$$TS = (c_1 - c_0)Q^* + \sqrt{2kd(h_s + ic_1)}\,\frac{Q^*}{d}$$

$$- (h_s + ic_0)\left[\frac{Q^*y(t^*)}{d} + \frac{Q^{*2}}{2d}\right] \qquad (3\text{-}20)$$

Equating the first derivative of TS with respect to Q^* to zero and solving for Q^* yields

$$Q^* = \frac{(c_1 - c_0)d}{h_s + ic_0} + \frac{h_s + ic_1}{h_s + ic_0}\sqrt{\frac{2kd}{h_s + ic_1}} - y(t^*) \qquad (3\text{-}21)$$

The time t^* at which the special order is placed depends on when knowledge of the impending price increase becomes available. If the price change is not known until after time t_0, then $t^* = t_1$. In this case, the solution procedure is as follows.

Step 1 Solve for Q^* using equation (3-21).
Step 2 Place a special order if $TS > k$, that is, if the total savings justifies the ordering cost of the special order.

If the price increase is known prior to time t_0, then one of three alternatives will be preferred:

1. No special order is placed.
2. A special order is placed at time t_0.
3. A special order is placed at time t_1.

(If alternative 3 is chosen, then the regular order placed at time t_0 could be reduced so that no inventory is held immediately prior to time t_1. This would result in an additional savings in holding cost which is ignored here. See problem 3-8.) The procedure now becomes the following.

Step 1 Solve for Q^* using equation (3-21), with $t^* = t_1$. Call this Q_1^*. Repeat to find Q_0^* when $t^* = t_0$.
Step 2 Evaluate TS for $t^* = t_1$, using equation (3-20). Call this TS_1. Repeat to find TS_0 when $t^* = t_0$.

Step 3 If max $\{TS_0, TS_1 - k\} > 0$, place a special order as in step 4. Otherwise, place no special order.

Step 4 If $TS_0 \le TS_1 - k$, place the special order at time t_1. Otherwise, place it at time t_0.

Example 3-5 Demands for an item occur at a uniform rate of 9 units per month. It costs \$4 to place an order for more stock and \$0.10 per month per unit stored. Capital costs 1 percent per month. On January 1, it becomes known that a price increase of \$3 per unit will become effective April 1. The current price per unit is \$10. The inventory level is 5 units as of January 1. Determine the timing and quantity of a special order, if any, to be placed. Assume that all months are of equal length and that units of stock are infinitely divisible.

The conditions stated translate notationally to $d = 9$, $k = 4$, $h_s = 0.10$, $i = 0.01$, $c_0 = 10$, and $c_1 = 13$. Let January 1 be $t = 0$ and April 1 be $t = 3$. The *EOQ* prior to the price increase is given by $\sqrt{2kd/(h_s + ic_0)} = 8.09$. The current inventory will be depleted at $t = \frac{5}{9} = 0.56$. The time between orders is $8.09/9 = 0.9$ month. Therefore successive orders will be placed at $t = 1.46, 2.36, 3.26$, etc., if no special order is placed. Evidently $t_0 = 2.36$.

By equation (3-21)

$$Q^* = \frac{(13 - 10)9}{0.10 + (0.01)(10)} + \frac{0.10 + (0.01)(13)}{0.10 + (0.01)(10)} \sqrt{\frac{(2)(4)(9)}{0.10 + (0.01)(13)}} - y(t^*)$$

$$= 155.34 - y(t^*)$$

The inventory level at time t_1 is $y(t_1) = 8.09 - (3 - 2.36)9 = 2.33$, so $Q_1^* = 153$. Also $Q_0^* = 155.34 - 8.09 = 147.25$. Using equation (3-20), $TS_1 = 260$ and $TS_0 = 241$. Since $TS_0 \le TS_1 - k$, a special order of size $Q_1^* = 153$ should be placed at time t_1.

An approximation to the above procedure has been applied [4] to the purchase of prescription drugs. The approximation is to consider only the first term in equation (3-21) and to ignore the storage cost component h_s of the holding cost. Thus equation (3-21) becomes (the order is placed at time t_1):

$$Q_1^* = \frac{(c_1 - c_0)d}{ic_0} \tag{3-22}$$

This approximation has the interpretation that the time Q^*/d covered by the special order is equal to the ratio of the percentage price increase $[100(c_1 - c_0)/c_0]$ to the percentage cost of capital $[100(i)]$. The effectiveness of this approximation can be investigated. See problem 3-7.

3-3 STOCHASTIC MODELS

The models in this section differ from those in the previous section primarily in that they recognize uncertainties in future demand quantities. This uncertainty will be expressed in the form of a demand probability distribution. That is, the models in this section require as input probability distributions of demand during a specified time interval, rather than actual demand quantities.

The next subsection lays the groundwork for the two that follow it by developing the cost and demand notation and properties which apply to section 3-3.

A General Continuous-Review Stochastic Model Framework

The distinguishing feature of most stochastic models is that orders are not placed to satisfy specific, known future demands. Rather, orders are placed in response to a comparison of current inventory status (stock on hand and on order) with the prospects of an uncertain future. It follows that orders are not planned for future release. A "wait and see" philosophy is more prevalent. Ordering decisions are deferred until the latest conditions reveal that it would not be economic to delay order placement any longer.

The uncertainty in demands causes trouble during the *lead time*, or time between placement and receipt of an order. It is during the lead time that demand variations cause stockouts or higher stock levels than desired. If the lead time were zero, no order would be placed until the inventory level dropped to zero, so that demand uncertainties would be of no consequence. Thus stochastic models always assume a positive lead time L.

The models in this section assume that it is possible to state the probability distribution of demand over any specified period. In particular, since the lead time is the usual period of concern, attention will be paid to the distribution of demand during lead time, denoted by $f_L(u)$. Specifically, the probability that demand during time L is between a and b is

$$\int_a^b f_L(u)\, du$$

The probability that demand during the lead time does not exceed some quantity γ is given by the cumulative distribution function $F_L(\gamma)$:

$$F_L(\gamma) = \int_0^\gamma f_L(u)\, du \qquad u \geq 0$$

These probability distributions are assumed to be independent both of the time at which an order is placed and of the inventory level. The average demand per unit time is assumed to be $\bar{d}$, so that the average demand during the lead time is $\bar{d}L$. Of course, this would be obtainable as an expected value from the probability distribution of demand:

$$\bar{d}L = \int_0^\infty u f_L(u) \, du \tag{3-23}$$

If the inventory level at the time an order is placed is s, then the average depletion of $\bar{d}L$ during the lead time would result in an average ending inventory of $s - \bar{d}L$. However, this does not account for the random variation in demand. If orders are repeatedly placed when the inventory level is s, then demand during the lead time will result sometimes in a (positive) residual inventory and sometimes in a shortage. Define $\bar{y}(s)$ as the average residual inventory when the initial inventory level s is depleted by demand during the lead time. Also, let $\bar{b}(s)$ be the average shortage under the same conditions. Then

$$\bar{y}(s) = \int_0^s (s - u) f_L(u) \, du \tag{3-24}$$

and

$$\bar{b}(s) = \int_s^\infty (u - s) f_L(u) \, du \tag{3-25}$$

If a discrete probability distribution is used, the integrals in equations (3-23) to (3-25) would be replaced by sums, as would all integrals in this section.

It is easy to show algebraically (see problem 3-9) that

$$\bar{y}(s) = s - \bar{d}L + \bar{b}(s) \tag{3-26}$$

The reader should pause to ascertain that equation (3-26) makes sense for the special cases $\bar{b}(s) = 0$, $\bar{y}(s) = 0$, and $s - \bar{d}L = 0$.

Unless otherwise stated, the following cost assumptions apply throughout this section. The holding cost is h per unit time per unit of stock held and is assessed on average inventory. The shortage cost is π per unit short. That is, if a shortage occurs, the cost is assumed to be π times the amount of the shortage. This implies that the shortage cost is assessed immediately before receipt of an order.

The next two subsections are distinct in that the first assumes that there is no cost associated with placing an order, while the second assumes an ordering cost k.

The revenue contribution $(r - c)$ per unit of stock sold is the difference between the selling price (r) and the cost (c) per unit.

Models Not Recognizing an Ordering Cost

If the cost of placing and receiving orders is negligible compared with other costs, then it is appropriate to order whenever any demand occurs. The combined holding and shortage costs can then be minimized. The model developed in this subsection assumes that a *base stock policy*, as defined in section 3-1, is used. Recall that this policy is to order (replenish) stock up to a level S whenever any demand (depletion) occurs. The value of S which minimizes TEC, the total expected holding and shortage costs per unit time, is sought.

The average residual inventory $\bar{y}(S)$ and the average shortage $\bar{b}(S)$ are given by equations (3-24) and (3-25) with s replaced by S:

$$\bar{y}(S) = \int_0^S (S - u) f_L(u)\, du \qquad (3\text{-}27)$$

$$\bar{b}(S) = \int_S^\infty (u - S) f_L(u)\, du \qquad (3\text{-}28)$$

In this case, the average inventory is synonymous with the average residual inventory. Therefore, the total expected cost per unit time is

$$TEC(S) = h\bar{y}(S) + \pi \frac{\bar{d}}{Q} \bar{b}(S) \qquad (3\text{-}29)$$

where $\bar{d}/Q$ is the number of orders placed per unit time, justified as follows. The average order size (number of units demanded per demand incident) is Q, and $\bar{d}$ is the average demand per unit time.

To find the value of S which minimizes $TEC(S)$, the latter is differentiated with respect to S and set equal to zero. Before this is done, equation (3-26) is used to eliminate $\bar{b}(s)$ from equation (3-29):

$$TEC(S) = h\bar{y}(S) + \pi \frac{\bar{d}}{Q} [\bar{y}(S) + \bar{d}L - s]$$

Differentiating with respect to S,

$$\frac{\partial TEC(S)}{\partial S} = 0 = \left(h + \pi \frac{\bar{d}}{Q}\right) \frac{\partial \bar{y}(S)}{\partial S} - \pi \frac{\bar{d}}{Q} \qquad (3\text{-}30)$$

Evaluation of the partial derivative $\partial \bar{y}(S)/\partial S$ in equation (3-30) involves differentiation of an indefinite integral. The general relationship governing this operation is usually treated at an advanced calculus level. The relationship is stated here without proof. A proof appears on pages 219 and 220 in [1]. For bounded, continuous functions $p(s)$, $q(s)$, and $g(s, y)$:

$$\frac{\partial}{\partial s} \int_{p(s)}^{q(s)} g(s, y)\, dy = \int_{p(s)}^{q(s)} \frac{\partial}{\partial s} g(s, y)\, dy - g(s, p(s)) \frac{\partial p(s)}{\partial s} + g(s, q(s)) \frac{\partial q(s)}{\partial s}$$

$$(3\text{-}31)$$

Applying equation (3-31) to our problem gives

$$\frac{\partial \bar{y}(S)}{\partial S} = \frac{\partial}{\partial S}\int_0^S (S-u)f_L(u)\,du$$

$$= \int_0^S f_L(u)\,du = F_L(S) \qquad (3\text{-}32)$$

Substitution of this result into equation (3-30) yields

$$0 = \left(h + \pi\frac{\bar{d}}{Q}\right)F_L(S) - \pi\frac{\bar{d}}{Q}$$

which rearranges to the key result of this subsection:

$$F_L(S) = \frac{\pi\bar{d}/Q}{\pi\bar{d}/Q + h} \qquad (3\text{-}33)$$

The following example illustrates the use of the base stock policy.

Example 3-6 Orders for an item are received one week after they are placed. Demand during this lead time is normally distributed with mean 8 and standard deviation 3. The average order size is 1 unit. The holding cost is $1 per unit held per week. The shortage cost is $10 per unit of demand not satisfied on time. Find the appropriate value of S for a base stock policy.

From the problem statement, $L = 1$, $h = 1$, $\pi = 10$, $\bar{d} = 8$, and $Q = 1$. From equation (3-33), $F_L(S) = 80/81 = 0.9877$. By using the table in appendix A, Prob $[Z \leq 2.25] = 0.9877$, where Z is normally distributed with mean 0 and standard deviation 1. Therefore $S = 8 + (2.25)3 = 14.75$. Rounding off yields $S = 15$. Thus the base stock level is 15. Every time demand occurs, an order is placed to replenish the stock to this level.

Models Recognizing an Ordering Cost

In this subsection it is assumed that a cost k is incurred every time an order is placed. The (s, Q) policy is assumed. Recall that under this policy an order for Q is placed whenever the stock level falls below s. Values of Q and s are sought which minimize the expected cost per unit time. Two models are developed. The first model assumes that unsatisfied demand is backlogged; the second treats the case where all shortages result in lost sales.

As in the previous subsection, the holding cost is assessed on the average inventory level, while the shortage cost is charged against the average shortage immediately prior to receipt of an order. This shortage was given by

60 PART II: INVENTORY CONTROL MODELS

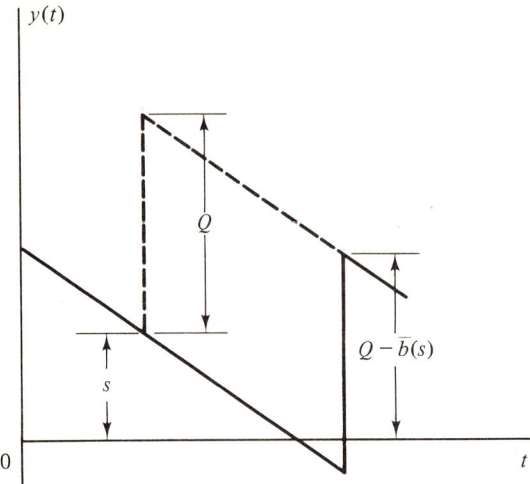

Figure 3-6 An inventory-time plot showing the amount added to stock when the average shortage $\bar{b}(s)$ occurs, and unsatisfied demand is backlogged.

equation (3-25). The average inventory is difficult to determine precisely and will be approximated for each model.

Consider first the case in which all unsatisfied demand is backlogged. The average inventory depends on both Q and s and will be designated $\bar{y}(Q, s)$. The approximation made here will be that $\bar{y}(Q, s)$ is equal to the expected residual inventory $\bar{y}(s)$ plus one-half of the average amount added to the inventory when an order is received. In referring to figure 3-6, it is seen that the average addition to inventory is $Q - \bar{b}(s)$. Therefore

$$\bar{y}(Q, s) = \bar{y}(s) + \tfrac{1}{2}[Q - \bar{b}(s)] \tag{3-34}$$

The total expected cost TEC per unit time can then be expressed as

$$TEC = \frac{k\bar{d}}{Q} + h\bar{y}(Q, s) + \pi \frac{\bar{d}}{Q} \bar{b}(s) \tag{3-35}$$

The penalty cost term is based on the fact that the cost $\pi \bar{b}(s)$ is incurred once each cycle of duration $Q/\bar{d}$. That is, the cost recurs at the rate of $\bar{d}/Q$ times per unit time.

By substituting for $\bar{y}(Q, s)$ from equation (3-34) and using equation (3-26) to eliminate $\bar{b}(s)$, equation (3-25) becomes

$$TEC = \frac{k\bar{d}}{Q} + \frac{hQ}{2} + \left(\frac{h}{2} + \frac{\pi \bar{d}}{Q}\right)\bar{y}(s) + \left(\frac{h}{2} - \frac{\pi \bar{d}}{Q}\right)(s - \bar{d}L) \tag{3-36}$$

The values of Q and s which minimize TEC are determined by differentiating equation (3-37) with respect to Q and s, equating to zero, and solving for the two unknowns. Differentiating with respect to Q gives

$$\frac{\partial TEC}{\partial Q} = \frac{h}{2} - \frac{k + \pi[\bar{y}(s) - s + \bar{d}L]\bar{d}}{Q^2} = 0$$

By using equation (3-26), this becomes

$$\frac{h}{2} - \frac{[k + \pi\bar{b}(s)]\bar{d}}{Q^2} = 0$$

which solves to yield

$$Q = \sqrt{\frac{2[k + \pi\bar{b}(s)]\bar{d}}{h}} \tag{3-37}$$

The reader should note the similarity between this value of Q and the classic EOQ value $Q = \sqrt{2k\bar{d}/h}$. It is as if the penalty cost $\pi\bar{b}(s)$ incurred each cycle were part of the ordering cost.

Differentiating with respect to s gives

$$\frac{\partial TEC}{\partial s} = \left(\frac{h}{2} + \frac{\pi\bar{d}}{Q}\right)\frac{\partial \bar{y}(s)}{\partial s} + \frac{h}{2} - \frac{\pi\bar{d}}{Q} = 0$$

From equation (3-32) (with S replaced by s), $\partial\bar{y}(s)/\partial s = F_L(s)$. So this becomes, after rearranging,

$$F_L(s) = \frac{\pi\bar{d}/Q - h/2}{\pi\bar{d}/Q + h/2} \tag{3-38}$$

The reader can pause to interpret equation (3-38) for the special cases $h = 0$ and $h/2 = \pi\bar{d}/Q$.

Anyone who researches the development of stochastic inventory models will discover that, for the same (s, Q) policy and the same cost assumptions, some authors obtain a result which varies from that of equation (3-38). The difference is likely to be due to the approximation made for $\bar{y}(Q, s)$. For example, see problem 3-13 and [3] and [5].

The solution procedure involves repeatedly cycling back and forth between equations (3-37) and (3-38) as follows:

Step 1 Assume $\bar{b}(s) = 0$. Solve for Q in equation (3-37).
Step 2 With the most recent value of Q, solve for s in equation (3-38).
Step 3 With the most recent value of s, solve for Q in equation (3-37).
Step 4 Return to step 2 unless two successive values of Q are sufficiently close together that further iterations would not result in any appreciable improvement.

PART II: INVENTORY CONTROL MODELS

Example 3-7 Suppose that the conditions of example 3-6 are in effect, except that now a cost of $8 is incurred every time an order is placed. Determine the appropriate values of s and Q for an (s, Q) policy.

From example 3-6, $L = 1$, $h = 1$, $\pi = 10$, $\bar{d} = 8$, and demand during the lead time is normally distributed with mean 8 and standard deviation 3 units. In addition, k now equals 8. Solving equation (3-37) with $\bar{b}(s) = 0$ gives

$$Q = \sqrt{\frac{2 \cdot 8 \cdot 8}{1}} = 11.31$$

Equation (3-38) then becomes

$$F_L(s) = \frac{10(8)/11.31 - 0.5}{10(8)/11.31 + 0.5} = 0.868$$

From appendix A, Prob $[Z \leq 1.1] = 0.868$, where Z is normally distributed with mean 0 and standard deviation 1. Therefore $s = 8 + 3(1.1) = 11.3$. Returning to equation (3-37), it is seen that it is necessary to calculate $\bar{b}(s)$. From equation (3-25),

$$\bar{b}(s) = \int_s^\infty (u - s) f_L(u) \, du$$

Since $f_L(u)$ is the normal probability density with mean μ and standard deviation σ, this becomes

$$\bar{b}(s) = \int_s^\infty (u - s) \frac{1}{\sigma\sqrt{2\pi}} e^{-[(u-\mu)/(2\sigma)]^2} \, du \qquad (3\text{-}39)$$

This integral can be evaluated by converting it to a standardized normal loss integral $I(\gamma)$ given by

$$I(\gamma) = \int_\gamma^\infty (u - \gamma) \frac{1}{\sqrt{2\pi}} e^{-u^2/2} \, du$$

Values of $I(\gamma)$ are tabulated in appendix B. The conversion of equation (3-39) is

$$\bar{b}(s) = \sigma I\left(\frac{s - \mu}{\sigma}\right) \qquad (3\text{-}40)$$

For this example this becomes (using appendix B)

$$\bar{b}(11.3) = 3I\left(\frac{11.3 - 8}{3}\right) = 3I(1.1) = 3(0.0686) = 0.2058$$

Returning then to equation (3-37), $Q = 12.7$. By equation (3-38), $F_L(s) = 0.872$ from which $s = 11.4$. Returning again to equation (3-37),

$Q = 12.6$. Since this is not significantly different from the previously obtained value of Q, the process is terminated with $Q = 12.6$ and $s = 11.4$. This translates into $(s, Q) = (12, 13)$, a policy under which 13 units are ordered whenever the stock level falls below 12 (that is, 11 or less).

The second model to be developed in this subsection treats the case in which all demand which cannot be satisfied is lost rather than backlogged. The development of the model parallels closely that of the backlog model.

The average inventory was defined earlier as being approximately equal to the average minimum inventory level plus one-half the average amount added to the inventory. In the lost-sales case, the addition to inventory is always Q, and so the average inventory level is

$$\bar{y}(Q, s) = \bar{y}(s) + \frac{Q}{2} \tag{3-41}$$

The total expected cost per unit time is then

$$TEC = \frac{k\bar{d}}{Q} + h\bar{y}(s, Q) + (\pi + r - c)\bar{b}(s)\frac{\bar{d}}{Q} \tag{3-42}$$

where the shortage cost $(\pi + r - c)$ includes the lost revenue contribution $r - c$. Equation (3-42) assumes that the order frequency is $\bar{d}/Q$, which is a simplification. This is because the effective demand rate is reduced to $\bar{d} - \bar{b}(s)/L$ because of lost sales, so that the order frequency is actually $[\bar{d} - \bar{b}(s)/L]/Q$.

Differentiating TEC with respect to Q, equating to zero, and solving for Q yields

$$Q = \sqrt{\frac{2[k + (\pi + r - c)\bar{b}(s)]\bar{d}}{h}} \tag{3-43}$$

By proceeding in the same way as for the backlog case, solving the equation $\partial TEC/\partial s = 0$ for s yields

$$F_L(s) = \frac{(\pi + r - c)\bar{d}/Q}{(\pi + r - c)\bar{d}/Q + h} \tag{3-44}$$

The reader should pause to interpret equation (3-44) for the special case $h = 0$.

The solution procedure involves repeatedly cycling back and forth between equations (3-43) and (3-44) as follows:

Step 1 Assume $\bar{b}(s) = 0$. Solve for Q in equation (3-43).

Step 2 With the most recent value of Q, solve for s in equation (3-44).

Step 3 With the most recent value of s, solve for Q in equation (3-43).
Step 4 Return to step 2 unless two successive values of Q are sufficiently close together that further iterations will not result in any appreciable improvement.

Example 3-8 Suppose the conditions of example 3-7 are in effect, except that all shortages result in lost sales. The revenue per unit is $70, and the cost per unit is $63. Determine the values of s and Q in this case.

From example 3-7, the demand during the lead time of one week is normally distributed with mean 8 and standard deviation 3 units. Thus $\bar{d} = 8$ and $L = 1$. Also, $h = 1$, $\pi = 10$, and $k = 8$. In addition, $r = 70$ and $c = 63$. Solving equation (3-43) with $\bar{b}(s) = 0$ yields $Q = 11.31$. Then, by equation (3-44), $F_L(s) = 0.923$. From appendix A, Prob $[Z \leq 1.43] = 0.923$, where Z is normally distributed with mean 0 and standard deviation 1. Therefore $s = 8 + 3(1.43) = 12.3$. Proceeding exactly as in example 3-7, we get

$$\bar{b}(12.3) = 3I\left(\frac{12.3 - 8}{3}\right) = 3I(1.43) = 3(0.0343) = 0.103$$

Solving equation (3-43) with $\bar{b}(s) = 0.103$ gives $Q = 12.5$. Returning to equation (3-44), $F_L(s) = 0.916$, from which $s = 12.1$. Then $\bar{b}(12.1) = 0.12$ and, from equation (3-43), $Q = 12.7$. Since Q has not significantly changed, the procedure terminates with $(s, Q) = (13, 13)$. Comparing this solution with that of example 3-7 shows that in the lost-sales case, s has increased from 12 to 13. This affords a slightly higher protection against stockouts, which is consistent with the fact that the penalty per unit shortage has been increased by the revenue contribution $r - c$.

The backlog case and the lost-sales case developed above represent two extreme consequences of shortages. In practical situations, it is likely that some fraction a, $0 \leq a \leq 1$, of shortages will be backlogged, so that $1 - a$ of the shortages will convert to lost sales. It turns out that the values of Q and s which minimize TEC in this case can be found as a linear interpolation of the values for the two extreme cases. Specifically, the minimal cost values of Q and s when a fraction a of shortages is backlogged are the solution to

$$Q = \sqrt{\frac{2\{k + [\pi + (1-a)(r-c)]\bar{b}(s)\}\bar{d}}{h}} \tag{3-45}$$

and

$$F_L(s) = \frac{[\pi + (1-a)(r-c)]\bar{d}/Q - ha/2}{[\pi + (1-a)(r-c)]\bar{d}/Q + h - ha/2} \tag{3-46}$$

The reader can readily verify that equation (3-45) reduces to equation (3-37) if $a = 1$ and to equation (3-43) if $a = 0$. Similarly, equation (3-46) reverts to equation (3-38) for $a = 1$ and to equation (3-44) for $a = 0$. The optimality of this linear interpolation is demonstrated in [3]. [Their version of equation (3-37), and therefore also of equation (3-46), differs from the ones above because of their slightly different approximation for $\bar{y}(Q, s)$. Their equation for Q is identical to equation (3-45).] They also show that the same interpolation can be made in the periodic-review case, which is the subject of the next chapter.

3-4 SUMMARY

Single-item models recognizing continuous-review ordering policies have been developed in this chapter. Two types of policies have been stressed. In the lot-size reorder-point policy an order for Q is placed when the stock level falls below s. This type of policy applies in the presence of an ordering cost k ($k > 0$). The base stock policy calls for ordering up to a level S whenever demands reduce the stock level below S. This policy is appropriate in the absence of an ordering cost ($k = 0$). Base stock policies are easily determined in the probabilistic case and trivial in the deterministic case.

Lot-size reorder-point policies are considered separately for deterministic and for probabilistic demand. The deterministic case is subdivided into a constant price, variable demand rate case and three variable price, constant demand rate cases. (The constant price, constant demand rate case was treated in chapter 2.) The variable price cases model the all-units quantity discount, the incremental quantity discount, and the imminent price increase. In these four cases lead times are taken to be zero and shortages are not permitted so that s is zero. Models for determining the minimal cost value of Q in each case are developed.

In the case of probabilistic demand, it is assumed that a fraction a of all shortages is backlogged. The lost-sales case ($a = 0$) and the pure backlog case ($a = 1$) represent the two extreme situations. For each of these situations an iterative scheme is used to find the least cost values of the parameters Q and s. It is then pointed out that a similar scheme could be used for any value of a between 0 and 1.

REFERENCES

1. Apostol, Tom M.: "Mathematical Analysis," Addison-Wesley, Reading, Mass., 1957.
2. Hadley, George, and T. M. Whitin: "Analysis of Inventory Systems," Prentice-Hall, Englewood Cliffs, N.J., 1963, chapters 2 and 4.

3. Montgomery, Douglas C.; M. S. Bazaraa; and A. K. Keswani: "Inventory Models with a Mixture of Backorders and Lost Sales," *Naval Research Logistics Quarterly*, vol. 20, no. 2, pp. 255–263, June 1973.
4. Myers, John E.; R. E. Johnson; D. Egan; and H. J. Schleef: "Determining Optimal Drug Purchase Quantities under Conditions of Increasing Prices," *American Journal of Hospital Pharmacy*, vol. 29, pp. 1035–1040, December 1972.
5. Wagner, Harvey M.: "Principles of Operations Research with Applications to Managerial Decisions," Prentice-Hall, Englewood Cliffs, N.J., 1969.

EXERCISES

3-1 Consider an item which will have a constant demand rate of 30 units per week for 40 continuous weeks. You are using continuous review. It costs you $10 to place an order and $0.20 per week per unit held in stock. You have 50 units in stock at present. Determine when and how much to order. Assume that you must have no inventory at the end of week 40 and that shortages are not allowed.

3-2 Suppose $d(t) = 1$ for t less than 2 and $d(t) = 0.5$ for t between 2 and 5. For the planning horizon $[0, T] = [0, 5]$, find the minimum cost timing of orders, given that exactly two orders must be placed. Assume no initial inventory. The holding cost is $1 per unit per time period. Show that the necessary conditions [equation (3-7)] for a minimum cost solution has two solutions in this case. Evaluate costs for both solutions.

3-3 Verify the results given for $n = 2$ and $n = 4$ in example 3-2.

3-4 Demands for a certain product occur steadily at the rate of 5 units per month. It costs $8 to place an order for stock. Storage space costs $2 per year per unit of stock. Capital costs amount to $1 per year for each unit of stock on hand. The material costs are $0.80 per unit if 19 or fewer are ordered and $0.70 per unit if more than 19 are ordered.

(*a*) Determine the minimum-cost order quantity.

(*b*) If shortages are permitted and it costs $1 per unit of unsatisfied demand per month (unsatisfied demand is backlogged), what is the ordering policy which minimizes costs per month? (Find the order quantity and the stock level just before an order is placed.) *Hint:* Equation (2-33) may be helpful.

3-5 Demands for a product occur at a uniform rate of 10 units per month. It costs $5 to place an order. Inventory costs amount to $3 per year per unit of stock. There are three possible suppliers of the product you are ordering. Their costs per unit of product are given as follows. Supplier A: $1 per unit for orders of 14 or less, $0.90 per unit for orders of 15 to 29, and $0.80 per unit for orders of 30 or more. Supplier B: $1 per unit for the first 15 units and $0.80 for each additional unit. Supplier C: $0.85 per unit regardless of the quantity ordered. From which supplier would you order, and what is the most economical order quantity?

3-6 You require 100 units per week of an item which costs $1 per unit. Capital cost is negligible, but storage costs are estimated to be 26 percent per year. It costs $18 to place an order. Your current inventory is 300 units. An impending price increase will change the material cost to $1.20 per unit. What is your response if this increase is to take place in one week? In four weeks?

3-7 Repeat example 3-5 using equation (3-22) in place of equation (3-21). What difference in total savings results?

3-8 (*a*) Derive the holding cost savings if a special order is placed at time t_1 in advance of a price increase and the order placed at time t_0 is decreased so that no inventory is held prior to the placement of the order at time t_1.

(*b*) Apply this to example 3-5. That is, add the holding cost savings from part (*a*) to TS_1. Does this affect the result previously obtained in example 3-5?

3-9 Use equations (3-23), (3-24), and (3-25) to show that

$$\bar{y}(s) = s - \bar{d}L + \bar{b}(s).$$

3-10 Demand during a lead time of two weeks is normally distributed with mean 20 and standard deviation 4. The average demand order size is 1 unit. The holding cost is $3 per unit held per week. The penalty for incurring a shortage is $18 per unit of demand not satisfied on time. Find the appropriate value of S for a base stock policy.

3-11 Assume the conditions of problem 3-10. Suppose that a cost of $20 per order placed is incurred. A fraction a of all shortages is backlogged; the remainder results in lost sales, for which the lost-revenue contribution is $25 per unit; however, the penalty of $18 per unit does *not* apply in the lost-sales case. Determine the appropriate (s, Q) policy for

(*a*) $a = 1$
(*b*) $a = 0$
(*c*) $a = 0.5$

3-12 Demand during a one-week lead time is uniformly distributed between 8 and 12 units. The average demand order size is 1 unit. The holding cost is $0.40 per unit per week. There is a penalty cost of $2 per unit of demand which occurs during a stockout period. Additionally, if sales are lost, there is a cost of $1.50 per unit which represents lost profit on these sales. A fraction a of all shortages are backlogged. It costs k per order placed. Determine the parameters of an (S) policy or an (S, Q) policy, whichever is appropriate, in the following cases:

(*a*) $k = 0$, $a = 1$
(*b*) $k = 3$, $a = 1$

(c) $k = 3, a = 0$
(d) $k = 3, a = \frac{1}{4}$

3-13 Show for the (s, Q) policy that if $\bar{y}(Q, s)$ is assumed to be $Q/2 + s - \bar{d}L$, instead of the assumption in equation (3-34), then equation (3-38) no longer follows, but instead

$$F_L(s) = \frac{\pi \bar{d}/Q - h}{\pi \bar{d}/Q}$$

3-14 Show that the integral in equation (3-39) can be converted to the equation for $I(y)$ which immediately follows it. *Hint:* Let $v = (u - \mu)/\sigma$ so that $dv = du/\sigma$.

CHAPTER
FOUR
PERIODIC-REVIEW ORDERING DECISION MODELS

The distinguishing feature between this chapter and the preceding one is that all positive actions with respect to inventory are taken periodically. In fact, it will be assumed throughout this chapter that such actions take place at the beginning of each of a number of time periods of equal length. At these times, it is assumed that the knowledge necessary to make a control decision is available. Thus, the inventory status (amount on hand and on order) together with forecast and cost information is reviewed, after which an order may or may not be placed.

As in the preceding chapter, the decision to order relates to a single item (stock-keeping unit) stored at a single stocking point. Extension to multiple items or multiple stocking points is considered in chapters 5 and 6. Most of the various cost and inventory behavior situations encountered in chapter 3 will be treated in this chapter also. The organization of this chapter resembles that of chapter 3, being subdivided primarily according to two model characteristics which can be chosen by the decision maker. The primary division is again between deterministic and probabilistic models. Given either of these model types, the next most important distinction is whether to recognize an ordering cost in the model. Before any models are developed, it is helpful to consider some of the forms which a periodic ordering policy can assume. Each model developed in the chapter is based on such an ordering policy.

4-1 PERIODIC ORDERING POLICIES

The majority of periodic ordering policies used in practice are of two basic types. In one type, the quantity ordered brings the inventory (on hand plus on order) exactly to a specified level, while the other type restricts the quantity ordered to be a multiple of a fixed quantity Q. An example of the first type is an (s, S) policy. To be specific, define y_k as the inventory level on hand plus on order at the end of period k and x_k as the amount ordered at the beginning of period k, for any k. Then under an (s, S) policy,

$$x_k = \begin{cases} S - y_{k-1} & \text{if } y_{k-1} < s \\ 0 & \text{if } y_{k-1} \geq s \end{cases}$$

The (s, S) policy is sometimes called an *optional replenishment policy*, since an order is not necessarily placed every review period. A special case of this policy is one for which $s = S$, and it may be denoted as an (S) *policy* and called an *order-up-to-S policy*. In this case, an order would be placed whenever there has been any demand during the preceding period. The use of the (s, S) policy (which implies $s < S$) avoids incurrence of ordering costs for small quantities of stock, and hence is preferred to the (S) policy if the cost of placing an order is significantly large.

An example of the second type of policy can be referred to as the (s, Q, S) *policy*. Under this policy, the quantity ordered is the smallest integer multiple of Q which will bring the inventory level up to at least S. Again, an order is placed only if the inventory level before ordering is less than s. Thus the amount ordered at the beginning of period k is

$$x_k = \begin{cases} nQ & \text{for } y_{k-1} < s \text{ and } S - nQ \leq y_{k-1} < S - (n-1)Q \\ 0 & \text{for } y_{k-1} \geq s \end{cases}$$

The (s, Q, S) policy would be used, for example, where the customary shipping unit (e.g., rail car or package) will hold Q stock units. Of course, for discrete items the special case $Q = 1$ reduces to an (s, S) policy.

All the above policies assume that the length T of each period is already specified. Many times it will be, because of the natural tendency for recurrent activities to be timed to coincide with natural time spans such as weeks, months, or fiscal periods. In fact, if this is the case, then for simplicity a time scale may be chosen so that $T = 1$ time unit. If T is not already specified, then the choice of T can become part of the policy. Thus, for example, if an (s, S) policy is to be used and the choice of T is at the discretion of the decision maker, then T becomes a parameter and the policy can be denoted as an (s, S, T) *policy*. Likewise, an (S) or an (s, Q, S) policy becomes, respectively, an (S, T) or an (s, Q, S, T) policy. The reader interested in policies involving the choice of T is referred to chapter 5, where multi-item decisions are considered, and to [1].

Table 3-1 Solutions and costs for example 3-2

Solution	t_1	t_2	t_3	t_4	HC	OC	TC
Approximate ($n = 3$)	3.00	5.78	8.56	—	$43.28	$30	$73.28
Optimal for $n = 3$	3.00	5.33	7.67	—	40.95	30	70.95
Optimal for $n = 2$	3.00	6.50	—	—	74.40	20	94.40
Optimal for $n = 4$	3.00	5.00	6.67	8.33	33.15	40	73.15

Models Recognizing No Ordering Cost

In a deterministic, continuous-review situation in the absence of ordering costs, no model can improve on the following rule of thumb: Order to exactly satisfy each demand as it occurs, thereby incurring no costs whatsoever.

Discounted Price Models

In this subsection, three types of price discounting will be modeled. The first two types reflect discounts based on the quantity ordered, while the third treats a discount based on timing of orders. All three types occur in practice regularly.

The following conditions are assumed to exist throughout this subsection. Demands occur at a constant rate d per unit of time, and no shortages are permitted to occur. An order for any quantity Q may be placed at any time at a cost k. The material cost per unit is designated as c, where c will be defined to reflect each of the three types of discount. The holding cost per unit held per unit time h will be assumed to consist of a component ic which depends on both the material cost (e.g., a cost of capital) and a component h_s which is independent of the material cost (e.g., a storage cost). Thus $h = h_s + ic$.

The first discounted price model to be considered is called the *all-units quantity discount* model. For this model, the material cost is defined as follows:

$$c = \begin{cases} c_0 & \text{for } 0 \equiv m_0 \leq Q < m_1 \\ c_1 & \text{for } m_1 \leq Q < m_2 \\ \vdots & \\ c_J & \text{for } m_J \leq Q \end{cases} \quad (3\text{-}10)$$

The discounted prices obey the relationship $c_0 > c_1 > \cdots > c_J$. The numbers $m_0, m_1, \ldots, m_J$ are assumed given and are called *breakpoints*. It is seen that the discount given for order quantities in excess of a breakpoint applies to all units in the order.

The problem is to find Q^*, the minimum-cost value of Q. To do this, the

CHAPTER 4: PERIODIC-REVIEW ORDERING DECISION MODELS 71

This chapter emphasizes ordering policies which do not restrict the order quantity to be a multiple of some fixed quantity Q. Thus policies such as the (S) and the (s, S) are stressed. It is possible (though not necessarily "optimal") to round off order quantities obtained, using these policies to the nearest multiple of Q if necessary. Determinations of the values of the parameters s and S are made on the basis of costs in the sections which follow.

4-2 DETERMINISTIC MODELS

The models in this section are based on the assumption that demands d_t are "known" for each future period $t = 1, 2, \ldots, n$ up through a planning horizon of n periods. In fact, demands may not be known, in which case demand estimates are used as model input in place of actual future demands. One can logically argue that the future is never really known with certainty, so that deterministic models do not reflect reality. The counterargument is that no model reflects the real world perfectly. What is sought is a model which reflects reality well enough to provide meaningful help to the decision maker, while not being so complicated as to be impractical. Deterministic models often fit this description, particularly if the (random) demand variation is small compared with the typical magnitude of demand.

Notation and Mathematical Background

In this subsection, the notation and mathematics for a fairly general situation will be developed. This will provide a perspective helpful in relating models in succeeding subsections.

Given known demands d_t for n future time periods $(t = 1, 2, \ldots, n)$, the problem is to determine an ordering schedule $x_t, t = 1, 2, \ldots, n$, indicating how much to order at the beginning of each period. The resulting inventory level at the end of period t will be denoted by y_t and is given by

$$y_t = y_0 + \sum_{j=1}^{t} (x_j - d_j) \qquad t = 1, 2, \ldots, n \qquad (4\text{-}1)$$

where y_0 is the initial (end-of-period-zero) inventory. Equation (4-1) implies that unsatisfied demand is backlogged rather than lost, which is the assumption made here unless otherwise indicated. When a backlog exists, equation (4-1) gives a negative value of y_t. In this section the amount of backlogged demand will be indicated by z_t. Thus if equation (4-1) yields a negative value of y_t, then y_t will be considered to have zero value and z_t will have a positive value equal to the quantity of backlogged demand. There is no loss of generality if y_0 is assumed to be zero since if $y_0 \neq 0, d_1$ can be reduced by y_0. Also, there is no loss of generality if the lead time between the placing and

Table 4-1 Example 4-1: An ordering schedule with associated inventory and shortage effects

t	1	2	3	4
d_t	3	2	5	6
x_t	8	0	0	8
y_t	5	3	0	0
z_t	0	0	2	0

receiving of an order is zero when demands are assumed known. The demand for period k in the model will be the demand occurring in the time interval $(k + L, k + 1 + L)$.

Example 4-1 The above situation will be visually represented in two ways. As an example suppose $n = 4$ and the situation in table 4-1 exists. One graphic equivalent of this situation appears in figure 4-1 as an inventory-time plot. The inventory level is drawn as if the demand is infinitely divisible and occurs continuously. This is done because it is an aid to visualization and because many models approximate inventory depletion in this manner. The other representation appears in figure 4-2. Notice that the demand for the entire planning horizon flows through

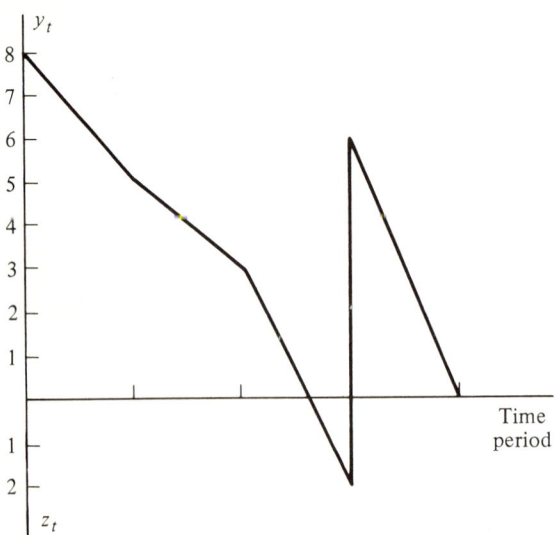

Figure 4-1 An inventory-time plot of the ordering schedule in table 4-1.

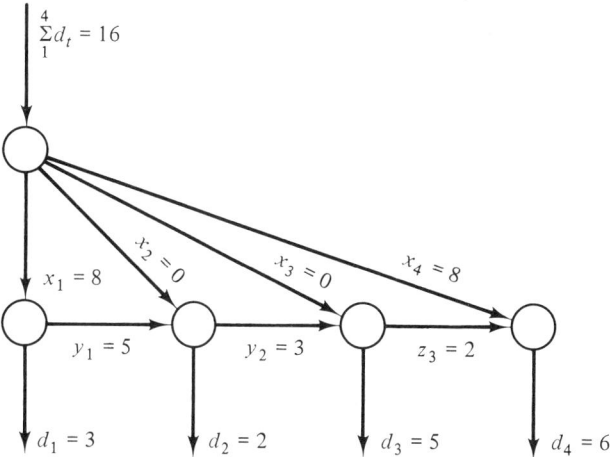

Figure 4-2 Network representation of the ordering schedule in table 4-1 and example 4-1.

the network from a single "source" to n ($= 4$) "sinks." Positive inventories ($y_t > 0$) flow to the right, while demand backlogs ($z_t > 0$) are satisfied by production in subsequent periods and are represented by flows to the left.

Associated with every ordering schedule $x = (x_1, \ldots, x_n)$ will be a cost $Z(x)$ of the form

$$Z(x) = \sum_{t=1}^{n} [c_t(x_t) + h_t(y_t) + p_t(z_t)] \qquad (4\text{-}2)$$

Here, $c_t(x_t)$ is the cost of ordering x_t units at the beginning of period t; $h_t(y_t)$ is the cost of holding y_t units in stock at the end of period t; and $p_t(z_t)$ is the cost of a backlog of z_t units at the end of period t. Use of this cost model implies that it is reasonable to assume that costs are *separable*, that is, that costs in any given period do not affect costs in any other period. The assumption may or may not be realistic, but it is made in the hope that the resulting ordering schedule comes close to minimizing the actual costs. The most important criterion is that three types of costs be recognized: ordering costs, holding costs, and penalty costs for shortages.

The behavior of the individual cost terms in equation (4-2) has a pronounced effect on the choice of an appropriate form of ordering policy. Most of the time, reality can be adequately reflected by model cost terms which are either concave or convex functions. A function $f(x)$ of a single variable x is *concave* if for any two values x' and x'' and any real number α, $0 \leq \alpha \leq 1$, the following relationship holds:

$$f[\alpha x' + (1-\alpha)x''] \geq \alpha f(x') + (1-\alpha)f(x'') \qquad (4\text{-}3)$$

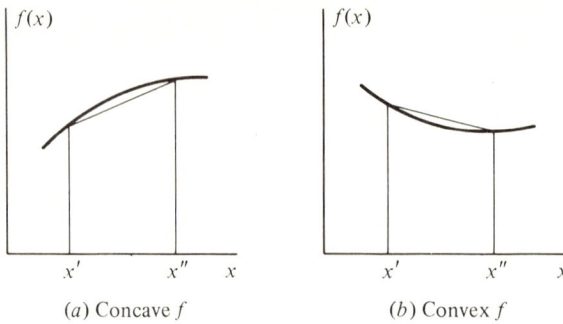

(a) Concave f (b) Convex f

Figure 4-3 Concave and convex functions.

Thus the value of a concave function never falls below a straight-line segment connecting any two points on the function. See figure 4-3(a). A function $f(x)$ is *convex* if the $\geq$ is replaced by $\leq$ in equation (4-3). Thus the value of a convex function never falls above a straight-line segment connecting any two points on the function. See figure 4-3(b). If a function f is concave, then $-f$ is convex. If f is a straight line, then f is both concave and convex.

In the context of inventory costs, consider the special case where it costs \$4 to place an order in any period; \$1 per unit ordered for the first 10 units ordered; \$0.80 per unit ordered in excess of 10 units; \$0.05 per unit held in inventory at the end of each period; and \$0.50 per unit of backlogged demand at the end of each period. This cost information is summarized as follows:

$$c_t(x_t) = \begin{cases} 0 & x_t = 0 \\ 4 + 1x_t & 0 < x_t \leq 10 \\ 14 + 0.08x_t & x_t > 10 \end{cases} \quad (4\text{-}4)$$

$$h_t(y_t) = 0.05 y_t \quad (4\text{-}5)$$

$$p_t(z_t) = 0.5 z_t \quad (4\text{-}6)$$

Now $h_t(y_t)$ and $p_t(z_t)$ are linear for $y_t \geq 0$ and $z_t \geq 0$, respectively. Hence, taken individually, both h_t and p_t are concave as well as convex. However, if one considers the functions $h_t(y_t)$ and $p_t(z_t)$ as two segments of one overall holding and penalty cost function $f_t(y_t)$ given by

$$f_t(y_t) = \begin{cases} h_t(y_t) & y_t \geq 0 \\ p_t(y_t) & y_t = -z_t < 0 \end{cases}$$

then $f_t(y_t)$ is convex but not concave. Figure 4-4(c), (d), and (e) illustrates these situations. If instead $p_t(z_t) = 0.5\sqrt{z_t}$, then p_t is still concave, but the combined holding and penalty cost is no longer convex.

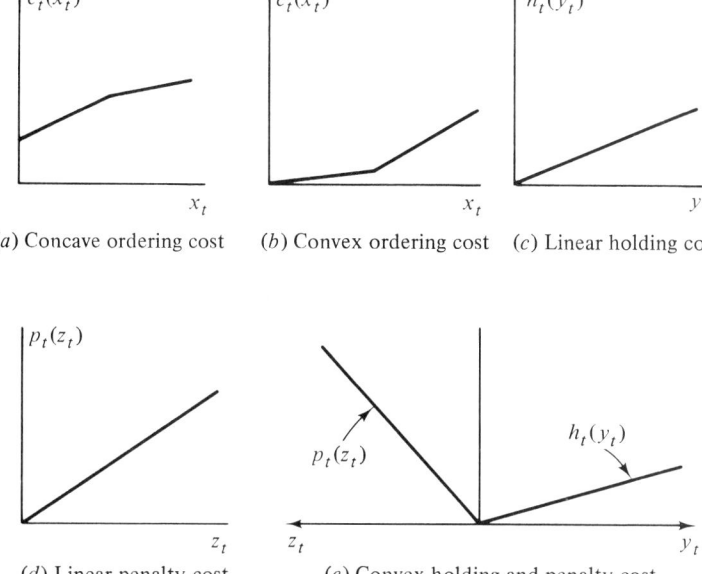

Figure 4-4 Typical concave and convex inventory cost functions.

The ordering cost defined by equation (4-4) is concave [see figure 4-4(a)]. It is possible that in another situation the ordering cost might be convex, as in figure 4-4(b). This could occur, say, if there were no fixed cost of placing an order such as the $4 cost in equation (4-4). In fact, it is usually the magnitude of the fixed cost of placing an order which leads one to choose one of the approaches in the next two subsections. The next subsection recognizes such a cost, while the following subsection assumes that it can be neglected.

Models Recognizing Concave Costs

The models in this subsection are designed to aid in making ordering decisions when the costs terms $c_t(x_t)$, $h_t(y_t)$, and $p_t(z_t)$ in equation (4-2) are each concave. Consider figure 4-5, which is a direct generalization of figure 4-2. The ordering schedule $(x_1, x_2, \ldots, x_n)$ is depicted as a flow through a network having a single source and multiple sinks, or destinations.

Thus, the problem of determining an ordering schedule $x = (x_1, \ldots, x_n)$ to minimize the cost

$$Z(x) = \sum_{t=1}^{n} [c_t(x_t) + h_t(y_t) + p_t(z_t)] \qquad (4\text{-}7)$$

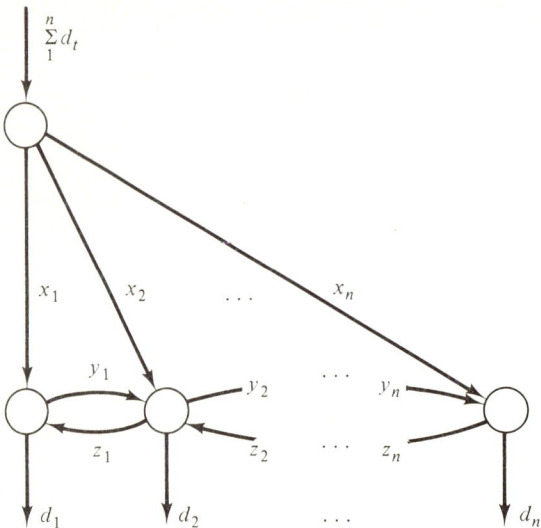

Figure 4-5 Representation of an ordering schedule as a flow through a network.

is equivalent to the problem of determining a flow through a network which minimizes the same costs. Each of the $3n$ cost terms in equation (4-7) is associated with one of the $3n$ arcs in the network. Each of these cost terms is a concave function. A network for which the cost associated with each arc is a concave function of the flow through that arc will be called a *concave-cost network*. The network in figure 4-5 fits this description.

A flow through a network with a single source is called an *extreme flow* if each node in the network has at most one positive inflow. Extreme flows are important because of the following property.

> **Theorem 4-1** For a concave-cost single-source network (in which there are no capacity constraints on arc flows) there exists a minimal cost flow which is an extreme flow.

Rather than rigorously proving this theorem (a proof appears in [7]), it will be demonstrated by example that from any nonextreme flow x there can be constructed extreme flows for at least one of which the total cost Z is no more than $Z(x)$. The construction is accomplished as follows. For the flow x, starting at the single source, trace the paths of positive flow until a node is reached which has two or more positive inflows (if the node has more than two positive inflows, consider only two of them; ignore the third for the time being). Make sure that the paths leading to the two inflows have not previously passed through any other node having two positive inflows. If

CHAPTER 4: PERIODIC-REVIEW ORDERING DECISION MODELS 77

there exists such a prior node, consider the prior node instead. Construct two flows $x^{(1)}$ and $x^{(2)}$ by alternately reducing each of the two positive inflows to zero. Then, in order to maintain conservation of flow, the flows along the two paths will have to be adjusted. This will decrease the flow along one path by the amount of a positive inflow to the node being considered and increase the flow along the other path by the same amount.

Example 4-1 (continued) Consider the example in figure 4-2. Evidently the flow $x = (8, 0, 0, 8)$ is not extreme since a node contains two positive inflows $y_2 = 3$ and $z_3 = 2$. Two flows $x^{(1)}$ and $x^{(2)}$ are generated from x by letting $y_2 = 0$ and $z_3 = 0$, respectively. Adjusting the other flow values to achieve conservation of flow results in the two flows $x^{(1)} = (5, 0, 0, 11)$ and $x^{(2)} = (10, 0, 0, 6)$. Now suppose the costs in equations (4-4) to (4-6) apply for each time period. Then the costs of the schedules x, $x^{(1)}$, and $x^{(2)}$ are tabulated as shown in table 4-2(a), (b), and (c). Note that the total cost of schedule $x^{(2)}$ is less than that of x.

By repeating the construction process as often as is necessary, a set of extreme flows can be generated from any nonextreme flow. Moreover, one or more of the extreme flows will have lower total cost than the original nonextreme flow. For the example above, the two flows $x^{(1)} = (5, 0, 0, 11)$ and $x^{(2)} = (10, 0, 0, 6)$ both happen to be extreme flows, so the construction process terminates. (If you are unsure that, say, $x^{(1)}$ is an extreme flow, draw a network for $x^{(1)}$ like the one in figure 4-2 and satisfy yourself that no node contains more than one positive inflow.)

The important consequence of theorem 4-1 is that in a search for the optimal ordering schedule, only extreme flows need be considered. Now extreme flows have the following properties.

Table 4-2 Costs for a nonextreme flow x and two extreme flows $x^{(1)}$ and $x^{(2)}$

	(a) $x = (8, 0, 0, 8)$				(b) $x^{(1)} = (5, 0, 0, 11)$				(c) $x^{(2)} = (10, 0, 0, 6)$			
t	1	2	3	4	1	2	3	4	1	2	3	4
d_t	3	2	5	6	3	2	5	6	3	2	5	6
x_t	8	0	0	8	5	0	0	11	10	0	0	6
y_t	5	3	0	0	2	0	0	0	7	5	0	0
z_t	0	0	2	0	0	0	6	0	0	0	0	0
c_t	12	0	0	12	9	0	0	14.80	14	0	0	10
h_t	0.25	0.15	0	0	0.10	0	0	0	0.35	0.25	0	0
p_t	0	0	1.00	0	0	0	2.50	0	0	0	0	0
$Z(\cdot)$		$25.40				$26.40				$24.50		

Property 1 Demand in each period is satisfied entirely from one order, whether the order is placed in the same period or in a different period. (This property follows from the fact that a node has at most one positive inflow.)

Property 2 From property 1 it follows that every order placed exactly satisfies the demands for some number of adjacent periods, including the order period. That is,

$$x_j = d_{i+1} + \cdots + d_k \qquad i+1 \leq j \leq k$$

Property 3 From property 2 it follows that between every two periods j and m in which an order is placed, there is a period k at the end of which the inventory level y_k is zero.

Properties 2 and 3 are illustrated schematically in figure 4-6. These properties make it possible to find an optimal ordering schedule fairly efficiently, using a dynamic programming algorithm. The procedure requires three cost definitions. Let c_{ijk} be the total cost in periods $i + 1, \ldots, k$ of placing an order in period j to satisfy demands in periods $i + 1, \ldots, k$. Then

$$c_{ijk} = \begin{pmatrix} \text{cost of} \\ \text{ordering in} \\ \text{period } j \end{pmatrix} + \begin{pmatrix} \text{shortage costs} \\ \text{in periods } i+1 \\ \text{through } j-1 \end{pmatrix} + \begin{pmatrix} \text{holding costs} \\ \text{in periods } j \\ \text{through } k \end{pmatrix}$$

$$c_{ijk} = c_j \sum_{t=i+1}^{k} d_t + \sum_{t=i+1}^{j-1} p_t \left(\sum_{m=i+1}^{t} d_m \right) + \sum_{t=j}^{k} h_t \left(\sum_{m=t+1}^{k} d_m \right)$$

$$1 \leq i + 1 \leq j \leq k \leq n \quad (4\text{-}8)$$

Let c_{ik} be the total cost associated with the least-cost choice of the period j in which to place this order. Then

$$c_{ik} = \min_{i+1 \leq j \leq k} c_{ijk} \qquad 0 \leq i < k \leq n \quad (4\text{-}9)$$

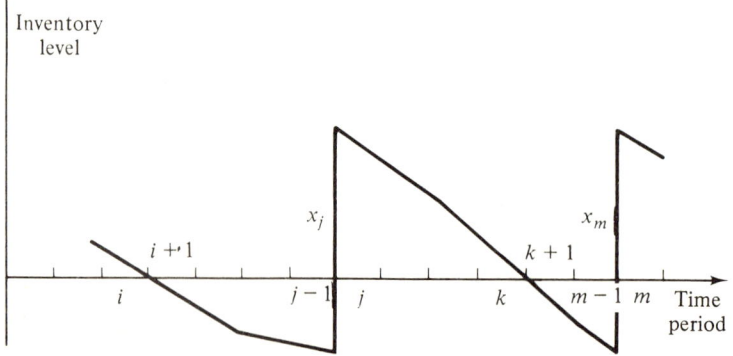

Figure 4-6 Illustration of properties 2 and 3 of extreme-flow ordering schedules.

CHAPTER 4: PERIODIC-REVIEW ORDERING DECISION MODELS 79

Let f_i be the minimum cost in periods $i + 1, \ldots, n$ given that $y_i = 0$. Then f_i can be found recursively using this equation:

$$f_i = \min_{i+1 \leq k \leq n} (c_{ik} + f_k) \qquad i = 0, \ldots, n - 1 \qquad (4\text{-}10)$$

The algorithmic procedure then consists of the following two steps.

Step 1 Use equations (4-8) and (4-9) to calculate all the c_{ik} for $0 \leq i < k \leq n$.
Step 2 Starting with $f_n = 0$, use equation (4-10) to calculate f_{n-1}, $f_{n-2}, \ldots, f_0$ in that order. The value of f_0 will be the cost of the optimal ordering schedule.

Example 4-1 Solved This procedure is illustrated using example 4-1, which was previously treated in table 4-2 and is repeated here for convenience. An ordering schedule $x = (x_1, x_2, x_3, x_4)$ is sought which satisfies the known demands $(d_1, d_2, d_3, d_4) = (3, 2, 5, 6)$ and which minimizes the costs given by

$$c_t(x_t) = \begin{cases} 0 & x_t = 0 \\ 4 + 1x_t & 0 < x_t \leq 10 \\ 14 + 0.8x_t & x_t > 10 \end{cases}$$

$$h_t(y_t) = 0.05 y_t$$

$$p_t(z_t) = 0.50 z_t$$

As an example, c_{14} will be calculated. Using equation (4-8), we obtain

$$c_{124} = 16.40 + (0.05)(17) = 17.25$$
$$c_{134} = 16.40 + (0.50)(2) + (0.05)(6) = 17.70$$
$$c_{144} = 16.40 + (0.50)(9) = 20.90$$

Then by equation (4-9)

$$c_{14} = \min (17.25, 17.70, 20.90) = 17.25$$

The c_{ik} values for all i and k are as follows:

i \ k	1	2	3	4
0	7	9.1	14.60	20.30
1		6	11.15	17.25
2			9	15.10
3				10

Finally, equation (4-10) is used to calculate the f_i values as follows:

$$f_4 = 0$$
$$f_3 = c_{34} = 10$$
$$f_2 = \min\,(c_{23} + f_3,\; c_{24} + f_4)$$
$$ = \min\,(9 + 10,\; 15.10 + 0)$$
$$ = 15.10 = c_{24} + f_4$$
$$f_1 = \min\,(c_{12} + f_2,\; c_{13} + f_3,\; c_{14} + f_4)$$
$$ = 17.25 = c_{14} + f_4$$
$$f_0 = \min\,(c_{01} + f_1,\; c_{02} + f_2,\; c_{03} + f_3,\; c_{04} + f_4)$$
$$ = 20.30 = c_{04} + f_4$$

The solution indicated is to order everything in period 1 and consequently to incur the cost $f_0 = c_{04} = c_{014} = 20.30$.

This procedure was originally developed for the case where no shortages are permitted. In this case, it is unnecessary to consider equation (4-9) since c_{ik} will necessarily equal $c_{i,i+1,k}$. Thus, the algorithm involves much less calculation in the no-backlog case and is usually referred to as the *Wagner-Whitin algorithm* after its authors [6]. An example of the use of this no-shortage procedure appears in section 6-4.

The results developed so far in this subsection can be summarized in a single sentence. Given known requirements and separable concave costs over an *n*-period planning horizon, an efficient dynamic programming procedure can be used to search the extreme-flow ordering schedules for an optimal schedule.

The above dynamic programming procedure was designed to handle the situation in which both costs and demands may vary over time. Such variations may be small enough to justify the use of a model which does not recognize them. Of course, if cost and demand conditions are time-invariant, the procedure will still work as outlined above. In fact, there would be no need to discuss the problem further if it were not for the fact that considerable computational savings can accrue in this case.

A model in which both costs and demands are time-invariant is called a *stationary* model. The demands and costs themselves may also be called stationary, and they are assumed to have the following properties:

1. $c_t(x_t) = c(x_t)$ for all *t*   3. $p_t(y_t) = p(y_t)$ for all *t*
2. $h_t(y_t) = h(y_t)$ for all *t*   4. $d_t = d$ for all *t*

In example 4-1 used above, the costs were stationary, but the demands were not.

The stationarity assumption simplifies the computations of c_{ik} in step 1 of the algorithmic procedure above, since c_{ik} depends only on the difference $k - i$. Thus $c_{01} = c_{12} \cdots = c_{n-1,n}$; $c_{02} = c_{13} = \cdots = c_{n-2,n}$; etc. This may give some relief if the computations are being performed manually, but since the procedure is customarily computerized, the savings here is modest for a finite planning horizon n. However, a considerable economy of computation accrues if the planning horizon is assumed to be infinite ($n = \infty$). (This assumption may appear artificial, but in fact it is not a harsh assumption at all, as you will see below.) With an *infinite horizon*, it would make no sense to calculate total costs according to equation (4-10); rather, the focus will be on the *average cost per period*, designated as A.

Consider the least cost c_{0k} in periods 1, ..., k of placing an order in some period j, $1 \leq j \leq k$, to satisfy demands in periods 1, ..., k. If this cost is incurred, then the average cost in periods 1, ..., k would be c_{0k}/k. Now consider finding k^*, a nonnegative integer value of k for which c_{0k}/k is a minimum:

$$\frac{c^*_{0k}}{k^*} = \min_k \frac{c_{0k}}{k} \qquad (4\text{-}11)$$

Then the least-cost ordering schedule over an infinite horizon will be one in which the costs c^*_{0k} are incurred every k^* time periods, yielding an overall average cost A of

$$A = \frac{c^*_{0k}}{k^*}$$

That is, the optimal ordering schedule will repeat itself during each k^*-period-long cycle. The procedure of finding the optimal ordering schedule is simply to evaluate c_{0k}/k for $k = 1, 2, \ldots$, until the k^* satisfying equation (4-11) is found. For any reasonable cost data, k^* will exist (that is, k^* will not be infinite).

Example 4-2 As an example, suppose $d = 4$:

$$c(x_t) = \$4 + \$1x_t \qquad h(y_t) = \$0.10y_t \qquad p(z_t) = \$0.50z_t$$

Using equations (4-8) and (4-9), the reader can verify that the resulting values of c_{0k} and j are as shown in table 4-3. Notice that it becomes economical to allow backlogging ($j > 1$) for $k \geq 6$. Notice also that the k-period average cost c_{0k}/k tends to decrease and then to increase as k increases. This is a typical pattern. The optimal solution appears from table 4-3 to be $k = 4$ or 5, for which $A = \$5.60$. Since $j = 1$, the solution is to order 16 every four periods (or 20 every five periods) and to permit no shortages.

Table 4-3 Values of c_{0k} and j for example 4-3

k	1	2	3	4	5	6	7	8
$c_{0k}(\$)$	8	12.40	17.20	22.40	28.00	34.00	40.00	46.40
j	1	1	1	1	1	(1 or 2)	2	2
c_{0k}/k	8	6.20	5.73	5.60	5.60	5.67	5.71	5.80

The situation described in example 4-2 is similar to that which gave rise to the economic order quantity models in chapter 2. In fact, the similarity is strong enough to make fruitful a comparison of results. Recall that under stationary conditions with continuous review and linear holding and penalty costs, the economic order quantity Q^* was found [equation (2-33)] to be

$$Q^* = \sqrt{\frac{2kd}{h}} \sqrt{\frac{p+h}{p}} \qquad (4\text{-}12)$$

The data in the above example applies to this equation as follows: $k = 4$; $d = 4$; $p = 0.50$; $h = 0.10$. In the continuous-review model, the holding and penalty costs were applied to the *average* inventory and shortage levels, rather than to the inventory or shortage occurring at the end of each period. However, the cost effects of increasing an already positive inventory y_t or shortage z_t by 1 unit will be reflected by the same increase in cost in either case. Substitution of the data values into equation (4-12) gives $Q^* = 19.6$. This converts to an optimal time between orders, t^*, of

$$t^* = \frac{Q^*}{d} = \frac{19.6}{4} = 4.9 \text{ periods}$$

This compares with the result obtained in table 4-3. A practical consequence of this comparison is that the value of k^* in equation (4-11) can be found more rapidly by using integers with values near t^* as trial values of k, rather than starting with $k = 1$.

It is now evident that the stationary infinite-horizon model is computationally far less demanding than a finite-horizon dynamic programming approach. Because of this, the author feels that except for fairly short horizons (say, $n \leq 10$), therefore, an infinite horizon should probably be assumed for the stationary case. In fact, if the actual finite horizon n happens to be an integer multiple of k^*, the same ordering schedule will result with either a finite- or an infinite-horizon stationary model [2].

Models Recognizing Convex Costs

In contrast to the preceding subsection, the models in this subsection are designed to aid in making ordering decisions when the cost terms in equation (4-2) are convex. Specifically, the ordering cost $c_t(x_t)$ will be considered to be convex on $(0, \infty)$, and the combined holding and penalty cost will be assumed to be convex on $(-\infty, \infty)$. Examples of these relationships were shown in figure 4-4(b) and (e).

Convexity of the ordering cost implies that any fixed ordering cost (exclusive of the cost of the ordered items themselves) is negligible. This would be the case when multiple items are ordered from each supplier and orders are placed regularly with these suppliers, so that inclusion of one more item in an order has an immaterial effect on the cost of the order. Also, convexity includes the case where the marginal cost of ordering one more unit of an item increases with the order size. This reflects a situation in which a single item may be obtained from more than one source and only a limited quantity is available from the low-cost sources, after which any additional amount ordered would have to come from a higher-cost source. Convexity of the holding and penalty cost reflects the widely held feeling that the marginal severity of one additional unit of an oversupply (or undersupply) of stock increases as the oversupply (or undersupply) increases in magnitude. For example, the holding cost per additional unit stored may become greater as the most convenient (and hence lowest cost) storage locations are filled to capacity.

The problem treated in this section, then, is to determine an ordering schedule $x = (x_1, \ldots, x_n)(x_t \geq 0)$ which minimizes the sum of convex cost terms over an n-period planning horizon:

$$Z(x) = \sum_{t=1}^{n} [c_t(x_t) + h_t(y_t) + p_t(z_t)] \qquad (4\text{-}13)$$

The following theorem is fundamental to some of the computational procedures to be used in this subsection. Implicit in the theorem is the fact that the known demands must be satisfied during the planning horizon.

Theorem 4-2 Assume that demands and order quantities must occur in integer amounts and that the costs are convex, as described above. Suppose that an optimal (i.e., minimum-cost) ordering schedule $x = (x_1, \ldots, x_n)$ has already been found for the given demand vector $d = (d_1, \ldots, d_n)$. Then if the demand is changed by 1 unit in a single period, there exists an ordering schedule $x' = (x'_1, \ldots, x'_n)$ which is optimal for the new demand vector d' and which differs from x by 1 unit in a single period.

Notationally, theorem 4-2 says that if u_k is a unit vector with a "1" in the kth position and $d' = d + u_k$, then $x' = x + u_j$ for some j. Also, if $d' = d - u_k$, then $x' = x - u_j$ for some j. The theorem will not be proved here. (A proof appears in [4].) The usefulness of the theorem will be demonstrated in the solution of the following example.

Table 4-4 Stages of the solution of example 4-3

(a) Cost matrix (table elements = c_{ij}^k)

i \ j	1	2	3	4	5	Order limit	k
1	3.00 3.90	3.25 4.15	3.50 4.40	3.75 4.65	4.00 4.90	3 ∞	0 1
2	4.00 5.20	3.00 4.20	3.25 4.45	3.50 4.70	3.75 4.95	3 ∞	0 1
3	5.00 5.90	4.00 4.90	3.00 3.90	3.25 4.15	3.50 4.40	3 ∞	0 1
4	6.00 7.30	5.00 6.30	4.00 5.30	3.00 4.30	3.25 4.55	3 ∞	0 1
5	7.00 8.70	6.00 7.70	5.00 6.70	4.00 5.70	3.00 4.70	3 ∞	0 1
demand d_j	4	6	2	3	2		

Example 4-3 Suppose a firm is faced with the demand schedule d = (4, 6, 2, 3, 2) over the next five time periods. In any period, one supplier will guarantee a supply of up to 3 units at a cost of \$3 per unit. If more than 3 units are ordered in any period t, they must be ordered from another supplier at a cost of c_t per unit. The values of c_t are \$3.90, \$4.20, \$3.90, \$4.30, and \$4.70, respectively, for t = 1, 2, 3, 4, 5. It costs \$0.25 per unit held over from one period to the next. Backlogged demand costs the firm \$1 per unit per period.

From these given data, the lowest cost c_{ij}^0 of ordering 1 unit in period i to satisfy 1 unit of demand in period j can be calculated. Assuming, for example, that nothing else has been ordered in period 3, the cost c_{34}^0 would be found as the cost of the item ordered plus the holding cost:

$$c_{34}^0 = \$3 + \$0.25 = \$3.25$$

This relationship would not change until 3 units have been ordered in period 3. After this the unit cost will increase from c_{34}^0 to a new value called c_{34}^1. Thus an additional unit ordered beyond the first 3 would cost

$$c_{34}^1 = \$3.90 + \$0.25 = \$4.15$$

These costs together with the other c_{ij}^k (k = 0 or 1) are shown in table 4-4(a).

Table 4-4 (continued)

(b) No backlog solution—obtained by an application of theorem 4-2 (solution details in table 4-5) (table elements = x_{ij}^k)

i	k	1	2	3	4	5	x_t	y_t	z_t
1	0	3					7	3	0
	1	1	3						
2	0		3				3	0	0
	1								
3	0			2			2	0	0
	1								
4	0				3		3	0	0
	1								
5	0					2	2	0	0
	1								

(c) A backlog solution obtained by an application of theorem 4-3; it could have been obtained by the transportation algorithm (table elements = x_{ij}^k)

i	k	1	2	3	4	5	x_t	y_t	z_t
1	0	3					6	2	0
	1	1	2						
2	0		3				3	0	1
	1								
3	0		1	2			3	0	0
	1								
4	0				3		3	0	0
	1								
5	0					2	2	0	0
	1								

It should occur to the reader who is familiar with the transportation algorithm that table 4-4(a) is in the proper format for solution by that technique. In fact, the solution shown in table 4-4(c) could be obtained in that manner. In this subsection, another approach will be developed which is potentially easier to use than the transportation algorithm. The approach has two steps:

Step 1 Solve the problem assuming that no backlogging is permitted.
Step 2 Relax the no-backlogging restriction and, if possible, improve the solution obtained in step 1 until an optimal solution is obtained.

Theorem 4-2 is applied to step 1 as follows: Demands in each period are artificially set to zero, for which the optimal solution is to order zero in each period. Then the demand in period 1 is increased by 1 unit at a time until the actual demand d_1 is reached. For each unit increase, an optimal solution is obtained by adding a unit vector to the previously optimal ordering schedule. Then the demand in period 2 is likewise increased 1 unit at a time until the actual demand d_2 is reached. This continues period by period, in order, until the n periods of demand are at their actual values. A new optimal solution is obtained for each unit increase in demand. By theorem 4-2, the resulting final ordering schedule is optimal for the given actual demands. This completes step 1.

For example 4-3, by using a transportation matrix format, the procedure just described leads to an optimal solution manually in a matter of a minute or so. For definiteness, let x_{ij}^k be the number of units ordered at a cost c_{ij}^k. Thus $x_{ij}^0 + x_{ij}^1$ will equal x_{ij}, the number of units ordered in period i to satisfy demand in period j. The procedure involves the steps shown in table 4-5. In executing the procedure, care must be taken that no more than 3 units are ordered at the lower cost in any period, i.e.,

$$\sum_j x_{ij}^0 \leq 3 \qquad \text{for all } i$$

The solution is given in the right-hand column of table 4-5 to be $x = (7, 3, 2, 3, 2)$. This solution is shown in transportation matrix format in table 4-4(*b*).

It is not necessary to write out the procedure in such detail, especially when the computations are performed manually. It is quite appropriate to use the short-cut line of reasoning: For each time period j, in order, increase demand to d_j and satisfy that demand as cheaply as possible, referring to the cost cells in column j of the cost matrix [figure 4-4(*a*)].

A very practical feature of theorem 4-2 is its ability to handle changes in the anticipated demands d_j. For example, if it is discovered that d_5, say, should be 3 rather than 2, very little effort is involved in revising the previously optimal (no-backlog) ordering schedule. Also, after each period expires, it is customary to extend the planning horizon by one period (say, to recognize $d_6 = 4$ or whatever). Again the old schedule can be updated in response to the new information (see problem 4-4).

The next step in dealing with the above example is to find an optimal

CHAPTER 4: PERIODIC-REVIEW ORDERING DECISION MODELS 87

Table 4-5 Generating an optimal no-backlog solution for example 4-3 (using theorem 4-2)

Set $j=$	Increase period j demand to	Increase x_{ij}^k to	Which increases x_{ij} to	Which increases x_i to
1	1	$x_{11}^0 = 1$	$x_{11} = 1$	$x_1 = 1$
	2	$x_{11}^0 = 2$	$x_{11} = 2$	$x_1 = 2$
	3	$x_{11}^0 = 3$	$x_{11} = 3$	$x_1 = 3$
	$4 = d_1$	$x_{11}^1 = 1$	$x_{11} = 4$	$x_1 = 4$
2	1	$x_{22}^0 = 1$	$x_{22} = 1$	$x_2 = 1$
	2	$x_{22}^0 = 2$	$x_{22} = 2$	$x_2 = 2$
	3	$x_{22}^0 = 3$	$x_{22} = 3$	$x_2 = 3$
	4	$x_{12}^1 = 1$	$x_{12} = 1$	$x_1 = 5$
	5	$x_{12}^1 = 2$	$x_{12} = 2$	$x_1 = 6$
	$6 = d_2$	$x_{12}^1 = 3$	$x_{12} = 3$	$x_1 = 7$
3	1	$x_{33}^0 = 1$	$x_{33} = 1$	$x_3 = 1$
	$2 = d_3$	$x_{33}^0 = 2$	$x_{33} = 2$	$x_3 = 2$
4	1	$x_{44}^0 = 1$	$x_{44} = 1$	$x_4 = 1$
	2	$x_{44}^0 = 2$	$x_{44} = 2$	$x_4 = 2$
	$3 = d_4$	$x_{44}^0 = 3$	$x_{44} = 3$	$x_4 = 3$
5	1	$x_{55}^0 = 1$	$x_{55} = 1$	$x_5 = 1$
	$2 = d_5$	$x_{55}^0 = 2$	$x_{55} = 2$	$x_5 = 2$

solution when backlogging is permitted. An effective approach is to start with the optimal no-backlogging solution and, if possible, perturb it in such a way that costs are lowered, until an optimal backlogging solution is obtained. Define a *pairwise perturbation* (*pp*) as a vector which, when added to an order schedule vector $x = (x_1, \ldots, x_n)$, produced another order schedule $x' = (x'_1, \ldots, x'_n)$ which differs from x by $+1$ in one period, -1 in another period, and 0 in all other periods. That is,

$$x' = x + u_j - u_k \qquad j \neq k$$

where u_j and u_k are unit vectors. Evidently the pairwise perturbation is given by

$$pp = u_j - u_k \qquad j \neq k$$

The procedure to be followed will consist of applying a series of pairwise perturbations to the no-backlog solution x until the optimal backlog solution x^* is obtained. Now the schedule x is feasible, since

$$\sum_{t=1}^{n} x_t = \sum_{t=1}^{n} d_t$$

If x is perturbed to $x' = x + pp$, then x' is clearly also a feasible schedule, provided, of course, that $x_j \geq 0$ for all j. The following theorem validates the procedure.

Theorem 4-3 Assume that the ordering cost and the combined holding and penalty cost are convex, as described in the first paragraph of this subsection, and that demands and order quantities are integers. Let x be any nonoptimal schedule and x^* be an optimal schedule so that the total costs Z obey the relation $Z(x) > Z(x^*)$. Then there exists a pp so that $x' = x + pp$ and $Z(x) > Z(x')$.

A proof of theorem 4-3 appears in [4] in general form. Its utility will be demonstrated here. The theorem implies the following reasoning. Let x be any current solution. If there is no pp yielding an x' for which $Z(x') < Z(x)$, then x ($= x^*$) is an optimal solution. Applying this to the no-backlog solution for example 4-3 yields the following procedure. Set $x = (7, 3, 2, 3, 2)$. Investigate all x' resulting from pp's of x. If $Z(x') \geq Z(x)$ for all x', stop. Otherwise, let an x' for which $Z(x') < Z(x)$ be designated as the new x and repeat the procedure until no further improvement is possible. We first try $pp = (-1, 1, 0, 0, 0)$, which yields $x' = (6, 4, 2, 3, 2)$. Thus x_1 and y_1 are decreased by 1, and x_2 is increased by 1. The cost effect of these changes is

$$Z(x') - Z(x) = -\$3.90 + \$4.20 - \$0.25 = +\$0.05$$

Thus, this pp is not profitable. A little reflection will reveal that this result could have been predicted without performing any cost calculations, since x' is another no-backlog solution and x is already known to be an optimal no-backlog solution. Being a bit wiser, we next try $pp = (-1, 0, +1, 0, 0)$ which yields $x' = (6, 3, 3, 3, 2)$. This does involve backlogging in period 2. The effect on costs is

$$Z(x') - Z(x) = -\$3.90 + \$3 - \$0.25 + \$1$$
$$= -\$0.15$$

Thus we let $x = (6, 3, 3, 3, 2)$. No pp of this x will reduce costs further, so an optimal solution is $x^* = (6, 3, 3, 3, 2)$. This is the solution shown in table 4-4(c), which could also have been obtained by using the transportation algorithm.

In summary, when costs are convex, as assumed in this subsection, a one-time (starting from scratch) solution may be obtained by using theorem 4-2 to find an optimal no-backlog solution and then theorem 4-3 to generate an optimal solution allowing backlogging. Moreover, if the costs $c(\cdot)$, $h(\cdot)$, and $p(\cdot)$ are piecewise linear, the transportation algorithm may be used. After an optimal solution (including backlogging) is obtained, theorem 4-2 may be used to update the schedule in response to any new information, including demand changes both within and subsequent to the initial planning horizon.

If demands over a given planning horizon are confidently known, extension of the horizon will only increase total demands. A practical implication of this is that the presently optimal order quantities will not decrease with extension of the planning horizon. Thus the currently optimal value of x_1 is a lower bound on the amount which would be ordered in period 1 if the horizon were extended. It may be effective to artificially extend the horizon until no further increases are occurring in x_1. Even though the demand quantities in the extended part of the horizon may not be confidently known, their approximation is sufficient for the purpose of making a final decision on the current order quantity x_1.

Finally, it is noted that in the stationary infinite-horizon case, in which costs and demands are time-invariant, the solution reduces to ordering $x_i = d$ in every period. This is true since there is no recognized fixed cost of placing an order. Ordering any more than d in a period would cause unnecessary holding costs to be incurred.

4-3 STOCHASTIC MODELS

In this section a variety of ordering models will be developed. They all have in common the fact that they give explicit recognition to uncertainties in future demands. In fact, for input they require probability distributions of demand over given time periods. These models are analogous to those of section 3-3, the primary difference being that in this chapter ordering is periodic. Comparison of the development here with that in section 3-3 will prove to be meaningful.

A General Periodic Stochastic Model Framework

Ordering decisions are to be made at the beginning of each of n periods of time, where each period is T time units in duration. At the beginning of period i, given an amount y_{i-1} of stock already on hand and on order, a decision is made regarding x_i, the quantity to be ordered. If y_{i-1} is negative, a shortage exists. Actually it is possible for y_{i-1} to be positive and to concurrently have a shortage exist since y_{i-1} may include stock on order. Nonetheless, x_i will be chosen based on y_{i-1}, not on the actual physical shortage at the beginning of period i. The amount ordered will be available (delivered) only after a delivery lag time L. If $L > T$, then any amount of x_{i-1} ordered at the beginning of the previous period will not have arrived yet.

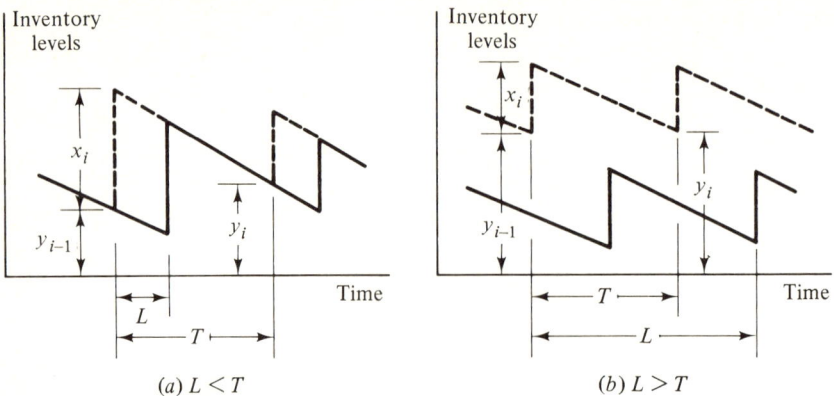

Figure 4-7 Inventory effects of periodic ordering decisions.

Figure 4-7 illustrates the above description for the two cases $L < T$ and $L > T$. It is helpful to account for both the inventory actually on hand (solid lines) and the total on hand and on order (dashed lines), as they change over time. The plots in figure 4-7 reflect the decision to place an order in every period, which will not necessarily always be done. A case where orders are not placed every period will be illustrated later (figure 4-8).

The curves in figure 4-7 depict the average rate of depletion of stock resulting from demands which vary randomly over time. It is supposed that the probability distribution of demand can be constructed for any time span of interest. In particular, the decision x_i will be based on the distributions of demand over one time period plus the lead time $T + L$. This is the amount of time until another (later) order can be *received*. Thus the latter $(T + L)$ is the amount of time over which demand should be satisfied by the present order x_i (plus existing stock y_{i-1}). Defining $f_\tau(u)$ as the probability density function of demand over the time interval τ, our interest, then, will be in $f_T(u)$ and $f_{T+L}(u)$. Equivalently, the cumulative distribution function $F_\tau(v)$ is the probability that demand during the time interval τ will not exceed v, and it is given (for continuous demand) by

$$F_\tau(v) = \int_0^v f_\tau(u)\, du$$

Again, the decision maker's concern is usually with $F_T(v)$ or $F_{T+L}(v)$. The above demand distributions are expressed as if demand were continuous. If demand is treated as discrete, then define $f_\tau(u)$ as the probability that demand is u over the time interval τ. In this case,

$$F_\tau(v) = \sum_{u=0}^{v} f_\tau(u)$$

It is customary to refer to any amount ordered in excess of the expected demand during the time $T + L$ as a *buffer stock* B. Explicitly, if $v_{0.5}$ is the value of v for which $F_{T+L}(v) = 0.5$, then B (≥ 0) is given by

$$B = y_{i-1} + x_i - v_{0.5}$$

Although the buffer stock is an indication of provision for uncertainty in demand, it is considered a consequence of the ordering decision models being developed here.

If the lead time L is not constant, the probability distribution of demand over $T + L$ is found by observing that

$$F_{T+L}(v) = \sum_{\substack{\text{all possible} \\ \text{values } L_0 \text{ of } L}} \{P[\text{lead time} = L_0]F_{T+L_0}(v)\}$$

The lead-time value is assumed to be independent of demands. For example, suppose $T = 1$ and $P[\text{lead time} = j]$ is $\frac{1}{3}$ for $j = 0.1$, $\frac{1}{2}$ for $j = 0.2$, and $\frac{1}{6}$ for $j = 0.3$. Also suppose that demand during a time interval is normally distributed with mean 10τ and standard deviation $\sqrt{\tau}$. Then the probability that demand over $T + L$ does not exceed, say, 13 is given by $F_{T+L}(13) = \frac{1}{3}\Phi[(13 - 11)/\sqrt{1.1}] + \frac{1}{2}\Phi[(13 - 12)/\sqrt{1.2}] + \frac{1}{6}\Phi[(13 - 13)/\sqrt{1.3}]$, where Φ is the cumulative distribution function for a normally distributed random variable with mean 0 and standard deviation 1. Thus using Appendix A,

$$F_{T+L}(13) = \tfrac{1}{3}\Phi(1.91) + \tfrac{1}{2}\Phi(0.91) + \tfrac{1}{6}\Phi(0)$$
$$= \tfrac{1}{3}(0.972) + \tfrac{1}{2}(0.818) + \tfrac{1}{6}(0.5)$$
$$= 0.816$$

The following cost structure will be inherent in the models in this section, unless otherwise specified. The cost of ordering x_i units is $c(x_i)$, which includes ordering and material costs. The usual assumption will be that

$$c(x_i) = k + cx_i \quad \text{for all } i \tag{4-14}$$

where k is an ordering cost and c is a unit purchase price. The cost of holding w units of stock in inventory will be given by $h(w)$, and this cost will be assessed immediately before the arrival of each order.

The common functional form is

$$h(w) = hw \quad w \geq 0 \tag{4-15}$$

where h is then a unit holding cost. The reason for assessing holding costs immediately before arrival of any order is that it is the point at which shortages (if any) are the most critical. If a shortage of w units exists just before an arrival of stock, a cost of $p(w)$ will be assessed. Again it is commonly assumed that this takes the form

$$p(w) = pw \quad w \geq 0 \tag{4-16}$$

Thus shortage and holding costs will be assessed at coincident points in time. The functional forms (4-14), (4-15), and (4-16) are not mandatory, but they are expedient because of their simplicity. There are many alternative cost assumptions made in inventory modeling. For example, the penalty cost $p(w)$ might have been modeled as a "shortage-no shortage" penalty:

$$p(w) = \begin{cases} \pi & w > 0 \\ 0 & w = 0 \end{cases}$$

or perhaps the penalty might have been assessed against the *average* shortage or against the number of unit-days short. Each of these leads to a possibly different model and to a possibly different decision. Similar variations are possible with respect to holding and ordering costs. The most important thing in any of these models is that all significant incremental costs be recognized. As discussed in chapter 2, these almost always fall in one or more of these three categories: ordering, holding, and penalty costs.

Additionally, it may be desirable to include a revenue $r(w)$ resulting from the sale of stock. If shortages lead to lost sales, this is handled by adding the lost-revenue contribution to the penalty cost term. If shortages result in backlogs, the effect on revenue, if any, can again be included with the penalty cost term.

The distinction between the approaches in the following two subsections is whether a cost k of placing an order is recognized in the model. This has a profound effect on any ordering decision. If $k = 0$, then an order might as well be placed every period, and the order quantity will be designed to balance holding and shortage costs. On the other hand, if k is materially nonzero, orders may not be placed in every period. When they are placed, they will tend to balance shortage, holding, and ordering costs. This fundamental difference warrants a separate and distinct treatment of the two cases.

Models Not Recognizing an Ordering Cost

As pointed out in section 4-2, the ordering cost (exclusive of the cost of the items themselves) would be negligible in the case where multiple items are ordered from each supplier and orders are placed regularly with these suppliers. This occurs quite often in large (multi-item) inventories.

For simplicity, assume that the functional forms in (4-14), (4-15), and (4-16) apply. (Extensions will be discussed later where appropriate.) In this case, there is no advantage to ordering large quantities since $k = 0$ and the unit cost c does not decrease as order size increases. Therefore it is reasonable to assume that the item will be ordered every period (unless there is no demand in a period). This means that the amount ordered x_i must bring the total on hand plus on order up to a level S_i, which provides a reasonable balance between holding costs and penalty costs.

The models in this section are stationary (the costs and demand distributions in the models are assumed not to vary as a function of time). It is not usually worth the computational effort to try to permit nonstationarity in stochastic ordering decision models when decisions must be made routinely for a large number of items. Thus in this development, S_i is considered to be a constant S for all i.

What is sought, then, is the value of S which minimizes ordering, holding, and penalty costs associated with placing an order for $S - y_{i-1}$ units of stock at the beginning of period i. Since demands vary randomly, costs cannot be predicted with certainty, so expected costs will be minimized.

Let ΔH be the marginal holding cost associated with holding one more unit in stock, and let ΔP be the marginal penalty cost associated with incurring one more unit of shortage, at the time that costs are assessed. Also let $\Delta TEC(S)$ be the marginal change in total expected cost as a function of S. For a given value of S, the probability of a shortage can be calculated as

$$\text{Prob [shortage]} = \int_{S}^{\infty} f_{T+L}(u)\, du = 1 - F_{T+L}(S)$$

The time interval $T + L$ is chosen because this is the period for which the quantity S of stock must satisfy demand, until the arrival of a subsequent order. Likewise, the probability of *no* shortage is given by $P[\text{no shortage}] = F_{T+L}(S)$. Thus for this value of S we have

$$\Delta TEC(S) = \Delta H F_{T+L}(S) - \Delta P[1 - F_{T+L}(S)]$$

Ordering costs appear to be excluded from this expression, but this apparent exclusion is not an actual one, as explained below.

At the optimal (minimal expected cost) value, S^* of S, $\Delta TEC(S)$ should equal zero. Thus

$$\Delta H F_{T+L}(S^*) - \Delta P[1 - F_{T+L}(S^*)] = 0$$

which solves to yield this *important result*:

$$F_{T+L}(S^*) = \frac{\Delta P}{\Delta P + \Delta H} \qquad (4\text{-}17)$$

Before the full power of equation (4-17) is examined, an example will clarify one way in which it may be applied to generate useful results.

Example 4-4 Suppose that orders are placed monthly for an item whose average demand is 40 units per month. Holding and penalty costs of $0.10 per unit and $1 per unit, respectively, are assessed immediately before the arrival of each order. It takes $\frac{1}{2}$ month to receive an order. The purchase price is $5 per unit. Unsatisfied demand is backlogged. Demand over a $1\frac{1}{2}$-month period is normally distributed with mean 60 and standard deviation 10. The units sell for $7 each. Stock on hand and on order is currently 24 units.

Since unsatisfied demand is backlogged, one may argue that the purchase price may be ignored, since demand will ultimately be satisfied by a purchase in some period. For the same reason, the revenue contribution may be ignored. The marginal holding and penalty costs are simply $\Delta H = \$0.10$ and $\Delta P = \$1$. Thus S^* is the solution to

$$F_{1.5}(S^*) = \frac{1.00}{1.10} = 0.9091$$

From a table of the standard normal distribution, $P[Z \leq 1.335] = 0.9091$. Therefore $S^* = 60 + (1.335)(10) = 73.35$. From this follows the decision to order $X = 74 - 24 = 50$ units.

The model indicated in example 4-4 was a stationary infinite-horizon model with backlogging of unsatisfied demand. The resulting marginal costs turned out to be $\Delta P = p$ and $\Delta H = h$, so that the optimal level S^* up to which to order was the solution to

$$F_{T+L}(S^*) = \frac{p}{p+h} \qquad (4\text{-}18)$$

The reader is invited to compare equation (4-18) to equation (3-33). To get a feel for equation (4-18), the reader should be satisfied that it makes sense when $p = 0$ or when $h = 0$. It turns out that a sharper insight will be gained by looking at a case in which the marginal costs ΔP and ΔH should include the cost effect of the purchase price of stock ordered. For example, if it is assumed that unsatisfied demand is lost, rather than backlogged, then ΔP should be reduced by the purchase price c of the unit of demand lost. In this case, the sales revenue is also lost. For consistency, p will continue to include penalty costs other than lost revenue, and the revenue per unit r will be added to ΔP. Thus, $\Delta P = p - c + r$, and S^* becomes the solution to

$$F_{T+L}(S^*) = \frac{p - c + r}{p - c + r + h} \qquad (4\text{-}19)$$

Thus, if sales are lost in example 4-4, the value of r would be $7. Suppose the $1 penalty cost represents a loss of goodwill or a fine for failure to deliver on time the stock demanded. Then, by using equation (4-19), S^* is the solution to

$$F_{1.5}(S^*) = \frac{1-5+7}{1-5+7+0.10} = \frac{3.00}{3.10} = 0.9677$$

Again, from a table of the standard normal distribution, $P[Z \leq 1.85] = 0.9678$. Therefore, $S^* = 60 + (1.85)(10) = 78.5$, and the amount ordered in this case would be $79 - 24 = 55$ units. This is higher than the amount ordered in the backlog case, which is to be expected in view of the more severe penalty associated with loss of sales.

Equation (4-17) finds application in another situation. Suppose that items ordered in any period are demanded only in that period. At the end of the period, any stock remaining will be disposed of at some salvage value v, which may be negative. For example, the item being ordered may be newspapers for sale on a streetcorner, Christmas trees for sale during December, or programs for sale at a football game. It is implicit in this case that unsatisfied demand is not backlogged, but lost. Thus, the marginal holding cost is increased by the difference between the purchase price and the salvage value: $\Delta H = h + c - v$. Also, as is always true in the lost-sales case, the marginal penalty cost is reduced by the purchase price and increased by the sales revenue: $\Delta P = p - c + r$. Thus, by equation (4-17), S^* is the solution to

$$F_{T+L}(S^*) = \frac{p-c+r}{p+h+r-v} \qquad (4\text{-}20)$$

In equation (4-20) the subscript $T + L$ is superfluous since demand occurs only during a single period in this case.

Example 4-5 Newspapers which sell for $0.20 cost the salesperson $0.15. With tips, the average revenue per paper sold is $0.23. During the rush hour, sales on a given street corner are uniformly distributed between 150 and 190. Determine how many papers should be acquired by the salesperson for sale during a particular rush hour. Evidently $r = 0.23$, $c = 0.15$, $h = 0$, $p = 0$, and $v = 0$. Thus, the solution is the value of S^* which satisfies

$$F(S^*) = \frac{0.23 - 0.15}{0.23} = 0.348$$

where $S^* = 150 + F(S^*)(190 - 150)$. This yields the value $S^* = 163.92$. Thus 164 papers should be ordered each day.

Models Recognizing an Ordering Cost

In this subsection the assumption $k = 0$ is relaxed, so that the cost definition equations (4-14), (4-15), and (4-16) apply as stated. Thus cost input to the models in this subsection will be values for c, k, h, and p.

Consider the stationary infinite-horizon ($n = \infty$) model with backlogging. In the previous subsection, with $k = 0$, it was seen that an (s) ordering policy was optimal in the sense that there was a single value S^* for S which minimized expected costs. This value was found by using equation (4-17). The important thing to note at this point is that when $k = 0$, S^* was chosen to minimize expected holding and shortage costs. In the present case, the ordering costs k must also be considered. It has been shown ([3], [5]) that the optimal form of an ordering policy for this situation is an (s, S) policy, as defined in section 4-1. The difficulty lies in determining the values of s and S. Ideally, one could choose s and S to minimize the expected holding, penalty, and ordering costs. No easy way has been found to do this. However, the procedure described below provides reasonable approximations to the optimal values of s and S.

The approximation procedure is based on the fact that the problem can be looked at differently for large k than it can for small k. For k near zero, the model of section 4-3 can be used. For large k, the number of periods between orders tends to increase. An illustration of the situation appears in figure 4-8, in which k is large enough to warrant order quantities that will satisfy demands for several time periods. The plot of inventory over time recognizes the lead time L between placing and receipt of orders. The plot is drawn as if demand occurred at its *expected* (i.e., average) rate of $\bar{d}$ units per period. Thus the solid line (inventory actually on hand) behaves as the deterministic backlogging model developed in chapter 2. The notations Q_D and s_D stand for the values which would be obtained if, in fact, that deterministic model

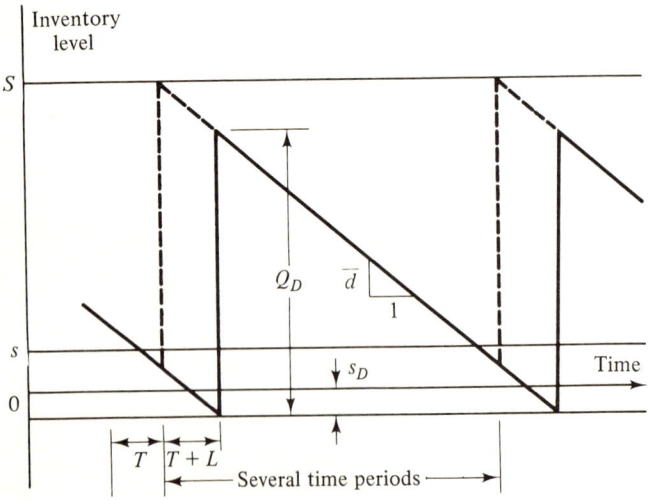

Figure 4-8 Behavior of expected inventory for large ordering costs.

(with $L = 0$) were used. The approach here is to infer from the optimal deterministic values Q_D and s_D what the (approximately) optimal stochastic-model values S and s should be.

Results from chapter 2 were that

$$s_D = \sqrt{\frac{2k\bar{d}}{h}} \sqrt{\frac{h^2}{(h+p)p}} \qquad (4\text{-}21)$$

and

$$Q_D = \sqrt{\frac{2k\bar{d}}{h}} \sqrt{\frac{p+h}{p}} \qquad (4\text{-}22)$$

From this it follows that

$$s_D = \frac{h}{h+p} Q_D \qquad (4\text{-}23)$$

Now since s_D is the shortage which will be incurred before receipt of each order, the value of s for the stochastic model will be chosen so that the expected shortage incurred (if an order is not placed until the stock level falls below s) is s_D. By using the demand probability distribution, this value of s satisfies

$$\int_{s-\bar{d}T/2}^{\infty} \left[u - \left(s - \frac{\bar{d}T}{2}\right)\right] f_{T+L}(u)\, du = s_D \qquad (4\text{-}24)$$

The quantity $s - \bar{d}T/2$ in equation (4-24) is the average inventory when an order is placed. By referring to the geometry of figure 4-8, the value of S can be seen to satisfy

$$S - \left(s - \frac{\bar{d}T}{2}\right) = Q_D \qquad (4\text{-}25)$$

Example 4-6 Suppose that the conditions of example 4-4 are repeated exactly, except that a cost of $8 is incurred every time an order is placed. Determine an approximately optimal ordering policy.

Equation (4-24) implies that in this example the value of s should satisfy

$$\int_{s-\bar{d}T/2}^{\infty} \left[u - \left(s - \frac{\bar{d}T}{2}\right)\right] \frac{1}{\sigma\sqrt{2\pi}} e^{-[(u-\mu)/2\sigma]^2}\, du = s_D \qquad (4\text{-}26)$$

since demand during time $T + L$ is normally distributed with mean μ and standard deviation σ. This integral can be evaluated by converting it to a *standardized normal-loss integral*:

$$I(\gamma) = \int_{\gamma}^{\infty} (u - \gamma) \frac{1}{\sqrt{2\pi}} e^{-(u/2)^2}\, du$$

Values of $I(\gamma)$ are tabulated in appendix B. The conversion of equation (4-26) is

$$I\left(\frac{s - \bar{d}T/2 - \mu}{\sigma}\right) = \frac{s_D}{\sigma} \qquad (4\text{-}27)$$

For this example

$$s_D = \sqrt{\frac{2 \cdot 8 \cdot 40}{0.10}} \sqrt{\frac{0.01}{(1.1)1}} = 7.6 \text{ units}$$

and $\sigma = 10$. From appendix B, $I(-0.6) = 0.76$, so $(s - \bar{d}T/2 - \mu)/\sigma = (s - 20 - 60)/10 = -0.6$ and $s = 74$. By equation (4-25), $S = s - \bar{d}T/2 + Q_D = 54 + 84 = 138$. Thus an approximately optimal policy for this example is to order up to 138 whenever the inventory level drops below 74.

A simpler approach, which avoids the need to use normal-loss integrals, is to set s_D equal to the average inventory level which would result if demand occurred at its average rate during the time $T + L$:

$$s - \frac{\bar{d}T}{2} - \bar{d}(T + L) = -s_D$$

For example 4-6, this would yield

$$s = 20 + 60 - 7.6 = 72.4 = 73$$

rather than 74.

Recall that the approximate procedure was developed based on "large" values of k. How large is "large"? A suggested rule of thumb is that if the economical ordering quantity Q_D will satisfy demand for more than 1.5 periods, then the approximation procedure may be used. This condition translates to a minimum value of k as follows:

$$Q_D > 1.5\bar{d} \Rightarrow \sqrt{\frac{2k\bar{d}}{h}} \sqrt{\frac{p+h}{p}} > 1.5\bar{d}$$

$$\Rightarrow k > \frac{1.125\bar{d}hp}{p+h} \qquad (4\text{-}28)$$

For example 4-6, this requirement is satisfied, since

$$k > \frac{1.125(40)(0.10)(1.0)}{1.1} = 4.09$$

If equation (4-28) is not satisfied, the model of section 4-3, which does not recognize an ordering cost, may be used. Of course, if $k = 0$, then this latter model will always be used, since equation (4-28) could not possibly be satisfied in this case. Further examples comparing these two models are presented in section 4-4.

The situation in which items ordered in any period are demanded only in that period was treated in the previous subsection. There it was shown [equation (4-20)] that when $k = 0$, the optimal level S^* up to which to place the single order is the solution to

$$F_{T+L}(S^*) = \frac{p - c + r}{p + h + r - v} \tag{4-29}$$

where v is the salvage value and the penalty cost p excludes the lost-sales revenue r. Assuming an initial stock level y_0 and a continuous demand distribution, adoption of this value of S^* yields total expected costs (TEC) of

TEC = ordering costs + holding costs + penalty costs − revenues

$$TEC(S^*) = k + c(S^* - y_0) + \int_0^{S^*} h(S^* - u) f_{T+L}(u)\, du$$
$$+ \int_{S^*}^{\infty} p(u - S^*) f_{T+L}(u)\, du - \int_0^{S^*} r(u) f_{T+L}(u)\, du$$
$$- rS^*[1 - F_{T+L}(S^*)] \tag{4-30}$$

Thus if an order is placed, it should bring the stock level up to S^* and yield costs indicated in (4-30). If an order is not placed, the total expected cost, written $TEC(y_0)$, depends on the initial stock level y_0 and is given by (4-30) with S^* replaced by y_0 and the ordering cost k deleted. These costs are shown graphically in figure 4-9. It can be seen by examining this graph that if y_0 is greater than s^*, no order should be placed. Thus an (s, S) policy is

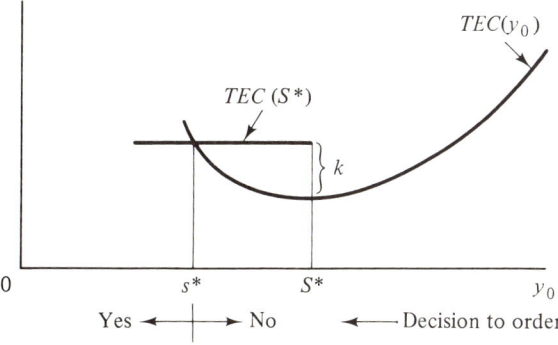

Figure 4-9 Effect of ordering on the total expected cost.

appropriate where S is determined by using equation (4-29) and s is found by solving for y_0 in the equation

$$TEC(y_0) = TEC(S^*) \qquad (4\text{-}31)$$

To return to the newspaper example (example 4-5), suppose now that it costs the salesperson an average of \$8 to sell newspapers during any given rush hour. This cost includes travel costs and lost income which would otherwise be earned through mowing lawns. This can be interpreted as an ordering cost, so $k = \$8$. How many papers should be ordered in this case?

Recall from example 4-5 that $r = 0.23$, $p = 0$, $h = 0$, and $S^* = 164$ papers. By using equation (4-30), the net cost of ordering 164 papers is

$$TEC(164) = \$8 + 0.5(164) - \int_{150}^{164} 0.23u \, \frac{1}{40} \, du - 0.23(164)\left(\frac{190 - 164}{190 - 150}\right)$$

$$= 8 + 24.60 - 12.64 - 24.52$$

$$= -\$4.56$$

This net cost (actually a net revenue) is compared with the cost of not ordering, which in this case is $TEC(y_0) = TEC(0) = 0$. Thus, the salesperson should continue to sell papers and to order 164 papers per day. If the ordering cost k increased to more than \$12.56 (which would reflect increased opportunities for the salesperson to earn more in some other endeavor), then no more papers should be ordered.

4-4 MODEL COMPARISON

This chapter has been concerned with a variety of periodic models. For the most part, these models are intended to aid in automatic decision making regarding ordering of a large number of routinely demanded items which collectively comprise the inventory. Thus the emphasis has been on straightforward model assumptions which may be only approximately correct, rather than more rigorously correct but complex models which would prove to be more cumbersome to use for a many-item inventory.

Any model is an approximation. Thus in choosing a model, the question is not whether reality is exactly reflected, but rather whether it is reflected well enough. Sometimes the choice of model will be apparent; the concern in this section is that it will not always be so. Demand is rarely really known with absolute certainty. Does this mean that a stochastic model is called for? There is always an ordering cost, albeit perhaps a very small one. Should the model chosen recognize an ordering cost? In this section, an example situation will be depicted for which the answers to these questions are not obvious. Then several models will be proposed as being appropriate for the situation. These models will be evaluated on the basis of expected costs, using the actual costs stated in the example.

Consider the following situation, many features of which are kept simple in order to highlight model differences. An item has demand during each period of 7, 8, or 9 with respective probabilities 0.2, 0.6, and 0.2. A holding cost of $h = \$1$ per unit of stock is assessed each period. Unsatisfied demand is backlogged at a penalty of $8 per unit per period. The lead time is negligible and is assumed to be zero. (This $L = 0$ assumption does not cause any loss of generality.) The purchase cost per unit will be neglected (assumed equal to zero) since demand will ultimately be satisfied anyway. There is an ordering cost of $8 per order placed.

The first model to be considered (which will be referred to as "model 1") will be the stochastic model recognizing the ordering cost $k = 8$. The values in the above situation were chosen so that relation (4-28) would be exactly satisfied, as the reader may verify. Therefore whether to recognize k in the model is at the discretion of the analyst.

By using equations (4-21) and (4-24), s is chosen so that

$$\sum_{u > s - \bar{d}T/2} \left[u - \left(s - \frac{\bar{d}T}{2} \right) \right] f_{T+L}(u) = s_D = \sqrt{\frac{2k\bar{d}}{h}} \sqrt{\frac{h^2}{(h+p)p}} = 1.33$$

The left-hand side (expected loss) is calculated for various values of s:

$s - \dfrac{\bar{d}T}{2}$	$\sum\limits_{u > s - \bar{d}T/2} \left[u - \left(s - \dfrac{\bar{d}T}{2} \right) \right] f_{T+L}(u)$
6	$1(0.2) + 2(0.6) + 3(0.2) = 2$
7	$1(0.6) + 2(0.2) = 1$
8	$1(0.2) = 0.2$

Therefore the value $s - \bar{d}T/2 = 7$, or $s = 11$ seems appropriate. Using equation (4-25), we have $S = s - \bar{d}T/2 + Q_D = 7 + 12 = 19$.

The second model (model 2) will also be stochastic, but will ignore the ordering cost k. Whether this is an advisable thing to do remains to be seen. (Do not trust your intuition if it tells you that it is not advisable.) In this case, the optimal value of S^* is obtained from equation (4-18):

$$F_{T+L}(S^*) = \frac{8}{8+1} = 0.88$$

This was solved in the table in the preceding paragraph to find $s - \bar{d}T/2$. For model 2, $S^* = 8$ or 9. Here, given an aversion to shortages, $S^* = 9$ is chosen.

Before proceeding with any more models, we will compare the two models already developed. The criterion to be used is the long-run expected cost of using each model. This is found according to the following procedure. For a given model solution:

Step 1 Define a set of mutually exclusive states which describe the possible inventory levels at a point in time when costs are assessed. In this case, this will be at the end of each time period.
Step 2 Determine the steady-state probability π_j of being in each possible state j.
Step 3 Calculate the cost c_j to be assessed whenever the inventory level is in state j.
Step 4 Calculate the expected cost per period

$$TEC = \sum_{\text{all } j} c_j \pi_j$$

This procedure will first be demonstrated for model 2.

Step 1 The states are 0, 1, and 2. This is because in each period an order is placed which brings the inventory level up to 9, after which the demand of 7, 8, or 9 depletes the inventory to 2, 1, or 0, respectively.
Step 2 The probability of being in each state j is, in this case, the probability that the demand is $9 - j$. Thus

$$\pi_0 = \text{Prob [demand} = 9] = 0.2$$

Similarly,

$$\pi_1 = 0.6 \quad \text{and} \quad \pi_2 = 0.2$$

Step 3 The cost c_j is the cost of ordering (which must now be considered in any comparison, even though it was ignored in model 2) plus the holding cost. Thus

$$c_j = k + h_j = 8 + j \quad j = 0, 1, 2$$

which yields $c_0 = 8$, $c_1 = 9$, $c_2 = 10$.
Step 4

$$TEC = c_0 \pi_0 + c_1 \pi_1 + c_2 \pi_2$$
$$= 8(0.2) + 9(0.6) + 10(0.2)$$
$$= \$10 \text{ per period}$$

Now the procedure can be followed for model 1.

CHAPTER 4: PERIODIC-REVIEW ORDERING DECISION MODELS **103**

Step 1 The possible states (levels of inventory) are 1, 2, 3, 4, 5, 10, 11, and 12. This can be seen more easily in step 2.

Step 2 The calculation of the probabilities π_j in this case requires a result from the theory of Markov chains, which is stated here without proof.

Let p_{ij} be the probability that the inventory level is j in any period given that the level was i in the preceding period. Let $P = [p_{ij}]$ be the matrix of such probabilities. If there are n possible states, P is an $n \times n$ matrix. Then $\pi = (\pi_1, \pi_2, \ldots, \pi_n)$ is the solution to $\pi = \pi P$. P is called a *transition matrix*. For the solution $(s^*, S^*) = (11, 19)$ for model 1, the transition matrix is given in table 4-6. A sample entry in the table is $p_{11,3} = 0.6$. This value follows from the fact that if the level i is 11, then no order is placed, so that the probability that the level j at the end of the next period is 3 is the probability that demand in that period is 8, which is 0.6.

The vector equation $\pi = \pi p$ can be written out as a series of linear equations:

$$\pi_2 = 0.2\pi_{11}$$
$$\pi_3 = 0.6\pi_{11} + 0.2\pi_{12}$$
$$\pi_4 = 0.2\pi_{11} + 0.6\pi_{12}$$
$$\pi_5 = \phantom{0.2\pi_{11} + {}} 0.2\pi_{12}$$
$$\pi_{10} = 0.2(\pi_2 + \pi_3 + \pi_4 + \pi_5 + \pi_{10})$$
$$\pi_{11} = 0.6(\pi_2 + \pi_3 + \pi_4 + \pi_5 + \pi_{10})$$
$$\pi_{12} = 0.2(\pi_2 + \pi_3 + \pi_4 + \pi_5 + \pi_{10})$$

Table 4-6 The transition matrix for the solution to model 1

i \ j	2	3	4	5	10	11	12
2					0.2	0.6	0.2
3					0.2	0.6	0.2
4					0.2	0.6	0.2
5					0.2	0.6	0.2
10					0.2	0.6	0.2
11	0.2	0.6	0.2				
12		0.2	0.6	0.2			

104 PART II: INVENTORY CONTROL MODELS

These, together with the requirement that

$$\sum_{\text{all } j} \pi_j = 1$$

can be solved to yield values of π_j:

j	2	3	4	5	10	11	12
π_j	$\dfrac{0.6}{9}$	$\dfrac{2.0}{9}$	$\dfrac{1.2}{9}$	$\dfrac{0.2}{9}$	$\dfrac{1.0}{9}$	$\dfrac{3.0}{9}$	$\dfrac{1.0}{9}$

Step 3 The cost c_j is the cost of ordering (if an order is placed) plus the holding cost:

j	2	3	4	5	10	11	12
c_j	10	11	12	13	10	11	12

Step 4

$$TEC = \sum_{\text{all } j} c_j \pi_j = \$11.11 \text{ per period}$$

The third model (model 3) to be considered will be a deterministic model which recognizes the ordering cost. By following the procedure in section 4.2, equation (4-11), using $\bar{d} = 8$ as the assumed deterministic demand,

$$c_{011} = 8 \qquad\qquad\qquad\qquad = c_{01} \qquad c_{01}/1 = 8$$
$$c_{012} = 8 + 1(8) \qquad\qquad\quad = 16 = c_{02} \qquad c_{02}/2 = 8$$
$$c_{022} = 8 \qquad\quad + 8(8) = 72$$
$$c_{013} = 8 + 1(24) \qquad\qquad\quad = 32 = c_{03} \qquad c_{03}/3 = 10.67$$
$$c_{023} = 8 + 1(8) \; + \; 8(8) = 80$$
$$c_{033} = 8 \qquad\quad + 64(8) = 520$$

The policy dictated by model 3 is then to order 8 every period or 16 every other period. However, one does not have to calculate an expected cost to realize that these are unsound policies. Because of the random variation in actual demand, any policy indicating a constant order quantity and no buffer stock will lead to excessive holding and shortage costs as time goes on. About the best modification in this case would be to order up to the *level* of 8 ($S = 8$) each period [or 16 every other period ($S = 16$)]. The long-run expected cost can be verified by the four-step procedure. For the $S = 8$ policy:

Step 1 The possible inventory levels j are $-1, 0, 1$.
Step 2 $\pi_{-1} = 0.2;\ \pi_0 = 0.6;\ \pi_1 = 0.2$.
Step 3 $c_{-1} = 16;\ c_0 = 8;\ c_1 = 9$.
Step 4 $TEC = \$9.80$ per period.

For the $S = 16$ policy:

Step 1 The possible inventory levels are 7, 8, 9.
Step 2 $\pi_7 = 0.2;\ \pi_8 = 0.6;\ \pi_9 = 0.2$.
Step 3 $c_7 = 15;\ c_8 = 16;\ c_9 = 17$.
Step 4 $TEC = \$16$ per period.

The final model (model 4) to be entertained is a deterministic model which does not recognize the ordering cost. The solution in this case (as discussed in section 4.2) is, by inspection, to order $\bar{d} = 8$ in every period. As in model 3, as a result of the random nature of demands, order up to *level* 8 in every period. This policy also accrued under model 3 and has $TEC = \$9.80$ per period.

The results of the four models of the example situation are summarized in table 4-7. A few observations may be gleaned from these figures:

1. Models ignoring the ordering cost outperformed those recognizing the cost, and with less computational effort. This is probably because the

Table 4-7 Cost results of several policies for a situation involving ordering costs and probabilistic demands

Model	s	S	$TEC(S)$
1	11	19	11.11
2	9	9	10.00
3	8	8	9.80
	16	16	16.00
4	8	8	9.80
—	9	17	9.98
—	8	17	9.18

ordering cost was not large enough to suggest ordering more than 1.5 periods' worth of demand per order.
2. Modified deterministic models performed better than the stochastic models, and with less computational effort. This is probably so because demand variability was not excessive in relation to average demand.
3. None of the models found the optimal solution. See the last solution indicated in table 4-7.
4. The above observations are based on a sample of 1 and should be discounted accordingly. To increase your experience to a sample of 2, see problem 4-15.

One conclusion transcends the sample of 1. In the general probabilistic demand case and in the presence of an ordering cost, the "optimal" solution involves burdensome computations which have not been treated here. In settling for an approximate answer, it might be well worth the effort to evaluate the policies suggested by several models before settling on one solution.

4-5 SUMMARY

Single-item models recognizing periodic-review ordering policies have been developed in this chapter. Two types of policies have been stressed. In an optional replenishment, or (s, S) policy, an order is placed to bring the inventory level up to S at the beginning of any period in which the level is below s. The second type of policy, called an (S) policy, is a special case of the first in which $s = S$. The (s, S) policy is appropriate when there is an ordering cost $(k > 0)$, while the (S) policy is used in the absence of such an ordering cost $(k = 0)$.

The deterministic models developed considered variable demands so that single values of s and S are not appropriate. Rather, special procedures are derived for determining order timing and quantity for the two cases $k > 0$ and $k = 0$. For $k > 0$ the properties of concave costs were exploited to yield such a procedure, while for $k = 0$ a convex-cost model was found to be more realistic.

In the stochastic demand case with no ordering cost, various (S) policies were derived, all of which relied on the notions of marginal costs of holding one more unit in stock, or of being short by one more unit, at the end of a time period. Equation (4-17) provided the important unifying link among the policies. When an ordering cost was included, an approximate procedure for determining policy parameter values was used for lack of a simple exact (i.e., cost-minimizing) procedure. Since the model for $k > 0$ is more complicated than the corresponding $k = 0$ model, a method of determining when to use the $k = 0$ model is given by equation (4-28).

A demonstration of model comparison showed some effects of applying four different models to the same situation involving ordering costs and probabilistic demands. For this demonstration it was seen that the model whose assumptions best matched the assumed situation did not necessarily yield the best cost results.

REFERENCES

1. Hadley, George, and T. M. Whitin: "Analysis of Inventory Systems," Prentice-Hall, Englewood Cliffs, N.J., 1963.
2. Love, Stephen F.: "A Facilities in Series Inventory Model with Nested Schedules," *Management Science*, vol. 18, no. 5, pp. 327–338, January 1972, pt. I.
3. Scarf, Herbert: The Optimality of (S, s) Policies in the Dynamic Inventory Problem, chapter 13 in K. Arrow, S. Karlin, and P. Suppes (eds.), "Mathematical Methods in the Social Sciences," Stanford University Press, Stanford, Calif., 1960.
4. Veinott, Arthur F., Jr.: "Production Planning with Convex Costs: A Parametric Study," *Management Science*, vol. 10, no. 3, pp. 441–460, April 1964.
5. Veinott, Arthur F., Jr.: "On the Optimality of (s, S) Inventory Policies: New Conditions and a New Proof," Technical Report No. 4, ONR Contract 225(77), I.E. Dept., Stanford University, July 15, 1965, 28 pp.
6. Wagner, Harvey, and T. M. Whitin: "Dynamic Version of the Economic Lot Size Model," *Management Science*, vol. 5, no. 1, pp. 89–96, October 1958.
7. Zangwill, Willard I.: "A Backlogging Model and Multi-Echelon Model of a Dynamic Economic Lot Size Production System—A Network Approach," *Management Science*, vol. 15, no. 9, pp. 506–527, May 1969.

EXERCISES

4-1 Demand for each of the next seven months, $t = 1$ to 7, is known and has values 6, 2, 0, 8, 1, 3, 5, respectively. No inventory is on hand at present, and none is desired at the end of the seventh month. It costs $6 to place an order. The cost of holding stock is $1 per unit held per month; the cost of a shortage is $3 per unit per month. Unsatisfied demand is backlogged.

(a) Find an optimal no-backlog solution.

(b) Find an optimal solution allowing backlogging.

4-2 Assume the conditions of problem 4-1, except that demand is constant at 4 units per month for an infinite horizon.

(a) Repeat problem 4-1(a).

(b) Repeat problem 4-1(b).

4-3 Suppose you are faced with demands $d = (4, 2, 3, 5)$ for the next four quarters. In any period you can obtain up to 3 units of stock at a cost C_1 per unit. Any additional amount obtained will cost C_2 per unit. In any period except the second, $C_1 = \$6$ and $C_2 = \$9$. In period 2, the corresponding values are $4 and $5. It costs $1 per unit held per period. Determine an optimal ordering schedule $x = (x_1, x_2, x_3, x_4)$.

4-4 Recall example 4-3, in which demands were given to be $d = (4, 6, 2, 3, 2)$. An optimal solution was found to be $x = (6, 3, 3, 3, 2)$. Suppose now that one period has elapsed and that information that demand in the sixth period will be for 5 units has been added to the forecast. Also recall from example 4-3 that $c_5 = \$4.70$. Assume c_6 also equals $\$4.70$. Thus you now face demands for the *next* five periods of $d = (6, 2, 3, 2, 5)$, with a current inventory of 2 units. Using as a starting point the optimal no-backlogging solution to example 4-3, find an optimal solution for the revised forecast for the next five periods.

4-5 Every year, the state Division of Motor Vehicles must order renewal stickers to be applied to the license plates of all passenger cars registered in the state. The stickers are self-adhesive and are imprinted with the year of issue. They cost $0.06 each. Excess stickers at the end of the year are disposed of. If a shortage of stickers occurs, extras can be rush-ordered at a cost of $0.20 per sticker. The number of cars which will require stickers is estimated to be normally distributed with mean 2,800,000 and standard deviation 70,000.

(a) How many stickers should be ordered at the beginning of each year?

(b) How much money would be saved per year if the stickers costing $0.06 could be used in subsequent years instead of being discarded? For this purpose, assume that a capital cost is charged on stickers held over to a future year because money is worth 6 percent to the Division of Motor Vehicles.

4-6 Suppose a discount factor α is applied to cash flows so that a flow of x dollars one period hence is valued at αx now, where α has a value slightly less than 1. Show how this affects the results in equations (4-18), (4-19), and (4-20).

4-7 An airport caterer prepares meals which are sold at a profit of $1 per meal. Demand for these meals is uniformly distributed between 1200 and 1400 per day. Any unsold meals are sold at the end of the day to a charitable organization at a *loss* of $1 per meal. How many meals should the caterer prepare each day?

4-8 Demand during a two-week period is normally distributed with mean 20 and standard deviation 4. The holding cost is $3 per unit held per week. The penalty for incurring a shortage is $18 per unit of demand not satisfied on time. Orders can be placed at the beginning of any week; orders arrive one week after they are placed. Unsatisfied demand is backlogged. Determine the value of the parameter for an (S) policy.

4-9 Repeat problem 4-8 under the following condition. All demand not satisfied on time results in lost sales for which the lost-revenue contribution is $25 per unit. In this case, the $18 penalty in problem 4-8 does not apply.

4-10 Repeat problem 4-8 if a cost of $20 per order placed is incurred. In this case, determine the parameter values for an (s, S) policy.

4-11 Demand during a two-week period is uniformly distributed between 8 and 12 units. The holding cost is $0.40 per unit per week. There is a penalty cost of $2 per unit of demand which occurs during a stockout period. Unsatisfied demand is backlogged. It costs k per order placed. Orders are placed at the beginning of any week and arrive at the beginning of the following week. Determine the parameter values of an (S) policy or an (s, S) policy, whichever is appropriate, when

(a) $k = 0$
(b) $k = 3$

4-12 Suppose the conditions of problem 4-11 are in effect, except that now sales are lost, resulting in a lost profit of $1.50 per unit in addition to the penalty cost.

(a) Repeat problem 4-11(a).

(b) Repeat problem 4-11(b). *Note:* Although no example in chapter 4 is exactly like problem 4-11(b), you should be able to handle it.

4-13 Suppose the conditions of problem 4-7 are in effect, except that the following additional facts are brought to light. The caterer incurs a fixed cost of $1250 for each day's meal preparation operations. The $1 profit per meal is the difference between a $2.50 selling price and a $1.50 variable cost per meal produced. How many meals should the caterer prepare per day in this case?

4-14 A growing company must provide additional capacity (measured in thousands of square meters) to house its operations which presently consume all available capacity. The *increase* in requirements each year (over the preceding year) are, for the next six years, 14, 20, 6, 12, 30, 20. It costs $400,000 to engage in any capacity expansion project regardless of its size. Idle (unused) capacity costs the company $10 per square meter per year. Capacity expansion is permitted to take place at the beginning of any year. The company has decided to meet the total of 102,000 square meters by the end of the sixth year, with no excess capacity at that time. Determine the number, timing, and size of capacity expansions over the six-year planning horizon to minimize costs if

(a) All requirements must be satisfied by company-financed construction projects.

(b) Requirements can be satisfied by leasing space at $30 per square meter per year.

4-15 Consider an item which has demand during each period of 7, 8, 9, or 10 with respective probabilities 0.2, 0.4, 0.3, and 0.1. A holding cost of $1.50 per unit is assessed each period. Unsatisfied demand is backlogged at a penalty of $10 per unit per period. There is an ordering cost of $12 per order placed. Assume that the lead time is zero.

(a) Find an optimal ordering policy under each of the following conditions:

1. Use a stochastic model which recognizes the ordering cost.
2. Use a stochastic model which ignores the ordering cost.
3. Use a deterministic model which recognizes the ordering cost.
4. Use a deterministic model which ignores the ordering cost.

(b) Compare the four policies found in (a) on an expected-cost basis, using the procedure developed in section 4-4.

CHAPTER
FIVE
COORDINATED REPLENISHMENT OF MULTIPLE ITEMS

In the preceding chapters, the models developed have recognized only single stock items. Likewise, all ordering policies have related to individual items. Now, forgive the understatement, but how many inventories contain but one item? The odd municipal water supply or grain elevator, perhaps. This chapter and the one following address concerns of controlling multi-item inventories.

The effective control of multiple items does not necessarily require procedures different from those in the preceding chapters. As an extreme case in point, suppose that a wealthy, eccentric merchant deals in three commodities—pet lizards, rubies, and extract of sauerkraut. Each item is obtained from a separate supplier. Demand for each item is unaffected by demand for either of the other two (lizards do not like sauerkraut). Each of these items can be controlled separately. The reason is that there is no *interaction* among the stocked items. Multiple-item ordering decision models ("multi-item models," for short) are useful simply because they recognize interactions among the items involved.

Item interactions as identified in this book are of three types: interactions resulting from costs, resources, and demands. An example of a *cost interaction* is a reduction in ordering costs because of simultaneous ordering of multiple items. Another example is a material cost saving as a result of quantity discounts applied to the total dollar amount purchased in one order. *Resource interaction* occurs when stock items compete for scarce resources. For example, the total amount of one order may be limited by the capacity (weight or volume) of a transport vehicle or vessel. A similar limitation may apply to the total quantity of material stored (e.g., warehouse capacity).

Demand interaction exists whenever the demand for one item can be affected by the demand for one or more other items being stocked. This can happen in a variety of ways. For example, if a stockout of one item occurs, some customers may select (substitute) another stocked item in its place. A different type of demand interaction takes place when two or more items under control bear a supply-demand relationship to each other. For example, an item may be under control at both the wholesale and retail levels. The item at the retail level, or *echelon*, is demanded externally and supplied internally, and the item at the wholesale echelon is supplied externally and demanded internally. Such *multiechelon* models are the subject of chapter 6.

This chapter is concerned with *single-echelon*, multi-item inventories. Each of the three types of item interaction considered above is treated in a separate section. However, there is a central concern common to all sections of this chapter. Regardless of the type of interaction involved, the cogent question is, What *degree* of interaction justifies the added complexity involved in the use of a multi-item model? The real world of inventories does not include very many wealthy, eccentric merchants. The truth is that it is almost impossible to find real-life multi-item inventory with no item interactions. Thus the question of justification of the use of multi-item control procedures needs to be addressed in essentially every practical instance.

In general, a policy for ordering multiple interactive items will be called a *coordinated replenishment* policy. Several types of such policies will be considered in the sections that follow. At this point, one such policy is defined, primarily for clarification. Sometimes the term "joint ordering policy" is used in the literature to mean what here is called a coordinated replenishment policy. In this book, joint ordering is defined as follows. Suppose that whenever any item is ordered, *every* item (for which there has been any demand since the previous order) is ordered. That is, every time an order is placed, every stock item is brought up to a specified inventory level. The policy specifying the levels up to which each item is ordered (as well as when to order) is called a "joint ordering policy" in this case. In a sense (as will be seen below), joint ordering is at the end of a spectrum of coordinated replenishment policies. At the opposite end is *independent ordering*, under which each item is ordered according to its own single-item policy. Other policies in the spectrum will be introduced as they are needed.

5-1 MODELS RECOGNIZING COST INTERACTION

As you have seen in earlier chapters, costs are usually modeled as belonging to four categories: ordering costs, material costs, holding costs, and shortage costs. It turns out that most cost interaction occurs in the first two categories. Ordering cost interaction occurs because such costs are reduced by coincident ordering of multiple items. This might be due to savings in freight, paperwork, or materials handling. This will be modeled by defining K to be the cost of placing any order and k_j to be the *additional* cost of ordering item j. Thus if items 2, 4, and 7 are ordered together, then the ordering cost will be $K + k_2 + k_4 + k_7$.

Material cost interaction occurs when, for example, a quantity discount applies to the total dollar amount of an order (from one supplier) regardless of which items are ordered. This section is subdivided by type of cost interaction.

Ordering Cost Interaction

In this subsection it is assumed that the cost of placing an order is K, plus k_j if item j is ordered. There are n items altogether, so that if every item is ordered in a single order, the ordering cost is $K + k_1 + k_2 + \cdots + k_n$. Two types of models will be developed. The first type will be deterministic, and the second stochastic. It will be seen that each model type gives rise to a different type of coordinated replenishment policy.

For the deterministic model, it is assumed that each item j ($j = 1, 2, \ldots, n$) has associated with it a holding cost h_j dollars per unit held per unit time and a demand rate d_j units per unit time. The ordering policy will specify for each item j a time t_j between orders for that item. Moreover, these times will be chosen in such a way that each time is an integer multiple of the minimum time. This will lessen the impact of incurring the cost K, because many items will be ordered whenever an order is placed. No shortages are permitted.

The model developed here seeks a solution which approximates a minimum-cost solution. The results are then compared with minimum-cost results. The heuristic relied on is that the relative ordering frequency of each item should resemble what it would be if each item were ordered with regard to only costs unique to that item. This statement is clarified as follows. Suppose item j was ordered on the basis of single-item economical order quantity considerations. Then, from equation (2-35), the time between orders would be

$$\tau_j = \sqrt{\frac{2k_j}{h_j d_j}} \tag{5-1}$$

The ordering cost in equation (5-1) is taken to be k_j rather than $K + k_j$, since the equation will be used only to determine relative ordering frequencies. The cost K will be taken into account in determining the absolute ordering frequencies. These τ_j are thus temporary times between orders, for establishing relative ordering frequencies. The final, absolute ordering frequencies will be based on t_j. For convenience, rank the n items in order of increasing time between orders: $\tau_1 \leq \tau_2 \leq \cdots \leq \tau_n$. Then define α_j by

$$\tau_j = \alpha_j \tau_1 \qquad j = 1, \ldots, n \tag{5-2}$$

where $1 = \alpha_1 \leq \alpha_2 \leq \cdots \leq \alpha_n$. *Note*: Let $\alpha_j = 1$ for any j for which $k_j = 0$. Now, in order to economize on ordering costs, the α_j must be integers. Let $[\alpha_j]$ be the integer resulting from rounding off α_j. Then, in the final policy, the absolute time between orders t_j will satisfy

$$t_j = [\alpha_j]t_1 \qquad j = 1, \ldots, n \tag{5-3}$$

The value of t_1 will be chosen to minimize the total cost TC per unit time:

$$TC = \frac{K}{t_1} + \sum_{j=1}^{n} \frac{k_j}{t_j} + \frac{1}{2} \sum_{j=1}^{n} h_j d_j t_j \tag{5-4}$$

which, by using equation (5-3), becomes

$$TC = \frac{1}{t_1}\left(K + \sum_{j=1}^{n} \frac{k_j}{[\alpha_j]}\right) + \frac{t_1}{2} \sum_{j=1}^{n} h_j d_j [\alpha_j] \tag{5-5}$$

Setting $\partial TC/\partial t_1$ equal to zero and solving for t_1 yields

$$t_1 = \sqrt{\frac{2\left(K + \sum_{j=1}^{n} \frac{k_j}{[\alpha_j]}\right)}{\sum_{j=1}^{n} h_j d_j [\alpha_j]}} \tag{5-6}$$

The solution procedure can be outlined as follows:

Step 1 Determine the values of τ_j by using equation (5-1).
Step 2 Determine α_j by using equation (5-2).
Step 3 Compute $[\alpha_j]$ by rounding off α_j.
Step 4 Calculate t_1 from equation (5-6).
Step 5 Calculate $t_2, \ldots, t_n$ from equation (5-3).

Example 5-1 As an example, assume that $K = 43.5, n = 15$, and the cost and demand data in the first four columns of table 5-1 apply. The time period for h_j and d_j is one year. After the calculations in table 5-1 are completed, t_1 is determined using equation (5-6) to be 0.0199 year (50.4 orders per year):

$$t_1 = \sqrt{\frac{2(43.5 + 71.88)}{585{,}500}} = 0.0199$$

The values of t_j for $j > 1$ can then be determined by using equation (5-3).
The total cost per year for controlling this inventory by using the coordinated replenishment policy above is calculated from equation

Table 5-1 Data and calculations for example 5-1

j	d_j	h_j	k_j	τ_j	α_j	$[\alpha_j]$	$h_j d_j [\alpha_j]$	$k_j/[\alpha_j]$
1	10,000	10	10	0.01414	1.00	1	100,000	10
2	35,000	2	8	0.0151	1.07	1	70,000	8
3	8,000	8	8	0.0158	1.12	1	64,000	8
4	9,000	5	6	0.0163	1.15	1	45,000	6
5	50,000	1	8	0.0179	1.27	1	50,000	8
6	15,000	2	5	0.0183	1.29	1	30,000	5
7	20,000	2	7	0.0187	1.32	1	40,000	7
8	12,500	1.6	4.5	0.0212	1.50	2	40,000	2.25
9	10,000	1.45	8	0.0327	2.31	2	29,000	4
10	4,250	2	5	0.0343	2.43	2	17,000	2.5
11	2,500	3	7	0.0432	3.06	3	22,500	2.33
12	10,000	1	10	0.0447	3.16	3	30,000	3.33
13	4,000	1.25	5	0.0447	3.16	3	15,000	1.67
14	2,000	3	6	0.0447	3.16	3	18,000	2.0
15	1,500	2	9	0.0775	5.48	5	15,000	1.8
Totals							585,500	71.88

(5-5) to be $TC = \$11,624$. To put this result in perspective, it will be compared with two other results. The value of TC, assuming that all items are controlled independently (with an ordering cost of $K + k_j$ for each item j), by using equation (2-36) is $23,034. Of course, this value may overestimate the true cost under independent ordering since it assumes that coincident ordering of more than one item never occurs.

Another result is due to Goyal [1], who has derived an iterative procedure for determining *optimal* (minimum-cost) values of t_1 and $\alpha_1, \ldots, \alpha_n$. His solution is $t_1 = 0.0215$ (46.6 orders per year) and $[\alpha_1]$ thru $[\alpha_{15}]$ given by 1, 1, 1, 1, 1, 1, 1, 2, 2, 2, 2, 2, 2, 4. This solution results in a total annual cost of $11,450.

We turn now to a model which recognizes some randomness in demands. The first thing to note is that the policy just completed would make no sense if any attempt were to be made to respond to stochastic demands. Even if all lead times are zero (so that stockouts are easily avoided), such a policy is unworkable. To see this, consider any point in time at which more than one item is scheduled to be ordered. Because of the randomness in demand, not all items will run out of stock simultaneously, as planned for. In fact, it will be necessary to place an order when the first of the items runs out of stock. At that time, a decision must be made regarding whether to order any other item—either one which was scheduled to be ordered together with the one being ordered or any other item whose inventory level is low, again because demand for that item has been higher than anticipated.

The type of policy which is suggested by the above situation is stated as follows. When any item reaches a zero inventory level, order that item together with any other items whose levels are "close to" zero. The "close to" criterion is formalized by defining for each item j a critical inventory level c_j. If any item is to be ordered, any other item j whose inventory level is below c_j will also be ordered. Now since demands vary randomly and a lead time L between order and receipt of stock is assumed, any item j will be ordered whenever its level reaches a reorder period s_j. Each item will be ordered up to a level S_j. The complete ordering policy will specify values for s_j, c_j, and S_j for $j = 1, 2, \ldots, n$. Such a policy is known as a *can-order policy*. The c_j values are known as *can-order levels*. Actually "can-order" is a misnomer; "must-include in the next order placed" would give a more proper connotation. The reorder points s_j can be thought of as "must place an order" points.

Although the concept of a can-order policy is straightforward and appealing to one's common sense, the specification of minimum-cost values for policy parameters is difficult. Several approaches to the specification of parameters will be discussed.

Suppose n items are under control. Each item j has associated with it an ordering cost $K + k_j$, a holding cost h_j, and randomly varying demands with average demand rate $\bar{d}_j$. Assume the standard deviation of demand per unit time is σ_j for item j. The cost K is, again, incurred only once per order regardless of the number of different items ordered. The delivery lead time is L. The following ratio (b_j) is useful in determining the relative desirability of ordering multiple items together. Define

$$b_j \equiv \frac{K}{K + k_j} \tag{5-7}$$

Clearly, $0 \leq b_j \leq 1$. If $b_j = 0$, then $K = 0$, in which case all items should be ordered independently. That is, $c_j = s_j$. At the other extreme, if $b_j = 1$, then $k_j = 0$. In this case, it costs nothing to order this item along with any other item already being ordered, so $c_j = S_j$. If $b_j = 1$ for all j, then $c_j = S_j$ for all j. This results in a policy known as *joint ordering*, under which all items are replenished to their S_j values whenever any item is ordered. In between the independent and joint ordering policies lies the whole spectrum of can-order policies.

The following approach is an attempt to make the determination of the parameter values s_j, c_j, and S_j, as simple as possible, consistent with model reality. The approach will then be compared with some results appearing in the technical literature.

Consider first the service level for item j resulting from selected values of s_j, c_j, and S_j. One way of defining "service level" is in terms of a specified probability α of running out of stock prior to a replenishment. If an item reaches its reorder point s_j before being ordered and the delivery lead time is L, then the probability of not running out of stock is $F_L(s_j)$, which is the cumulative distribution function of demand during the lead time for item j. The service level requirement then becomes

$$F_L(s_j) = 1 - \alpha \qquad j = 1, 2, \ldots, n \tag{5-8}$$

The value of $1 - \alpha$ may be determined using economic considerations [as it was in equation (3-33)], or it may be specified arbitrarily. The latter approach is taken in this subsection, because the emphasis is on a policy designed to economize on ordering costs. If penalty costs are available, an approach such as the use of equation (3-33) could be substituted here without affecting the remainder of the procedure.

The use of equation (5-8) to determine s_j, $j = 1, 2, \ldots, n$, is extremely conservative. To see this, define the *average remnant stock* R_j to be the average stock level of item j immediately prior to placement of an order for that item. The true service level for item j is actually more closely related to R_j than to s_j. The remnant stock prior to any particular order will vary randomly between s_j and c_j, as illustrated in figure 5-1. Some possible alternatives to the blind use of equation (5-8) to determine s_j would be any one of the following.

1. Use the desired service level to determine the average remnant stock:

$$F_L(R_j) = 1 - \alpha \qquad j = 1, 2, \ldots, n$$

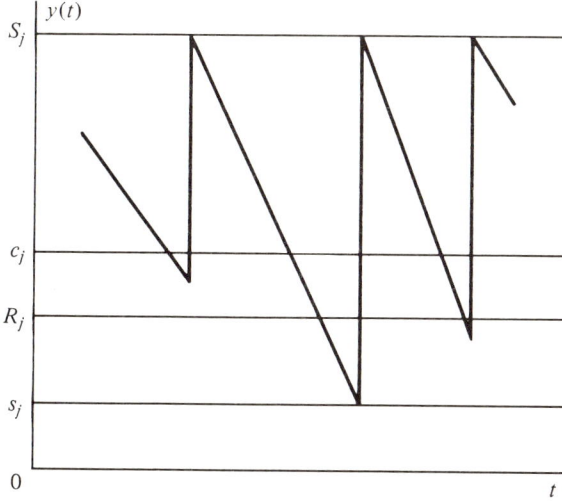

Figure 5-1 An inventory-time plot of item j under a can-order policy.

Then relate s_j to R_j in some way. Unfortunately, this is not a straightforward task. The discussion involving equations (5-16) through (5-20) below would be one approach. This may be dangerous in that when the actual remnant stock is less than R_j, a serious shortage will occur. The risk that this will occur cannot be readily determined, but depends in a complex way on the number of items being controlled, on their demand distributions, and on all the parameter values s_j, c_j, and S_j, $j = 1, 2, \ldots, n$.
2. Choose s_j to be some fraction, say $\frac{8}{10}$, of that determined from equation (5-8).
3. Increase the allowed probability of stockout α to some higher value α' [say $\alpha' = 0.08$ instead of $\alpha = 0.05$ in equation (5-8)].

More research is needed into this as well as many other facets of the can-order policy.

A preview of the complete procedure used here to determine the parameter values of the can-order policy is in order. Step 1, which is to determine s_j, $j = 1, \ldots, n$, has already been discussed. The remaining steps are as follows.

Step 2 Determine the desired time between orders t_j for each item j ($j = 1, 2, \ldots, n$). This will be done with the objective of attempting to minimize the associated holding and ordering costs.

Step 3 Determine S_j in such a way that the times determined in step 2 will (approximately) occur when the model is implemented.

Step 4 Determine c_j by relating it to the previously determined parameters, as described below.

Step 2 is based heavily on concepts used in the deterministic model earlier in this subsection. Recall that in that model, first a set of relative times τ_j between orders was determined based on holding costs and "line item" ordering costs k_j. Then absolute times t_j were chosen on the basis of the "header" ordering cost K. The items were ordered so that $t_1 \leq t_2 \leq \cdots \leq t_n$. In the deterministic model, the values t_j/t_1 were required to be integers, but that is not necessary in this case. Step 2 will be executed as follows. First determine the τ_j according to equation (5-1), which is repeated here for convenience:

$$\tau_j = \sqrt{\frac{2k_j}{h_j d_j}} \qquad (5\text{-}1)$$

Then order the items so that $\tau_1 \leq \tau_2 \leq \cdots \leq \tau_n$. Let $\alpha_j = \tau_j/\tau_1$ as before. Now the value of t_1 will be determined by minimizing the following estimate

CHAPTER 5: COORDINATED REPLENISHMENT OF MULTIPLE ITEMS

of the total cost TC per unit time:

$$TC = \frac{K}{t_1} + \sum_{j=1}^{n} \frac{k_j}{t_j} + \frac{1}{2}\sum_{j=1}^{n} h_j \bar{d}_j t_j + \frac{1}{2}\sum_{j=1}^{n} \frac{h_j b_j \sqrt{n\sigma_j}\sqrt{t_j}}{2.3} \tag{5-9}$$

The equation for TC reflects only holding and ordering costs related to the time between orders. Holding costs related to the necessity of carrying safety stocks are not included here; they are considered only in determining the reorder points s_j. Equation (5-9) differs from equation (5-4) only in that the last term has been added. This term reflects the holding cost which occurs because of the spacing $(S_j - s_j)$ between S_j and s_j required to help ensure that the desired values of t_j actually occur when the model is implemented. Thus this term is clarified below in the discussion of step 3. By accepting the term for the moment and using the relation $t_j = \alpha_j t_1$, equation (5-9) becomes

$$TC = \frac{1}{t_1}\left(K + \sum_{j=1}^{n} \frac{k_j}{\alpha_j}\right) + t_1\left(\frac{1}{2}\sum_{j=1}^{n} h_j \bar{d}_j \alpha_j\right) + \sqrt{t_1}\left(\frac{1}{2}\sum_{j=1}^{n} \frac{h_j b_j \sqrt{n\sigma_j}\sqrt{\alpha_j}}{2.3}\right) \tag{5-10}$$

Equation (5-9) has the form $TC = A/t_1 + Bt_1 + C\sqrt{t_1}$. Setting $\partial TC/\partial t_1 = 0$ gives the equation

$$\frac{-A}{t_1^2} + B + \frac{C}{2\sqrt{t_1}} = 0 \tag{5-11}$$

This equation is solved for t_1 by first evaluating "y" as follows:

$$y = \sqrt[3]{\frac{C^2}{8A^2} + \sqrt{\frac{C^4}{64A^4} + \frac{64B^3}{27A^3}}} + \sqrt[3]{\frac{C^2}{8A^2} - \sqrt{\frac{C^4}{64A^4} + \frac{64B^3}{27A^3}}} \tag{5-12}$$

Then substitute y into the following equation to find t_1:

$$t_1 = \frac{4}{C/(A\sqrt{y}) + \sqrt{-y^2 + C\sqrt{y/A}}} \tag{5-13}$$

A simpler procedure results if the last term of equation (5-10) can be ignored. If the demand of each item during t_1 is much larger than 1 (say, at least 10) and the number of items under control is not too large (say, no more than 20), then the exclusion of the last term will not have much effect on the value of t_1. In this case, equation (5-10) can be approximated by

$$TC = \frac{1}{t_1}\left(K + \sum_{j=1}^{n} \frac{k_j}{\alpha_j}\right) + t_1\left(\frac{1}{2}\sum_{j=1}^{n} h_j \bar{d}_j \alpha_j\right) \tag{5-14}$$

Setting $\partial TC/\partial t_1$ equal to zero and solving for t_1 yields

$$t_1 = \sqrt{\frac{2\left(K + \sum_{j=1}^{n} \frac{k_j}{\alpha_j}\right)}{\sum h_j \bar{d}_j \alpha_j}} \qquad (5\text{-}15)$$

The remaining t_j are calculated according to $t_j = \alpha_j t_1$, to complete step 2.

Step 3 is designed to yield values for the order-up-to levels S_j. This is done by choosing the S_j values in a manner which supports the t_j values determined in step 2. The value of S_j is allowed to vary according to the value of $b_j = K/(K + k_j)$. The value of S_j chosen for a given value β of b_j is designated by the use of a superscript: $S_j^{(\beta)}$. When $b_j = 0$ (for $j = 1, 2, \ldots, n$), independent ordering is appropriate, so $S_j^{(0)}$ is chosen as

$$S_j^{(0)} = s_j + \bar{d}_j t_j \qquad (5\text{-}16)$$

At the other extreme, if $b_j = 1$ (for $j = 1, 2, \ldots, n$), joint ordering is appropriate. Under joint ordering, all items are ordered up to their S_j levels whenever an order is placed. In this case, the average time between orders is t_1 for all items. In practice, the time between any two adjacent orders will be the time at which one of the n items *first* reaches its reorder point s_j. To ensure that this time is approximately t_j, we will choose $S_j^{(1)}$ according to the heuristic

$$\text{Prob [demand for item } j \text{ during time } t_j \leq S_j^{(1)} - s_j] = \frac{n}{n+1} \qquad (5\text{-}17)$$

In terms of the cumulative distribution function F of demand for item j during time t_j, this is

$$F_{t_j}(S_j^{(1)} - s_j) = \frac{n}{n+1} \qquad (5\text{-}18)$$

For example, if demand for item j during time t_j were normally distributed with mean 10 and standard deviation 4 and 8 items were under control, then since Prob $[Z \leq 1.22] = \frac{8}{9} = 0.889$ (where Z is a normally distributed random variable with mean 0 and standard deviation 1), the value of $S_j^{(1)}$ chosen would satisfy

$$S_j^{(1)} - s_j = 10 + 4(1.22) = 14.88$$

Then for item j, for which b_j has the value β,

$$S_j^{(\beta)} = S_j^{(0)}(1 - \beta) + \beta S_j^{(1)} \qquad (5\text{-}19)$$

This completes step 3.

We are now in a position to justify the last term in equation (5-9). The reader may desire to proceed directly to step 4 below. For normally dis-

CHAPTER 5: COORDINATED REPLENISHMENT OF MULTIPLE ITEMS 121

tributed demand, $S_j^{(1)} - s_j$ will vary roughly as $\mu_j(t_j) + \sqrt{n}\,\sigma_j(t_j)/2.3$, where $\mu_j(t_j)$ and $\sigma_j(t_j)$ are the mean and the standard deviation of demand during t_j, and $S_j^{(1)}$ is determined by using equation (5-18). Then, by employing the rule of thumb that $\sigma_j(t_j)$ is proportional to the square root of t_j, $S_j^{(1)}$ would vary as $\bar{d}_j t_j + \sqrt{n}\,\sigma_j\sqrt{t_j}/2.3$. The average inventory would vary by half as much as $S_j^{(1)}$, or

$$\frac{1}{2}\left(\bar{d}_j t_j + \frac{\sqrt{n}\,\sigma_j\sqrt{t_j}}{2.3}\right)$$

Interpolating between $b_j = 0$ and $b_j = 1$, the average inventory will vary as

$$(1 - b_j)\left(\frac{1}{2}\bar{d}_j t_j\right) + b_j\left(\frac{1}{2}\bar{d}_j t_j + \frac{1}{2}\frac{\sqrt{n}\,\sigma_j\sqrt{t_j}}{2.3}\right) = \frac{1}{2}\bar{d}_j t_j + \frac{b_j}{2}\frac{\sqrt{n}\,\sigma_j\sqrt{t_j}}{2.3}$$

This gives rise to the last two terms in equation (5-9).

Step 4 leads to the determination of values of c_j, $j = 1, 2, \ldots, n$. The approach taken here is to relate c_j to the average remnant stock R_j. On the average, the remnant stock for item j will be based on the time between orders for item j:

$$R_j = S_j - \bar{d}_j t_j \tag{5-20}$$

Similarly, once the inventory level for item j enters the "can-order zone," i.e., falls below c_j, the average time until the next order should be $t_1/2$, so

$$c_j - R_j = \bar{d}_j \frac{t_1}{2} \tag{5-21}$$

Substituting equation (5-20) into equation (5-21) yields

$$c_j = S_j - \bar{d}_j\left(t_j - \frac{t_1}{2}\right) \tag{5-22}$$

The complete procedure for determining the parameters of the can-order policy, then, is as follows.

Step 0 Collect the required data. These are n, K, L and $\bar{d}_j$, σ_j, h_j, and k_j for each item j, $j = 1, \ldots, n$.
Step 1 Determine s_j by using equation (5-8) or one of the alternatives 1 to 3 above.
Step 2 Determine t_1 by using either equation (5-13) or (5-15). Then find the remaining $t_j = \alpha_j t_1$.
Step 3 Derive S_j by using equations (5-16), (5-18), and (5-19).
Step 4 Calculate c_j from equation (5-22).

Figure 5-2 illustrates the general relationships between the parameter values obtained with this procedure.

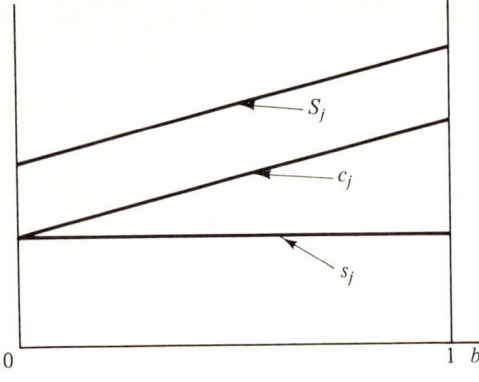

Figure 5-2 General relationships among values of parameters of the can-order policy determined using the heuristic procedure of section 5.1.

Example 5-2 This example provides the opportunity to pace through the calculations. Suppose $n = 4$, $K = 50$, $\alpha = 0.95$, and $L = \frac{1}{12}$ year. The remaining data and calculations are shown in table 5-2. It is assumed that demand during the lead time is normally distributed and that the standard deviation of demand during the lead time is equal to the square root of the average demand per period. Equation (5-8) is used to obtain s_j. Equation (5-15) is used to determine t_1. Results are included in table

Table 5-2 Data and calculations for example 5-2

j	$\bar{d}_j$	$\sigma_j = \sqrt{\bar{d}_j}$	h_j	k_j	τ_j	α_j
1	290	17.03	1.38	10	0.2235	1.00
2	41	6.4	0.24	10	1.426	6.38
3	77	8.77	0.78	10	0.577	2.58
4	122	11.04	0.46	10	0.597	2.67

j	$h_j d_j \alpha_j$	$\dfrac{k_j}{\alpha_j}$	t_j	s_j	$\bar{d}_j t_j$
1	400.2	10	0.4245	32.26	123.1
2	62.78	1.567	2.71	6.46	111.1
3	154.95	3.876	1.095	10.58	84.3
4	149.84	3.745	1.133	15.41	138.2

j	$S_j^{(0)}$	$S_j^{(1)}$	S_j	c_j
1	155.36	164.7	163.13	101.58
2	117.57	126.42	124.94	22.53
3	94.90	102.61	101.32	33.35
4	153.64	163.52	161.87	49.54

5-2. A few sample calculations help to fill in between the lines of the table. For item 1:

$$t_1 = \sqrt{\frac{2(50 + 19.188)}{767.77}} = 0.4245$$

$$s_1 = 24.17 + 1.645(4.92) = 32.26$$

$$S_1^{(1)} = 32.26 + 123.1 + 9.32 = 164.7$$

$$c_1 = 163.13 - 290(0.2123) = 101.58$$

The proof of effectiveness of a heuristic procedure such as the one above lies in its performance against a measure of effectiveness. It would be nice if an accurate cost equation could be formulated so that the above policy could be evaluated. Any cost model for a can-order policy is necessarily approximate because of the complex interactions involved. Simulation is one possible means of evaluation. The following equation is another. It reflects total ordering and holding costs per unit time.

$$TC = \frac{K}{t_1} + \sum_{j=1}^{n} \frac{k_j}{t_j} + \sum_{j=1}^{n} h_j \left(\frac{S_j + R_j}{2} - L\bar{d}_j \right) \qquad (5\text{-}23)$$

where $L\bar{d}_j$ is the reduction in inventory level because of the lag in receiving material. Substitution for R_j by using equation (5-20) yields

$$TC = \frac{K}{t_1} + \sum_{j=1}^{n} \frac{k_j}{t_j} + \sum_{j=1}^{n} h_j \left[S_j - \bar{d}_j \left(\frac{t_j}{2} + L \right) \right] \qquad (5\text{-}24)$$

Evaluation of equation (5-24), with the results of example 5-2 (table 5-2), yields a value of \$345.81 for TC. This is compared with two other results in the next paragraphs.

Example 5-2 was adapted from a paper by Silver [4] who used it to illustrate an iterative procedure for determining the parameters of a can-order policy. Within each iteration, a one-dimensional search is used to determine c_j. The calculations involved are more cumbersome than those developed above.

Thus a computer is required to determine the parameter values. Also, his algorithm assumes that item demands are Poisson-distributed. His results, summarized in table 5-3, invite comparison with those of example 5-2. It would be hasty to draw any strong conclusion related to the general effectiveness of the two approaches. For one thing, it would be based on but a single example. For another, the cost equation (5-24) is not exact. In particular, it assumes that the remnant stock levels R_j and the ordering intervals t_j are those which would actually occur if the policy were implemented. A well-executed simulation (see problem 5-9) is about the only way to obtain more conclusive results.

Table 5-3 Parameter values and total costs for three control policies applied to example 5-2

	Independent control $(c_j = s_j)$		Coordinated control [4]			Coordinated control (heuristic)		
j	S_j	s_j	S_j	c_j	s_j	S_j	c_j	s_j
1	192	33	184	119	32	163	102	32
2	150	7	100	41	4	125	23	6
3	120	11	97	52	9	101	33	11
4	194	16	156	82	13	162	50	15
TC	$441.21		$383.12			$345.81		

In a related work, Thompstone and Silver [7] have described an algorithm which treats the case of compound Poisson item demand distributions. An application of a can-order policy is cited in [6].

Material Cost Interaction

As pointed out earlier, one example of material cost interaction involves a quantity discount offered by a supplier on the total (dollar) amount of an order. The case where a vendor offers a fractional reduction δ on the invoice cost C of any invoice, totaling at least B dollars, is considered briefly here. The cost for the invoice would be $C(1 - \delta)$ if it qualified for the discount.

Assume that there are n items regularly ordered from the supplier. Associated with each item j is an ordering cost k_j, a holding cost per unit held per unit time of h_j, and an average demand rate d_j. Also let G be any group of items from among the n items. Such a group could range in size from a single item to all n items. For any such group, if the d_j are assumed known and constant, it is easy to derive the group joint economic order quantity Q_G, as in equation (2-34):

$$Q_G = \sqrt{\frac{2 \sum k_j \sum d_j}{\sum h_j d_j / \sum d_j}}$$

where all sums ($\sum$) are over all items in the group. The denominator under the radical is the weighted average holding cost when all items in G are jointly ordered. Then for any item j in G, the understood policy is to order $Q_j = Q_G(d_j / \sum d_j)$.

At this point, for any given G, if the invoice cost $\sum c_j Q_j \geq B$, no further modification is needed. If $\sum c_j Q_j = \alpha B$, where $\alpha < 1$, then the methods of section 3-2 can be invoked to determine whether the group quantity Q_G or the *stretched group quantity* Q_G / α, which would qualify for the vendor discount, would result in less total cost per unit time.

The real problem is the determination of a set S_G of groups G for which each and every item is in exactly one group, and for which total costs per unit time are minimized. The number of possible sets S_G which can be formed is, of course, a huge combinatorial quantity which gets large quickly as n increases. In practice, the groups are likely to comprise items whose individual economic order quantities Q_j are approximately the same. In fact, a reasonable approach is to rank the n items in order of their economic order quantities (so that $Q_1 \leq Q_2 \leq \cdots \leq Q_n$) and only allow adjacent items to be in one group. This greatly reduces the number of combinations which would be looked at in practice.

In the stochastic case, such precise planning of order timing and quantity is impossible. Instead, an approach such as the can-order policy of the previous subsection is used to trigger placement of an order for one item in a group, and therefore for some (or all) other items in the same group. At this point, a judgment is made of whether sufficient material should be ordered to qualify for the discount. Based on the existing stock levels and order-up-to levels of the items designated for inclusion in the order, if the group order quantity is insufficient to qualify for the discount, should the order be *stretched* in order to qualify? If the answer is affirmative, the stretched quantity (Q_G/α) must be *allocated* among the items in the group. This might be done so that service levels among the items in the group individually or collectively meet some criterion. Or it might be done as it would be in the deterministic case: $Q_j = (Q_G/\alpha)(d_j/\sum d_j)$. The reader is referred to [8] for a discussion of how this decision is actually made in some applications.

5-2 MODELS RECOGNIZING RESOURCE INTERACTION

The second type of multi-item model to be treated in this chapter is one which recognizes interaction among multiple items because the items share resources in common. Such resources include capital, storage capacity, and delivery vehicle capacity. If the items are being produced rather than ordered from an external supplier, then the items may share productive capacity as well. Both of these types of capacity-based item interaction are discussed below.

The fact that resources are shared is of no consequence until the capacity of that resource is fully used, i.e., until the resource becomes scarce. The finite capacity of the resource then acts as a constraint which restricts the actions of the ordering decision maker.

The first type of model to be considered is one in which inventory levels are constrained. Specifically, suppose n items are stocked. Each item j has known demand rate d_j, unit holding cost h_j per unit time, and material cost c_j. All demands are satisfied; no shortages are permitted. Lead times are taken to be zero. The ordering cost is k_j per order for item j. The ordering policy is to order Q_j units of item j whenever the stock of that item is depleted. The items do not interact in any way except through a constraint of the form

$$\sum_{j=1}^{n} \alpha_j Q_j \leq M \qquad (5\text{-}25)$$

There are numerous instances in which such an equation might apply. For example, α_j might be the square (or cubic) meters of space required per unit of item j stored, and M the storage capacity in square (cubic) meters. Note that this could apply to the capacity of the delivery medium as well as the storage medium. Or, a constraint on average investment can be reflected by setting $\alpha_j = 2c_j$ and making M the upper limit of average investment. If the items are produced rather than ordered, α_j might represent the time required per unit of item j produced, and M the allowed time to fill an order.

The average cost TC per unit time is (ignoring material cost which is not affected by Q_j)

$$TC = \sum_{j=1}^{n} \left(\frac{h_j Q_j}{2} + \frac{k_j d_j}{Q_j} \right) \qquad (5\text{-}26)$$

The problem at hand is to determine values of Q_j ($j = 1, 2, \ldots, n$) which minimize TC subject to the constraint (5-25). This will be done by using the method of Lagrange multipliers, which is reviewed graphically in the following paragraph.

The problem stated above is a special case of a more general problem: Choose values x_j ($j = 1, 2, \ldots, n$) to minimize $f(x_j)$ subject to $g(x_j) \leq 0$. Here, f and g are assumed to be continuous and differentiable. In this discussion, assume $n = 2$ since that case can be graphed. The derivation would be handled the same way for larger n. The gradient $\nabla f(x_1, x_2)$ is defined as the vector of partial derivatives of f with respect to x_1 and x_2:

$$\nabla f(x_1, x_2) = \left(\frac{\partial f}{\partial x_1}, \frac{\partial f}{\partial x_2} \right)$$

The gradient of g is defined the same way. The gradient of a function points in the direction of steepest ascent of the function. Now suppose the minimum point being sought is at (x_1^0, x_2^0). If this point is at an interior point of the set of feasible points defined by $g(x_j) \leq 0$, then $\nabla f(x_1^0, x_2^0) = 0$. This says no more than that the first derivatives of f with respect to the decision variables x_1 and x_2 are equal to zero, which is as expected. However, suppose (x_1^0, x_2^0) is on the boundary of the feasible region, i.e., at a point so that $g(x_1^0, x_2^0) = 0$. Such a point is illustrated in figure 5-3. At this point, the gradients of f and g point in opposite directions. This means that there exists a number λ ($\lambda \leq 0$ in this case) which satisfies

$$\nabla f(x_1^0, x_2^0) = \lambda \nabla g(x_1^0, x_2^0) \qquad (5\text{-}27)$$

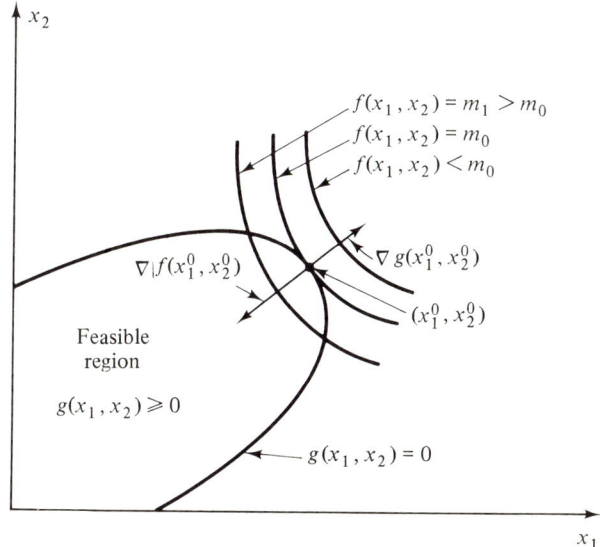

Figure 5-3 Graphical justification of the Lagrange multiplier approach for two decision variables.

Equation (5-27) is a vector form of two equations:

$$\left.\frac{\partial f}{\partial x_1}\right|_0 - \left.\frac{\lambda \, \partial g}{\partial x_1}\right|_0 = 0$$

$$\left.\frac{\partial f}{\partial x_2}\right|_0 - \left.\frac{\lambda \, \partial g}{\partial x_2}\right|_0 = 0$$

These, together with the equation $g(x_1^0, x_2^0) = 0$, result in three equations in three unknowns (x_1^0, x_2^0, and λ) which can hopefully be solved for x_1^0 and x_2^0. These same equations result from forming the so-called *Lagrangian* function L, defined by

$$L = f(x) - \lambda g(x) \tag{5-28}$$

and setting the derivatives of L with respect to x_1, x_2, and λ all equal to zero.

To return to the problem at hand, from equations (5-26) and (5-25) it is seen that

$$f(x) = \sum_{j=1}^{n} \left(\frac{h_j Q_j}{2} + \frac{k_j d_j}{Q_j} \right) \tag{5-29}$$

and

$$g(x) = M - \sum_{j=1}^{n} \alpha_j Q_j \leq 0 \tag{5-30}$$

128 PART II: INVENTORY CONTROL MODELS

The Lagrangian function becomes

$$L = \sum_{j=1}^{n} \left(\frac{h_j Q_j}{2} + \frac{k_j d_j}{Q_j} \right) - \lambda \left(M - \sum_{j=1}^{n} \alpha_j Q_j \right) \tag{5-31}$$

from which

$$\frac{\partial L}{\partial Q_j} = 0 = \frac{h_j}{2} - \frac{k_j d_j}{Q_j^2} + \lambda \alpha_j \qquad j = 1, 2, \ldots, n \tag{5-32}$$

and

$$\frac{\partial L}{\partial \lambda} = 0 = M - \sum_{j=1}^{n} \alpha_j Q_j \tag{5-33}$$

From equation (5-32)

$$Q_j = \sqrt{\frac{2k_j d_j}{h_j + 2\alpha_j \lambda}} \tag{5-34}$$

Substituting equation (5-34) into equation (5-33) yields

$$\sum_{j=1}^{n} \alpha_j \sqrt{\frac{2k_j d_j}{h_j + 2\alpha_j \lambda}} = M \tag{5-35}$$

Thus, to obtain a solution, λ must first be solved for in equation (5-35), after which the Q_j can be obtained from equation (5-34). The solution of (5-35) is a tedious, trial-and-error process; a more satisfactory closed-form solution is presented later (problem 5-6).

Example 5-3 Three items are customarily ordered from a supplier at a cost of $64 per order placed. Demand rates and costs for the items are shown in table 5-4. Total dollar investment in these items is restricted to be no more than $10,600. Determine the least-cost order quantities Q_j, $j = 1, 2, 3$.

The constraint is of the form

$$\sum_{j=1}^{3} c_j Q_j \leq 10,600$$

Table 5-4 Data and calculations for example 5-3

Item j	d_j	$c_j = \alpha_j$	k_j	h_j	Q_j
1	800	$40	$64	$8	89.44
2	900	30	64	6	109.54
3	1000	35	64	7	106.91

If the constraint were ignored, then each item would be ordered according to its economic order quantity $Q_j = (2k_j d_j / h_j)^{1/2}$. These values would be $Q_1 = 113.1$, $Q_2 = 138.6$, and $Q_3 = 135.2$, which violate the constraint since $Q_1 d_1 + Q_2 d_2 + Q_3 d_3 = 13{,}415$.

Equation (5-35) becomes, in this case,

$$40 \sqrt{\frac{(2)(64)(800)}{8 + (2)(40)(\lambda)}} + 30 \sqrt{\frac{(2)(64)(900)}{6 + (2)(30)(\lambda)}} + 35 \sqrt{\frac{(2)(64)(1000)}{7 + (2)(35)(\lambda)}} = 10{,}600$$

By trial and error, $\lambda = 0.06$. Then substitution into equation (5-34) yields the Q_j values in table 5-4.

Additional insight into the solution derived by using the above equations is obtainable. Define the "total investment" TI as that function of inventory [as defined by the left-hand side of inequality (5-25)] which is being constrained. Then

$$TI = \sum_{j=1}^{n} \alpha_j Q_j \qquad (5\text{-}36)$$

Also define "total order cost" TO as the number of orders per unit time, weighted by the ordering costs, being placed. Thus

$$TO = \sum_{j=1}^{n} \frac{k_j d_j}{Q_j} \qquad (5\text{-}37)$$

Then the minimal cost values of Q_j will satisfy

$$(TI)(TO) = \left(\sum_{j=1}^{n} \sqrt{\alpha_j k_j d_j} \right)^2 \qquad (5\text{-}38)$$

The relationship defined by equation (5-38) is called the *optimal policy curve* and is illustrated in figure 5-4. For the results of example 5-3, it is easily verified that $TI = 10{,}600$, $TO = 1697$, and $(TI)(TO) = 17{,}997{,}000$, which also equals the right-hand side of equation (5-38). Note that equation (5-38) can be used to check the accuracy of the computations. Also illustrated in figure 5-4 is the unconstrained solution: $Q_1 = 113.1$, $Q_2 = 138.6$, $Q_3 = 135.2$. For this solution, $TI = 13{,}415$, $TO = 1342$, and $(TI)(TO)$ again equals 17,997,000.

Thus the problem which has been solved can be viewed as the problem of minimizing TO subject to $TI \leq M$. This approach enables the Q_j to be obtained in closed form, thus avoiding the trial-and-error solution of λ in equation (5-35). This is carried out in problem 5-6.

Another source of resource interaction occurs when the inventory items are being produced on common facilities which have finite capacity. A pro-

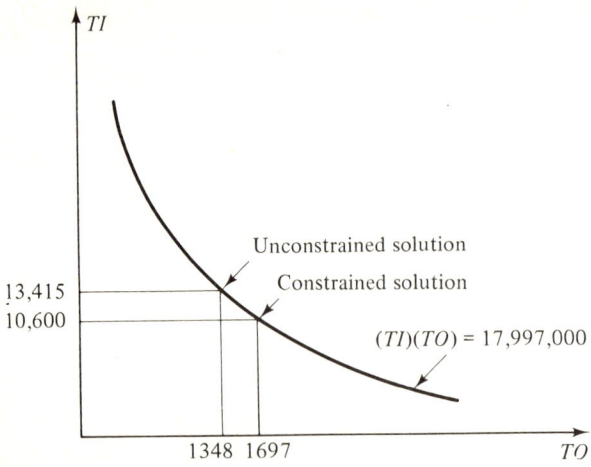

Figure 5-4 The optimal policy curve with numerical results from example 5-3.

totype of this sort of interaction is considered here. Suppose n items are being produced on a common facility (machine). Each item j has known demand rate d_j, holding cost h_j per unit held per unit time, and ordering cost (setup cost, in this case) of k_j per setup. Item j can be produced on the facility at a rate of P_j items per unit time. No shortages are permitted.

An example will be used to illustrate the concepts being introduced. Data for the example appear in table 5-5. Notice that the machine is used 92.5 percent of each week to produce the five items shown: this is the sum of the d_j/P_j column. Additional time required for setups will be ignored here, although the cost of those setups will not. The problem at hand is to determine the time t_j between runs or batches of each item j and thereby to determine the batch sizes Q_j in such a way that costs are at least approximately minimized.

A naive approach to this problem would be to attempt to produce each item j according to its economic production quantity EPQ_j. From problem 2-5, it is seen that this is given by

$$EPQ_j = \sqrt{\frac{2k_j d_j}{h_j}} \sqrt{\frac{P_j}{P_j - d_j}} \qquad (5\text{-}39)$$

The time to produce a batch of size EPQ_j is EPQ_j/P_j. Also, the time between production runs for item j would be EPQ_j/d_j. Referring to table 5-5, note that some items would run out of stock before the machine became available, since their batch sizes would not satisfy demand for as long as the cycle time of 0.77 week. Thus the EPQ's are infeasible batch sizes.

The approach recommended here is to use the line of reasoning

Table 5-5 Data and calculations for the example used to illustrate item interaction resulting from common use of a productive facility

Item j	$ per unit per week h_j	$ per setup k_j	Production capacity per week P_j	Demand per week d_j	Machine utilization d_j/P_j	Independent EPQ_j
1	0.20	40	16,000	3000	0.188	1215.3
2	0.30	25	5,200	1000	0.192	454.3
3	0.50	40	1,400	250	0.178	220.7
4	0.90	20	200	40	0.200	47.1
5	0.50	30	600	100	0.167	120.0
Totals					0.925	

j	$\dfrac{EPQ_j}{P_j}$	$\dfrac{EPQ_j}{d_j} = \tau_j$	$\dfrac{\tau_j}{\tau_1} = \alpha_j$	$[\alpha_j]$	$h_j d_j [\alpha_j] \dfrac{(P_j - d_j)}{P_j}$	$\dfrac{k_j}{[\alpha_j]}$
1	0.08	0.41	1.00	1	487.5	40
2	0.09	0.45	1.10	1	242.3	25
3	0.16	0.88	2.15	2	205.4	20
4	0.24	1.18	2.88	3	86.4	6.7
5	0.20	1.20	2.92	3	125.0	10
Totals	0.77				1146.6	101.7

j	t_j	Q_j	π_j	n_j	$n_j \pi_j$	$h_j d_j \dfrac{(P_j - d_j)}{P_j}$
1	0.42	1260	0.079	6	0.474	487.5
2	0.42	420	0.081	6	0.486	242.3
3	0.84	210	0.150	3	0.450	102.7
4	1.26	50.5	0.252	2	0.504	28.8
5	1.26	126	0.210	2	0.420	41.67
Totals					2.334	903

developed in the first section of this chapter. There, in the deterministic model developed to economize on ordering costs, each item j was ordered in a quantity which lasted an integer multiple $[\alpha_j]$ of a basic time t_1. The use of integer multiples here will ensure that no item runs out of stock before it is run again. The values of EPQ_j/d_j in table 5-5 are the analog of the τ_j of table 5-1 and equation (5-2). Then $\alpha_j = \tau_j/\tau_1$ and $[\alpha_j]$ are calculated in table 5-5 just as they were in table 5-1.

To determine t_1, equation (5-6) must be altered to fit the present situation. There is no "header" setup cost K; t_1 must be chosen to minimize total costs TC per unit time, which consist of the setup and holding costs:

$$TC = \sum_{j=1}^{n} \left(\frac{k_j}{t_j} + \frac{1}{2} h_j d_j t_j \frac{P_j - d_j}{P_j} \right) \tag{5-40}$$

By using equation (5-3) this becomes

$$TC = \frac{1}{t_1} \sum_{j=1}^{n} \frac{k_j}{[\alpha_j]} + \frac{t_1}{2} \sum_{j=1}^{n} h_j d_j [\alpha_j] \frac{P_j - d_j}{P_j} \tag{5-41}$$

Setting $\partial TC/\partial t_1$ equal to zero and solving for t_1 yields

$$t_1 = \sqrt{\frac{2 \sum_{j=1}^{n} \frac{k_j}{[\alpha_j]}}{\sum_{j=1}^{n} h_j d_j [\alpha_j] \frac{P_j - d_j}{P_j}}} \tag{5-42}$$

For the data in table 5-5,

$$t_1 = \sqrt{\frac{2(101.7)}{1146.6}} = 0.42 \text{ week}$$

The other t_j are shown in table 5-5, along with Q_j, the batch sizes, and π_j, the production times to run a batch of item j. It remains to define a feasible sequence of batch runs which avoid machine interference and stockouts. The "pattern cycle time" will be defined as the length of time between repetition of the identical production run sequence, or *pattern*. The pattern cycle time is t_1 times the least common multiple of the $[\alpha_j]$. For the example, the pattern cycle time is $(0.42)(6) = 2.52$ weeks. A pattern is a sequence of item numbers in which each item number j appears n_j times, where $n_j = $ the pattern cycle time divided by $[\alpha_j]$. That is, n_j is the number of times item j will be run during one pattern cycle time. The n_j appear in table 5-5. Also to be scheduled once during each pattern cycle is the machine idle time I per cycle. The idle time per cycle is the difference between the pattern cycle time and the total productive time per cycle $\sum (n_j \pi_j)$. For the example being followed, $I = 2.52 - 2.334 = 0.186$ week. This idle time can be split and scheduled at more than one point in the cycle.

Now a pattern must be specified. This pattern should arrange the item numbers so that successive batches of the same item are run at approximately equally spaced points in time. The placement of idle time in the sequence can help to accomplish this objective. For the example, the following sequence is chosen:

5, 1, 2, I_1, 3, 1, 2, 4, 1, 2, 5, 1, 2, I_2, 3, 1, 2, 4, 1, 2, 3

where $I_1 = 0.10$ and $I_2 = 0.086$. The number of entries in the pattern will, of course, equal $\sum n_j$ plus the number of idle periods scheduled.

The final test of the above solution is its total cost TC per unit time. This cost is the sum of the ordering cost plus the holding cost, for each of the n items. Defining the average inventory for item j by $\bar{y}_j$, this is

$$TC = \sum_{j=1}^{n} \left(\frac{k_j}{t_j} + h_j \bar{y}_j \right) \qquad (5\text{-}43)$$

To determine the average inventory, it is necessary to recognize that the inventory level of an item does *not necessarily* drop to zero prior to the production of each batch. This is due to the unequal time intervals between successive batch runs for the item. Generally, the inventory level will reach zero only prior to the start of one batch production run for an item. For example, an inventory-time plot for item 3 in the example of table 5-5 appears in figure 5-5. Define the "average residual stock" $\bar{y}_{rj}$ as the average inventory level of item j immediately prior to start of a batch run. For example, figure 5-5 shows $\bar{y}_{r3} = (85 + 0 + 30)/3 = 38.33$. The average inventory level $\bar{y}_j$, then, is given by

$$\bar{y}_j = \frac{Q_j}{2} \frac{P_j - d_j}{P_j} + \bar{y}_{rj} \qquad j = 1, 2, \ldots, n \qquad (5\text{-}44)$$

By using equations (5-43) and (5-44), the value of TC for the example of table 5-5 can be calculated (problem 5-12) to be \$548.55.

Another approach to this problem is to simply determine an economic batch size for the group, as in equation (2-34):

$$Q = \sqrt{\frac{2 \sum k_j \sum d_j}{\sum [h_j d_j (P_j - d_j)/P_j]/\sum (d_j)}} \qquad (5\text{-}45)$$

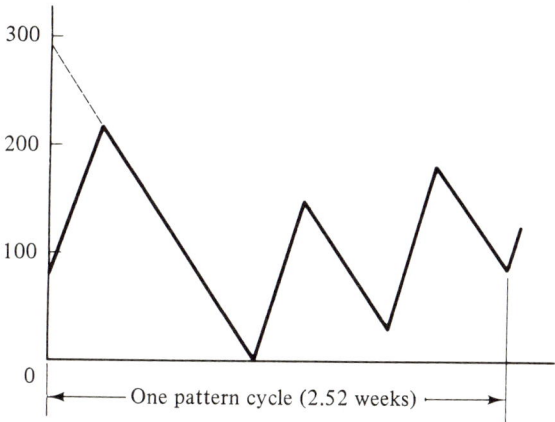

Figure 5-5 An inventory-time plot for item 3 for the example of table 5-5.

Then the pattern cycle time is given by

$$t = \frac{Q}{\sum d_j} = \sqrt{\frac{2 \sum k_j}{\sum [h_j d_j (P_j - d_j)/P_j]}} \qquad (5\text{-}46)$$

In this case, each item is ordered once during each pattern cycle. Derivation of the policy and the total costs for the example of table 5-5 would enable comparison with the result for the first policy above. This is left as a problem (5-13).

A third approach to the machine interference multi-item batch size problem is suggested by Saipe [3]. His approach allows only two values for $[\alpha_j]$, $+1$ or 2. Thus the n items are placed into two groups—one with a time between batches twice that of the other. His approach, then, is a compromise between the two given above.

5-3 MODELS RECOGNIZING DEMAND INTERACTION

The third and final type of multi-item model to be considered in this chapter is one recognizing certain interactions among item demands. As discussed early in this chapter, the type of interactions included in this section involve the effects of demand of one item on the demand for another item at the same echelon. This means that the items themselves do not have supply-demand relationships to one another. Those types of relationships are common, say, in an assembly process. Demands related in this way are called *dependent* demands. Models for dependent demands are discussed in chapter 6. A more appropriate term for the nature of demand interaction treated in this section is "correlation."

Correlated demands arise from the existence of options. Options are recognized here as being of two basic types. The first type is an either-or option. A straightforward example is that of color, say, of a new automobile. The second type is an "add on" option, such as the inclusion of a luggage rack on that new car. It should be recognized that the two types are not entirely distinct. Depending on the form in which the inventory is stocked, the option may be of either type. For example, from the point of view of the automobile assembly plant that builds cars to customer order, the luggage rack is an add-on option. However, the automobile dealer maintaining a stock of cars for immediate sale from the lot views the luggage rack as an either-or option. The difference is, of course, that for the dealer the luggage rack is already an integral part of the car, just as is the finish color. Perhaps it would be stretching a point to think of the color as an add-on option at the assembly plant level. Thus, any option may be thought of alternatively as either an add-on or an either-or type of option. Also, an add-on option may be a "take away" or a "negative add-on" option.

At the plant level, the color option, though a very real concern, is not as critical a problem as it is at the dealer level. The plant will maintain an adequate supply of all the color options so that any customer order can be filled. However, the dealer cannot stock enough cars of every color to ensure that every request can be satisfied. The dealer is faced with the need to respond to the marketing phenomenon of *substitution*. Lacking the desired color, the dealer may or may not have a customer who is willing to accept a substitute color.

Sometimes an option may be bidirectional in nature. That is, two items may be options for each other. The marketing phenomenon occurring here is one of *reinforcement*. In many cases, appeal is being made to impulsive demands. The retailer who stocks peanut butter next to jelly is attempting to induce sales of the add-on option. In this case, either item is an option for the other. Is that true of luggage racks and automobiles?

Before possible models for dealing with demand substitution are discussed, one should point out one option of the inventory controller which is always available: to ignore the demand interaction entirely. This is an especially attractive alternative in a stable situation in which no option changes have been made recently nor are any imminent. Take, for example, the demand for peanut butter and jelly. Suppose the natural demand for each one individually is 10 units per week, but because of reinforcement 12 units per week of each are actually sold. If such a pattern has persisted, the inventory controller need not know about the underlying 10 units per week. In fact, the forecasting procedure being used (see chapter 7) may well be intrinsic, i.e., may well be based solely on historical demand. However, if some change in the status quo is due (e.g., plans are made to discontinue sales of peanut butter), then knowledge of the demand interaction is valuable.

Similarly, demand naturally occurring before substitution may be ignored and attention paid only to the demand resulting from substitution. For example, suppose that demand for red cars is six per month, and three per month for green, but four of each color are made available for sale each month. If 50 percent of those people desiring a green car will settle for a red one, sales will reflect demands equal to supplies. The conclusion to be drawn from this is that blindness with respect to substitution has more serious consequences than blindness with respect to reinforcement.

Consider the following periodic-review model, to reflect demand substitution for two items. Each item j ($j = 1, 2$) is replenished up to level S_j at the beginning of each period. Demand d_j during the period obeys probability distribution function $f_j(d_j)$. Holding costs are h_j per unit per unit time. Shortage costs are p_j per unit per unit time. Unsatisfied demand is backlogged, and lead time is zero. Both of these last two assumptions can be relaxed, but they are maintained for simplicity of exposition.

If item 1 runs out of stock, then a fraction f_{12}, $0 \le f_{12} \le 1$, of the unsatisfied demand can be satisfied by supplying an equal amount of item 2, provided it is available. The fraction f_{21} is similarly defined. Thus if item 1 runs out of stock first, demand for item 2 becomes $d_2 + f_{12}(d_1 - S_1)$, which is satisfied subject to the availability of stock.

Let $S_1^*(f_{12}, f_{21})$ and $S_2^*(f_{12}, f_{21})$ be the minimum-cost values of S_1 and S_2 for specified values of f_{12} and f_{21}. Also define $S^*(f_{12}, f_{21}) = (S_1^*(f_{12}, f_{21}), S_2^*(f_{12}, f_{21}))$. If $f_{12} = f_{21} = 0$, then no substitution is possible. In this case, the items have no demand interaction, and $S^*(0, 0)$ can be found by using techniques discussed in chapter 4.

If $f_{12} = 1$ and $f_{21} = 0$, then item 2 will completely substitute for item 1. In this case, item 1 need not be stocked at all $[S_1^*(1, 0) = 0]$. Then $S_2^*(1, 0)$ can also be found in the conventional (chapter 4) manner for the aggregate demand $d_1 + d_2$. The case $f_{21} = 1$ can be dealt with similarly. Figure 5-6 illustrates the three solutions indicated up to this point. Clearly $S_1^*(0, 1) = S_2^*(1, 0)$ and $S_2^*(0, 1) = S_1^*(1, 0)$. Also if $f_{12} = f_{21} = 1$, then any solution on the straight-line segment between $S^*(0, 1)$ and $S^*(1, 0)$ is optimal (i.e., minimum-cost).

The solutions $S^*(0, 0)$, $S^*(0, 1)$, and $S^*(1, 0)$ are seen to be the extreme points of a triangle. This suggests that the solution for any values of f_{12} and f_{21} should lie within this triangular region. The following heuristic algorithm provides a solution of this type.

$$S^*(f_{12}, 0) = S^*(0, 0) + f_{12}[S^*(1, 0) - S^*(0, 0)] \qquad (5\text{-}47)$$

$$S^*(0, f_{21}) = S^*(0, 0) + f_{21}[S^*(0, 1) - S^*(0, 0)] \qquad (5\text{-}48)$$

Let $S^*(f_{12}, f_{21})$ lie at the intersection of the two line segments $(S^*(f_{12}, 0), S^*(0, 1))$ and $(S^*(0, f_{21}), S^*(1, 0))$. (See the dashed lines in figure

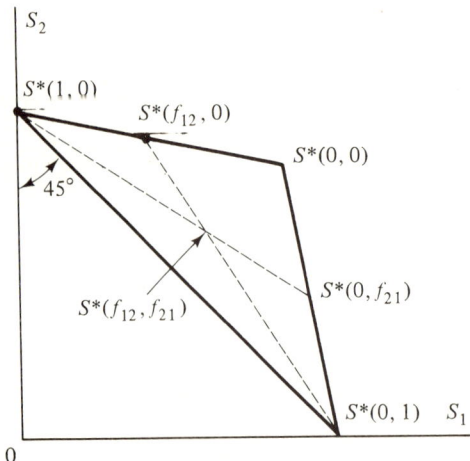

Figure 5-6 Relationships between minimal-cost solutions to the two-item substitution model.

5-6.) It is left as a geometric/algebraic problem (5-14) to show that this intersection point is defined as follows:

$$S^*(f_{12}, f_{21}) = S^*(f_{12}, 0) + \alpha[S^*(0, 1) - S^*(f_{12}, 0)] \quad (5\text{-}49)$$

or

$$S^*(f_{12}, f_{21}) = S^*(0, f_{21}) + \beta[S^*(1, 0) - S^*(0, f_{21})] \quad (5\text{-}50)$$

where

$$\alpha = (f_{21} - f_{12} f_{21})/(1 - f_{12} f_{21})$$
$$\beta = (f_{12} - f_{12} f_{21})/(1 - f_{12} f_{21})$$

This heuristic is, of course, a form of linear interpolation. A similar algorithm is proposed by Kamat [2], whose approach gives favorable results. The following example is the one he used to compare his heuristic to a minimum-cost solution.

Example 5-4 Two products have demand which is Poisson-distributed with a mean of 6 per period. The holding cost h is \$1 per unit held per unit time. The cost of a shortage is $p = \$49$ per unit per unit time. Three cases of the substitution fractions are tested: (a) $f_{12} = f_{21} = 0.5$; (b) $f_{12} = 0.6, f_{21} = 0$; (c) $f_{12} = 0.75, f_{21} = 0$.

By using equation (4-18), the extreme-point solutions are obtained as follows:

$$F(S_1^*) = F(S_2^*) = \frac{p}{p + h} = 0.98$$

For $f_{12} = f_{21} = 0$, demand averages 6 per period. By using a table of the Poisson distribution, $S_1^*(0, 0) = S_2^*(0, 0) = 11$. If $f_{12} = 1$ or $f_{21} = 1$, then the aggregate demand of 12 per period gives a result of $S_1^*(0, 1) = S_2^*(1, 0) = 19$. Of course, $S_2^*(0, 1) = S_1^*(1, 0) = 0$. Thus the three extreme solutions (corners of the triangle) are $S^*(0, 0) = (11, 11)$, $S^*(0, 1) = (19, 0)$, and $S^*(1, 0) = (0, 19)$.

For case (a), using equations (5-47) and (5-48), $S^*(f_{12}, 0) = (5.5, 7)$ and $S^*(0, f_{21}) = (7, 5.5)$. Then $\alpha = \beta = \frac{1}{3}$, so that by equation (5-49)

$$S^*(0.5, 0.5) = (5.5, 7) + \tfrac{1}{3}[(19, 0) - (5.5, 7)]$$
$$= (10, 4.67)$$

Cases (b) and (c) yield, respectively, $S^*(0.6, 0) = (4.4, 15.8)$ and $S^*(0.75, 0) = (2.75, 17)$.

Extension of the above heuristic to more than two items is possible, but the computations increase rapidly as the number of items n increases. For $n = 3$, a solution could be obtained as an interpolation of the four extreme points of a tetrahedron: $S^*(0, 0, 0)$, $S^*(0, 0, 1)$, $S^*(0, 1, 0)$, and $S^*(1, 0, 0)$.

If substitution is not recognized as a possibility, then enough of each option must be provided individually. As pointed out earlier, it is possible to estimate needs for each option as if its demand were independent of that for other options. Option demand interactions can be explicitly accounted for in a variety of ways, including the following.

The total demand for all options and percentages for each option can be monitored. Several variations of this are possible. Total demand may be known, but the option percentages unknown. An example of this is a production plan which is constrained to meet a given dollar budget, but within that budget may vary with respect to individual items produced. Or, options may be specified by a customer after the total demand is known. For example, the total number of meals for an airline flight is known, but it is not known which menu item will be selected by each patron. Conversely, the total demand may be uncertain, but the option percentages known fairly accurately. For example, a certain percentage of a part may be defective. Total demand for the part may not be known, but the "option" of requiring two (or more) parts to satisfy demand for one part is known from the reliability history of the part.

There appears to be little need for elaborate models recognizing demand interaction when no substitution is possible. The primary problem in this case is one of forecasting, rather than ordering decision making.

5-4 SUMMARY

Models involving more than one item are appropriate whenever there is a significant interaction among these items. Three types of interactions have been modeled in this chapter. Cost interactions occur commonly as reductions in ordering costs or in material costs through inclusion of more than one item in an order. Resource interactions appear as competition among items for the common use of resources. Demand interactions reflect the effect of demand for one item upon demand for other items.

Ordering cost interaction was modeled by assuming that the cost of placing an order consisted of a fixed cost plus a variable cost for each item included in the order. In the deterministic case a procedure for determining a time interval between successive orders for each item was introduced. These time intervals are integer multiples of the shortest interval. In the stochastic case, a can-order policy was suggested. In this policy, whenever an order is placed for any item, all other items whose inventory levels have fallen below their can-order levels are included in the order.

Two forms of resource interaction were considered. In the first, two items competed for a common resource such as storage space. A limit on the availability of the resource imposed a constraint on the allowable inventory levels. The minimum-cost ordering quantities were therefore obtained using a constrained optimization technique. A second form of resource interaction involved the common use of a productive facility to supply the items. Order quantities for the items must then reflect a feasible production schedule.

Demand interaction was modeled by allowing a fraction of demand for one item to be satisfied by substituting a second item. The order-up-to levels of the two items were determined in such a way that the risk of not being able to satisfy demand was controlled.

In some of the above cases it was possible to compare results of multi-item (coordinated replenishment) models with those of single-item models. In cases where significant item interaction occurred, the multi-item models yielded lower costs.

REFERENCES

1. Goyal, S. K.: "Optimum Ordering Policy for a Multi-Item Single Supplier System," *Operational Research Quarterly*, vol. 25, no. 2, pp. 293–298, 1973.
2. Kamat, Satish J.: "A Two-Product Inventory Control Model with Substitution," Presented at the 39th National O.R.S.A. Meeting, May 5–7, 1971, New Mexico State University.
3. Saipe, Alan L.: "Production Runs for Multiple Products: The Two-Product Heuristic," *Management Science*, vol. 23, no. 12, pp. 1321–1327, August 1977.
4. Silver, Edward A.: "A Control System for Coordinated Inventory Replenishment," *International Journal for Production Research*, vol. 12, no. 6, pp. 647–671, 1974.
5. Starr, Martin K., and D. W. Miller: "Inventory Control: Theory and Practice," Prentice-Hall, Englewood Cliffs, N.J., 1962.
6. Taylor, William: "Production, Payroll, Inventory, Delivery—All on One Small Computer," *Industrial Engineering*, vol. 1, no. 7, pp. 36–39, July 1969.
7. Thompstone, Robert M., and Edward A. Silver: "A Coordinated Inventory Control System for Compound Poisson Demand and Zero Lead Time," *International Journal for Production Research*, vol. 13, no. 6, pp. 581–602, 1975.
8. "System/360 Consumer Goods System (COGS)—Allocation (DOS)(OS) Application Description," publication no. GH20-0721-3, IBM Corp., White Plains, N.Y., 40 pp.

EXERCISES

5-1 Suppose that four items are under control and have the costs and demands given in the following table.

Item j	Demand/year d_j	Ordering cost k_j	Holding cost per unit per year h_j
1	1,800	$40	$0.45
2	6,400	40	0.45
3	14,000	40	0.45
4	30,000	40	0.45

An additional cost $K = \$80$ is incurred every time an order is placed. Find the minimum-cost time between orders and the total annual cost:
  (a) If each item is controlled independently
  (b) If a coordinated replenishment policy is used

5-2 Repeat problem 5-1(b) using the relevant data in table 5-2 in place of the table in problem 5-1. (Of course, $\bar{d}_j \equiv d_j$.)

5-3 Demand during a lead time L for each of n items ($j = 1, 2, \ldots, n$) is normally distributed with standard deviation equal to the square root of the mean demand. Each item has associated with it a demand rate d_j, a holding cost h_j, and an ordering cost k_j. Also an additional cost K is incurred whenever an order is placed. For a 95 percent service level ($\alpha = 0.05$), you are to determine the parameter values of a can-order policy and to evaluate the total cost per time period for the policy. Use equation (5-8) to determine the reorder points s_j. Use $L = 1$ week. Solve using the appropriate data from table 5-5 with $K = \$1$.

5-4 Repeat problem 5-3 using the appropriate data from problem 5-1. Assume $K = \$100$.

5-5 For the data of problem 5-1, suppose that the total investment in an inventory $\sum c_j Q_j$ is not to exceed \$10,000. Find the minimum-cost values of Q_j and the associated total cost per unit time, where the material cost per unit is \$2. Also find the total cost per year and compare with problem 5-1(a) if you have worked that problem.

5-6 Use the Lagrange multiplier approach to show that the values of Q_j, $j = 1, 2, 3$, which minimize TO subject to $TI \leq M$ are given by

$$Q_j = \sqrt{\frac{k_j d_j}{\alpha_j}} \frac{M}{\sum_{j=1}^{n} \sqrt{k_j d_j \alpha_j}}$$

5-7 The allowed maximum investment in three items is \$15,000. Find the order quantities Q_j which minimize total cost per unit time. The ordering cost is \$50 for any item. The demands and material costs are given by

j	d_j	c_j
1	1000	50
2	1000	20
3	2000	80

Hint: The result of problem 5-6 will be useful.

5-8 Use the result of problem 5-6 to verify the values of Q_j found in example 5-3.

5-9 Although computer simulations are beyond the scope of this text, your instructor may wish you to write a simulation program to compare the heuristic can-order policy with that of Silver referred to in table 5-3.

5-10 Suppose several items under control are all produced on a common machine having a production rate of 250 units per day for any item. Using the data in problem 5-1, find a feasible, cost-effective cycle pattern for production of batches of the items. Assume a 250-working-day year. Calculate the total cost per year for the pattern. What is the batch size for each item?

5-11 Repeat problem 5-10, except that each item is produced only once per cycle. Calculate total annual cost and compare with that of problem 5-10. What is the batch size for each item?

5-12 Using equations (5-43) and (5-44), show that the total cost of the solution to the example based on table 5-5 is $548.55.

5-13 Determine a minimum-cost solution to the example represented in table 5-5 if each item can be ordered only once per pattern cycle. Calculate the total cost per week for this policy, and compare it with the value verified in problem 5-12.

5-14 Using algebraic and/or geometric arguments, verify the validity of equations (5-49) and (5-50).

5-15 Two items under periodic review are coordinated using base stock policies which replenish their stock levels up to values S_1^* and S_2^* each time period. It costs $1 for each unit of either item remaining in stock at the end of a period, and $7 per unit of demand unsatisfied. Demand for each item is Poisson-distributed with a mean of 14 units per period. The substitution fractions (confer section 5-3) are $f_{12} = 0.25$ and $f_{21} = 0.20$. Determine the values of S_1^* and S_2^*.

5-16 Repeat problem 5-15 where demand for each item is normally distributed with mean 10 and standard deviation 2, $f_{12} = 0.15$, and $f_{21} = 0.10$.

CHAPTER
SIX

CONTROLLING MULTIECHELON INVENTORIES

This chapter, like the previous one, addresses problems associated with the coordinated control of multiple inventory items. As was discussed early in the last chapter, the only reason for coordinated control is that there is interaction among the items being controlled. The interactions considered in the previous chapter were of three types: cost interactions, demand interactions, and interactions resulting from a sharing of common resources. In this chapter, the primary interaction is a supply-demand relationship between items.

It is important to recognize at the outset that the supply-demand relationship can exist between two physically identical items. Thus cases of beans may be stored at the cannery, the regional warehouse, and the retail supermarket. Of course, the supply-demand relationship exists twice in this case. Suppose, though, for sake of discussion, that the inventories at the warehouse and at the supermarket are under common control, while the cannery inventory is under the control of an entirely different management. In this case, we will say that the cannery is an *external* supplier. From the supermarket's point of view, the warehouse will be an internal supplier. The warehouse then faces a situation of external supply and internal demand. In general, internal supplies and demands are under common control. Moreover, throughout this chapter, items bearing an internal supply-demand relationship will be considered to be distinct (different) items, even though they may be physically identical. Items under common control, among which internal supply-demand relationships exist, are said to belong to echelons. An *echelon* can be considered one stage, among several under common control, in the flow of material, at which items are inventoried. The supermarket warehouse system is a two-echelon system.

Figure 6-1 illustrates several notions which will be employed in this chapter. First note that there are five items in three echelons. The arrows represent the direction of flow of material. All material need not visit (be stored at) every echelon. (The flow from item 1 to item 5 demonstrates this.) Items for which external demands exist will be called *retail*, even though they may not be stored in what is normally thought of as a retail store. Nonretail items will be called *wholesale*. Wholesale items are *not* items which have a wholesale price; in fact, they are not for "sale" at all in this context. In figure 6-1, items 1, 2, and 4 are wholesale.

Each *internal* supply-demand relationship has associated with it a predecessor item and a successor item. Thus item 2 precedes item 4, and item 4 succeeds item 2. External supplies and demands are *not* termed "predecessors" *or* "successors." If every item in an inventory network has at most one successor, the network will be called a *coalescence*. Figure 6-1 is a coalescence. This structure is common in assembly situations. It is not hard to imagine that items 1, 2, and 3 in figure 6-1 could be raw materials, item 4 a subassembly, and item 5 a finished product or final assembly. The retail (external) demand for item 3 could arise if it was demanded as a spare part. A reverse situation is one in which every item in the network has at most one predecessor, in which case the network will be called an *arborescence*. An arborescence structure is common in the distribution of items from, say, a single point of production to geographically dispersed customers.

A special type of multiechelon network is a *series* structure. In a series network, every item has at most one predecessor and at most one successor.

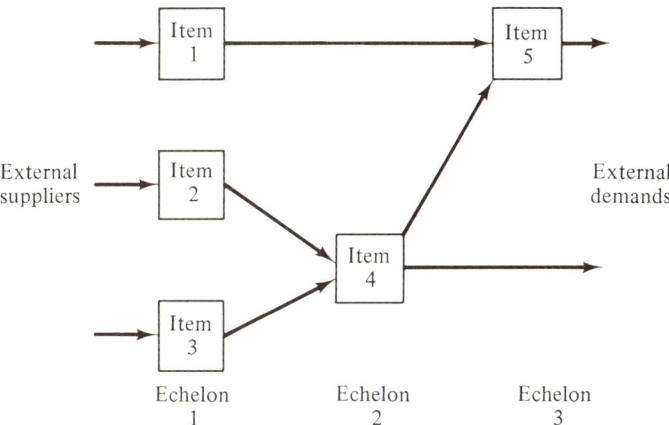

Figure 6-1 A multiechelon (coalescence) inventory network.

In this case, if there are m items, then there are also m echelons. An additional requirement usually associated with a series network is that only the first item is externally supplied and only the mth (last) item is retail. This requirement will also be imposed here, so that a series network will appear as in figure 6-2.

The following notation will make it possible to succinctly describe multiechelon concepts. In this chapter, it will be assumed that there are m items and n echelons. Each item j, $j = 1, 2, \ldots, m$, has a known external demand during period t of d_t^j for $t = 1, 2, \ldots, n$, where n can be considered as the number of time periods constituting a planning horizon. For each item j ($j = 1, 2, \ldots, m$), let $A(j)$ be the set of predecessors and $B(j)$ the set of successors. Thus, for example, in figure 6-1, $A(4) = \{2, 3\}$ and $B(4) = \{5\}$.

Denote the amount of item j ordered (for purchase or production) at the beginning of period t by $x_t^j \geq 0$ and the inventory level of item j (amount on hand at the end of period t) by y_t^j. The number of units of item j which must be supplied to satisfy 1 unit of demand of item k $[k \in B(j)]$ is assumed to be g_{jk}. When echelons are different locations of the same item, then $g_{jk} = 1$. Finally, assume that the lead time between placement of an order for item j and receipt of stock is given by $L(j) \geq 0$, where $L(j)$ is an integer. Then a fundamental relationship which must be satisfied is

$$y_t^j = y_{t-1}^j + x_{t-L(j)}^j - \sum_{k \in B(j)} (g_{jk} x_t^k) - d_t^j \tag{6-1}$$

The "(gross) requirements" r_t^j for item j in period t are defined to be the sum of internal and external demands for item j in period t:

$$r_t^j \equiv \sum_{k \in B(j)} (g_{jk} x_t^k) + d_t^j \tag{6-2}$$

Substituting equation (6-2) into (6-1) yields the relationship

$$y_t^j - y_{t-1}^j = x_{t-L(j)}^j - r_t^j \tag{6-3}$$

which is simply a mathematical way of saying that the change in inventory level from one period to the next equals the receipts minus the requirements. Clearly inventory levels can be negative, representing unsatisfied requirements. Such requirements are backlogged until they can be satisfied.

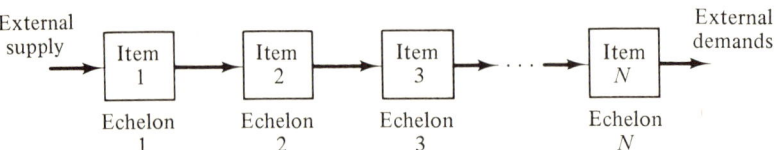

Figure 6-2 A series inventory network.

6-1 THE BEHAVIOR OF MULTIECHELON INVENTORIES

When supply-demand relationships exist among items under common control, some phenomena occur which would not occur in the single-echelon case. The example which follows will illustrate these phenomena by using a series network; however, the same results would be evident if a more general multiechelon inventory structure were used instead.

Example 6-1 Suppose that a series structure consists of three items under common control. Also suppose that exactly 1 unit of supply is required for 1 unit of demand, so that $g_{jk} = 1$ for all j, k. The ordering decision rule in use is one which attempts to satisfy requirements and to maintain an on-hand inventory of 12 units as insurance against unforeseen production or supply problems. More precisely, the ordering rule is

$$x_t^j = x_{t-1}^{j+1} + \tfrac{1}{2}(12 - y_{t-1}^j) \qquad j = 1, 2, 3 \tag{6-4}$$

where $x_t^4 \equiv d_t$ for all t. The value of x_t^j is rounded up to an integer. This rule may not be the most effective one, but it is used here to illustrate some features of multiechelon control. Equation (6-4) assumes that one time period elapses between the occurrence of a requirement x_t^{j+1} and knowledge of that requirement at the preceding echelon j. Thus x_t^j in equation (6-4) depends on x_{t-1}^{j+1}, not on x_t^{j+1}. Now assume further that there is a two-period delay between placement of any order and receipt of that order. In this case, equation (6-3) becomes

$$y_t^j = y_{t-1}^j + x_{t-2}^j - x_t^{j+1} \qquad j = 1, 2, 3 \tag{6-5}$$

The results of applying equations (6-4) and (6-5) to example 6-1 appear in table 6-1. The demand pattern for a 25-period time horizon is shown in the top row. The demands are deliberately shown to be constant for the first 10 periods and varying thereafter. A graph of the demand pattern together with resulting inventory levels is shown in figure 6-3. Of particular interest is the way in which the inventory levels fluctuate. Notice that when demands are constant, the inventory levels are also; and when the demands vary, so do the inventory levels. However, the inventory levels vary more widely than the demands themselves; and the larger the number of echelons between an inventory and the demands, the more widely the level of that inventory fluctuates. Thus a multiechelon inventory control system can exhibit some rather unstable behavior, even when demands are moderately varying. Note that production (order) rates are varying similarly.

Table 6-1 Demands, order quantities, and inventory levels for example 6-1

t	1	2	$\cdots$	9	10	11	12	13	14	15
d_t	6	6	$\cdots$	6	6	7	8	9	10	9
x_t^3	6	6	$\cdots$	6	6	6	8	10	12	14
y_t^3	12	12	$\cdots$	12	12	11	9	6	4	5
x_t^2	6	6	$\cdots$	6	6	6	6	9	13	18
y_t^2	12	12	$\cdots$	12	12	12	10	6	0	-5
x_t^1	6	6	$\cdots$	6	6	6	6	6	11	18
y_t^1	12	12	$\cdots$	12	12	12	12	9	2	-10

t	16	17	18	19	20	21	22	23	24	25
d_t	8	7	6	5	4	5	6	7	8	9
x_t^3	13	10	5	2	0	0	0	2	7	12
y_t^3	9	16	23	28	29	26	20	13	5	-2
x_t^2	23	22	15	1	0	0	0	0	0	0
y_t^2	-5	3	21	41	56	57	57	55	48	36
x_t^1	29	40	41	27	0	0	0	0	0	0
y_t^1	-22	-26	-12	27	68	95	95	95	95	95

This phenomenon of "amplification of oscillations" was examined extensively by Forrester in his "Industrial Dynamics" [3] in which he modeled multiechelon production and inventory systems. Among other things, he showed that these oscillations are characteristic of the system, in much the same way as the oscillations of a mass on the end of a spring. Thus in example 6-1, even if the demand pattern had been random rather than gently oscillating, the inventory levels, especially those several echelons removed from the demand source, would still oscillate. See problem 6-2 for a demonstration of this.

The magnitudes of the oscillations in a multiechelon system depend on the ordering policies used, the number of echelons, and the lengths of lead times in the system. Forrester demonstrated that a reduction in lead times tended to reduce the magnitude of oscillations occurring in the system, thereby "stabilizing" the system. Lead times are of particular concern because they tend to cumulate, or "stack," in a multiechelon system. Consider the fact that in example 6-1, an increase in demand in period t is not detected until period $t + 1$ at echelon 3, not until period $t + 2$ at echelon 2, and not until period $t + 3$ at the first echelon. This accumulation of time between occurrence and detection of an event is a primary reason why echelon j fluctuates more widely than echelon $j + 1$ ($j = 1, 2$).

The above lead time is informational in nature. There is also a production/delivery lead time in example 6-1. The following example illus-

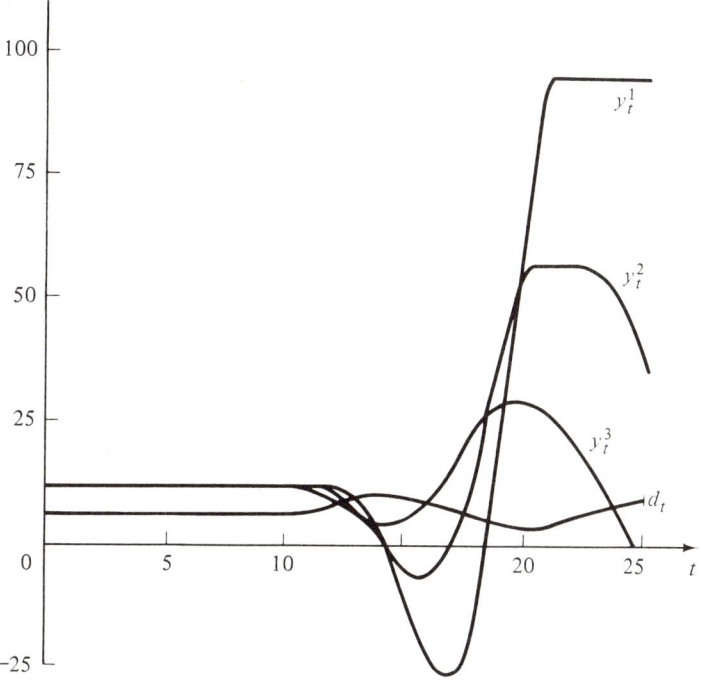

Figure 6-3 Graphs of demands and multiechelon inventory levels for example 6-1.

trates the effect of removing some of this latter type of lead time from the system.

Example 6-2 In example 6-1, suppose that the lead times for delivery of orders are reduced from two periods to one period. Then equation (6-5) must be modified to read

$$y_t^j = y_{t-1}^j + x_{t-1}^j - x_t^{j+1} \qquad j = 1, 2, 3 \qquad (6\text{-}6)$$

Equations (6-4) and (6-6) are applied to the demands of example 6-1, resulting in the values shown in table 6-2 and the graphs in figure 6-4. Notice that the reduction in delivery lead time resulted in reduced fluctuations in inventory levels. Note also that echelon 1 still has the most widely varying inventory level.

Still further reductions in inventory fluctuations can be attained if either of the two types of lead times remaining in example 6-2 are reduced. See problem 6-3.

Another important way to reduce the magnitude of oscillations in a

Table 6-2 Demands, order quantities, and inventory levels for example 6-2

t	1	2	...	9	10	11	12	13	14	15
d_t	6	6	...	6	6	7	8	9	10	9
x_t^3	6	6	...	6	6	6	8	10	11	12
y_t^3	12	12	...	12	12	11	9	8	8	10
x_t^2	6	6	...	6	6	6	6	9	13	15
y_t^2	12	12	...	12	12	12	10	6	4	5
x_t^1	6	6	...	6	6	6	6	8	13	19
y_t^1	12	12	...	12	12	12	8	5	0	−2

t	16	17	18	19	20	21	22	23	24	25
d_t	8	7	6	5	4	5	6	7	8	9
x_t^3	10	7	5	3	2	2	4	7	10	11
y_t^3	14	17	18	18	17	14	10	7	6	7
x_t^2	16	11	4	0	0	0	0	1	8	15
y_t^2	10	19	25	26	24	22	18	11	2	−1
x_t^1	22	22	11	0	0	0	0	0	0	0
y_t^1	1	12	30	41	41	41	41	40	32	17

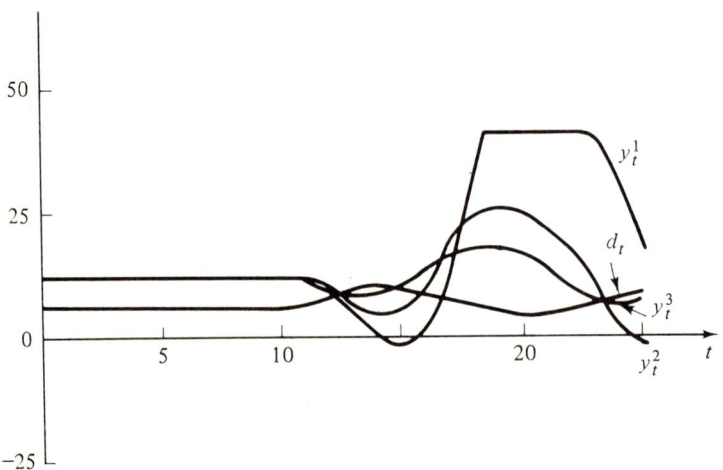

Figure 6-4 Graphs of demands and multiechelon inventory levels for example 6-2.

multiechelon inventory network is by altering the ordering decision rule. Problem 6-4 demonstrates that this can easily be done in the case of example 6-1.

Fluctuations in inventory levels and production or order rates are not necessarily undesirable. In fact, they are sometimes deliberately induced. The following example illustrates such a situation.

Example 6-3 Suppose three items form a series inventory network in which $g_{j,j+1} = 1$ for $j = 1, 2, 3$. External demand for item 3 occurs at a known constant rate of 2 units per period. Because of economic lot size considerations, it has been decided that items 1, 2, and 3 should be ordered in batches of 24, 12, and 4, respectively. (Because of its higher value, item $j + 1$ is ordered in smaller batches than item j.) The lead time $L(j)$ equals 1 for all j. The timing of the placement of orders remains to be specified. One possible situation appears in table 6-3(a). Here, the timing of order placement at each echelon is made without regard to its relation to other echelons. In contrast, table 6-3(b) illustrates the results obtained if care is taken in deciding when to order at each echelon. In

Table 6-3a Example 6-3 with arbitrary relative timing among echelons

t	1	2	3	4	5	6	7	8	9	10	11	12	13	14	15	16	17	18	19
d_t	2	2	2	2	2	2	2	2	2	2	2	2	2	2	2	2	2	2	2
x_t^3	4	0	4	0	4	0	4	0	4	0	4	0	4	0	4	0	4	0	4
y_t^3	0	2	0	2	0	2	0	2	0	2	0	2	0	2	0	2	0	2	0
x_t^2	12	0	0	0	0	0	12	0	0	0	0	0	12	0	0	0	0	0	12
y_t^2	0	12	8	8	4	4	0	12	8	8	4	4	0	12	8	8	4	4	0
x_t^1	0	0	0	24	0	0	0	0	0	0	0	0	0	0	0	24	0	0	0
y_t^1	0	0	0	0	24	24	12	12	12	12	12	12	0	0	0	0	24	24	12

Table 6-3b Example 6-3 with relative timing which follows the principle of delayed timing

t	1	2	3	4	5	6	7	8	9	10	11	12	13	14	15	16	17	18	19
d_t	2	2	2	2	2	2	2	2	2	2	2	2	2	2	2	2	2	2	2
x_t^3	4	0	4	0	4	0	4	0	4	0	4	0	4	0	4	0	4	0	4
y_t^3	0	2	0	2	0	2	0	2	0	2	0	2	0	2	0	2	0	2	0
x_t^2	0	12	0	0	0	0	0	12	0	0	0	0	0	12	0	0	0	0	0
y_t^2	0	0	8	8	4	4	0	0	8	8	4	4	0	0	8	8	4	4	0
x_t^1	24	0	0	0	0	0	0	0	0	0	0	0	24	0	0	0	0	0	0
y_t^1	0	12	12	12	12	12	12	0	0	0	0	0	0	12	12	12	12	12	12

particular, the timing of each order at echelon j is *delayed* so that the arrival of the order coincides in time with a positive requirement, x_t^{j+1}. In general, the "principle of delayed timing" will be defined as follows: *An order is never timed to arrive before at least a portion of that order is required.* Thus the timing in table 6-3(*b*) conforms to the principle of delayed timing. Adherence to this principle ensures that for the given lot sizes and given the stipulation that no planned shortages are permitted, the minimum possible inventory levels are obtained. This principle is invoked in the remaining sections of this chapter.

6-2 MATERIAL REQUIREMENTS PLANNING (MRP)

The concepts discussed in this section have collectively been given the label "material requirements planning," or MRP for short. The concepts are drawn from almost all facets of inventory control including forecasting, order points, lot sizes, and computerized control. However, the concepts have been fused into a fairly unified approach to determine when and how much to order for each item in a many-item, multiechelon inventory structure. Thus, what appears to be a technique is, in fact, the application of a philosophy of how to tie together many techniques.

The philosophy is buried right in the title. Recall that *requirements* for an item are taken to be the sum of internal plus external demands placed on that item. In MRP, these requirements are segregated into periods of time (weeks, say) called *time buckets*. The duration of time covered by these time segments extends from the current time out to the end of a *planning horizon*. Then, in each time bucket and for each item, the requirements for that item are *planned* by determining a number r_t^j defined by

$$r_t^j = \sum_{k \in B(j)} (g_{jk} x_t^k) + MPS_t^j \tag{6-7}$$

Equation (6-7) is a modified form of equation (6-2). The right-hand term will be explained later. The time buckets t do not have to be of equal length. For example, there might be 56 buckets—the first 52 being weeks and the last 4 quarters, making a two-year planning horizon. From equation (6-7) it is seen that the requirements can be planned only because the *orders* are planned. This is perhaps the most distinguishing feature of MRP—that orders are planned long before they are actually released. Before the applicability of MRP is elaborated, the mechanics of the approach will be described. An example will be used to illustrate the concepts involved. The example is kept as simple as possible, consistent with the need to demonstrate the major features of MRP.

Example 6-4 Suppose a product (item 7) has the multiechelon network shown in figure 6-5. Two assemblies (items 5 and 6) are required to form

CHAPTER 6: CONTROLLING MULTIECHELON INVENTORIES **151**

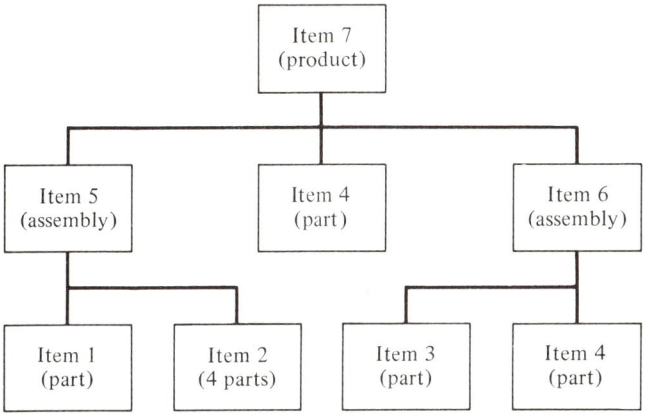

Figure 6-5 Bill of material for example 6-4

the product, along with one part (item 4) which is a spare part that accompanies each product shipped. One assembly requires five parts, four of which (item 2) are identical. The other assembly requires two parts. It takes one week to complete either assembly as well as one week to prepare (i.e., assemble, test, and package) the final product, given the assemblies. Items 1 and 2 can normally be obtained without any delay, but items 3 and 4 require two weeks' time between placement (release) and receipt of an order. Item 5 also has an external demand since it is sold to another manufacturer at the rate of 6 to 8 (average 7) units per week for use in another product. Management's policy is to maintain enough stock to be able to ship the assembly to the customer without delay. Demand for the product has been a steady 10 units per week. This rate is expected to continue. Item 1 has been experiencing a quality problem; 10 percent of these units have been defective and have hence been returned to the vendor (and replaced free of charge).

The present inventory status of each of the items is as follows:

Item	1	2	3	4	5	6	7
On hand	16	0	20	−7	5	6	0

Evidently item 4 is in a shortage condition.

The problem is to determine order timing and quantity for each of the seven items. The MRP approach requires that for each end (retail) item, a *master production schedule* (*MPS*) be specified. The MPS is a statement of the number MPS_t^j of each end item j which is planned to be made available

Table 6-4 Master production schedules for the retail items of example 6-4

t	1	2	3	4	5	6	7	8	9	10
MPS_t^5	7	7	7	7	7	7	7	7	7	7
MPS_t^7	10	10	10	10	10	10	10	10	10	10

to satisfy external demand in each time bucket t. Given the information in example 6-4, a reasonable MPS for each end item appears in table 6-4.

Notice that the MPS satisfies only the external demand portion of the total requirements for item 5. This provides the explanation for the right-hand term in equation (6-7).

The heart of the MRP process is an arithmetic computation called *netting*. The netting calculations involve repeated application of equations (6-7) and (6-3), together with a third relationship called the *netting relationship*:

Net requirements in period t
$\quad$ = gross requirements in period t which cannot be
$\quad\quad$ satisfied by units on hand or by scheduled receipts $\quad$ (6-8)

The computations, usually performed on a computer, are customarily displayed in tabular form for each item and for every time bucket in the planning horizon. Table 6-5 shows the netting computations for item 7. The computations are performed from the top row of the table down. The "P.D." column corresponds to period zero, or the period just ended. The table is always viewed in time as if period 1 is just about to begin. Evidently an order was placed in period 0 which is scheduled to arrive in period 1, in time to satisfy requirements of period 1. The lead time, $L(7) = 1$ week, is recognized here. Net requirements begin in the first period in which a shortage is projected. Notice that a lot size of $Q_7 = 20$ is being used. Lot size values are arbitrary in this example; more is said in section 6-4 about the choice of lot sizes.

The planned order releases for any item contribute to the gross requirements for each predecessor item. This is reflected in table 6-6. Requirements are said to be *exploded* from end items backward through the predecessors until raw material or parts having no predecessors are reached. Since item 6 (table 6-6) has no lot size requirement, material is never planned to arrive in advance of need.

Table 6-7 illustrates the combination of internal and external demands to create the requirements for item 5. It also illustrates one way of treating

Table 6-5 Netting computations for item 7 of example 6-4 that illustrate the basic netting process

Period (week) t	P.D.	1	2	3	4	5	6	7	8	9	10	11
Gross requirements (r_t^7)		10	10	10	10	10	10	10	10	10	10	10
Scheduled receipts (x_{t-1}^7)		20										
Projected on hand	0	10	0	−10	−20	−30	−40	−50	−60	−70	−80	−90
Net requirements				10	10	10	10	10	10	10	10	10
Planned order releases (x_t^7)		20		20			20			20		
Revised on hand (y_t^7)	0	10	0	10	0	10	0	10	0	10	0	10

Table 6-6 Netting computations for item 6 of example 6-4 that illustrate explosion of requirements

Period (week) t	P.D.	1	2	3	4	5	6	7	8	9	10	11
Gross requirements (r_t^6)		0	20	0	20	0	20	0	20	0	20	0
Scheduled receipts (x_{t-1}^6)		6										
Projected on hand	6	6	−14	−14	−34	−34	−54	−54	−74	−74	−94	−94
Net requirements			14		20		20		20		20	
Planned order releases (x_t^6)		14		20		20		20		20		
Revised on hand (y_t^6)	6	6	0									

Table 6-7 Netting computations for item 5 of example 6-4 that illustrate external demands and safety stock

Period (week) t	P.D.	1	2	3	4	5	6	7	8	9	10	11
Gross requirements (r_t^5)		7	27	7	27	7	27	7	27	7	27	7
Scheduled receipts (x_{t-1}^5)		40	10	3								
Projected on hand	4	37		3	−24	−31	−58	−65	−92	−99	−126	−133
Net requirements					24	7	27	7	27	7	27	7
Planned order releases (x_t^5)			40			40		40		40		
Revised on hand (y_t^5)	4	37	10	3	16	9	22	15	28	21	34	27

153

the fact that a safety stock of 1 unit is to be maintained. Here, the actual inventory on hand is artificially reduced by 1 unit, after which the netting computations are performed as usual. Thus the extra unit of safety stock is "buried," only to resurface in a shortage situation.

Another approach is to allow the safety stock to be explicitly recognized in the netting process by timing order releases in such a way that an order *arrives* in the time bucket in which the inventory level would otherwise fall below the safety stock level. This is mathematically equivalent to the first approach and will produce identical results. This approach is called *time-phased order point* and is similar to conventional order point except that order *arrivals* are triggered by a stock level rather than order *releases*. This is in keeping with the MRP philosophy, which is to defer receipt of an order until it is needed. Time-phased order point differs from conventional order point in that it includes recognition of requirements which occur *between* order release and arrival. Thus any unusual requirement during such a lead time can change the timing of order release.

Table 6-8 provides an example of another element of MRP logic. Observe (figure 6-5) that item 4 is required at two echelons. Therefore it could potentially appear twice in the explosion of requirements. This, however, would not be the neatest way of informing the buyer of item 4 of the requirements for that item. He or she would have to remember that the item's requirements are segregated. This is overcome by the technique, called *low-level coding*, in which all requirements for an item are accumulated at the lowest level (echelon) at which that item appears. Note that they could not be accumulated at the highest echelon since not all requirements for the item are known at that point. Thus item 4 appears as if it were at the lowest echelon. However, the requirements are generated from the planned order releases of the two successor items 6 and 7, as shown in table 6-8.

Table 6-8 also indicates that a scheduled receipt of 40 units of item 4 is past due. The presumption is that those 40 units will arrive in period 1, in time to satisfy period-1 demands as well as the past-due unsatisfied demand for 7 units. Therefore the negative on-hand in the past-due column generates no net requirements.

Note that an order release for 41 units of item 4 is planned for week 2. This means that the order is planned to arrive in week 4, resulting in an inventory level of 40 at the end of week 4. It would be possible to allow a shortage of 1 unit to occur in period 4 by planning the order release for period 3 instead of period 2. Even though this would be likely to save holding costs in period 4, it would violate the philosophy of MRP, which is never to plan a shortage.

To illustrate the complete explosion of requirements for example 6-4, it would remain to display the netting computations for the remaining items, 1, 2, and 3. Since no new concepts are introduced in the netting for item 3, it is not displayed. For item 2, since four parts are required for each assembly (item 5), the gross requirements for item 2 are obtained for each time bucket by multiplying the corresponding planned order releases of item 5 by 4. The net requirements for item 2 are then calculated in the usual manner.

The gross requirements for item 1 also differ numerically from the planned order releases of item 5, but for a different reason. Recall that 10 percent of the units of item 1 are defective. This means that (roughly) 1100 units must be ordered for every 1000 required. Actually, slightly more than 1100 would be needed, since there is a probability of $\frac{1}{10}$ that each of the extra 100 items would be defective. In general, if the probability that an item is defective is p, then for every good unit required, the number of units which must be ordered is

$$1 + p(1 + p(1 + p(\ldots))) = \sum_{k=0}^{\infty} p^k = \frac{1}{1-p}$$

Thus if $p = \frac{1}{10}$ and 1000 good units are required, an order should be placed for 1111. The extra 111 units are called *reject allowance*. Thus for item 1, table 6-9 shows gross requirements which include reject allowances. Fractional units are not shown here although theoretically they could be. Instead, every time the cumulative fractional parts of the reject allowances add up to (or exceed) 1, another unit is added to the gross requirements. In table 6-9, this occurs in weeks 7 and 11.

A second complication accrues from the fact that defective units of item 1 are being received. Suppose the defectives occur randomly. (That is, the probability that a unit is defective is p for each unit received.) Then it is likely that for some orders, less than the required number of good items will be received. In fact, this will occur in around half of the orders received. This means that in order to provide protection against resulting shortages, a safety stock should be carried. To determine an appropriate safety stock level, use is made of the fact that the number v of defectives in an order of size n is binomially distributed with mean np and standard deviation $\sqrt{np(1-p)}$. Therefore, 3 standard deviations of v for item 1 is

$$(3)\sqrt{(44)(0.1)} \times \sqrt{(1-0.1)} = 5.97$$

So, assuming that 3 standard deviations of v will provide sufficient protection against stockouts, a safety stock of 6 units of item 1 will be maintained. This is reflected in table 6-9, in which the stock on hand is reduced by 6 units, after which the netting computations are performed as usual.

The above discussion has demonstrated the way in which requirements for externally demanded end items are exploded into requirements for lower-echelon items via the MRP netting process. The procedure is predicated on the existence of requirements for all end items which are assumed to be planned as they appear in a master production schedule.

Table 6-8 Netting computations for item 4 of example 6-4 that illustrate low-level coding and past-due receipts

Period (week) t	P.D	1	2	3	4	5	6	7	8	9	10	11
Gross requirements (r_t^4)		14	20	20	20	20	20	20	20	20	20	20
Scheduled receipts (x_{t-2}^4)	40	0	40									
Projected on hand	-7	19	39	19	-1	-21	-41	-61	-81	-101	-121	-141
Net requirements					1	20	20	20	20	20	20	20
Planned order releases (x_t^4)			41		40	40		40		40		40
Revised on hand (y_t^4)	-7	19	39	19	40	20	0	20	0	20	0	20

Table 6-9 Netting computations for item 1 of example 6-4 that illustrate reject allowance and quality-related safety stock

Period (week) t	P.D.	1	2	3	4	5	6	7	8	9	10	11
Gross requirements (r_t^1)				44		44		45		44		45
Scheduled receipts (x_t^1)												
Projected on hand	~~16~~ 10	10	10	-34	-34	-78	-78	-123	-123	-167	-167	-212
Net requirements				40		44		45		44		45
Planned order releases (x_t^1)				40		44		45		44		45
Revised on hand (y_t^1)	~~16~~ 10	10	10	0	0	0	0	0	0	0	0	0

Now, as every one knows, plans change. The ensuing discussion addresses the effects of changes in the MPS.

The MPS can be divided into two portions. The earlier time buckets constitute the *firm* portion, while the later ones comprise the *tentative* portion. In any time bucket within the tentative portion, requirements can be increased indefinitely, and shortages can still be avoided without changing any orders which have already been released. The dividing line between the firm and tentative portions is found by calculating the longest cumulative (stacked) lead time between satisfaction of a requirement of the MPS and order of any item needed to satisfy that requirement. Another way of putting this is that if an additional requirement occurs in a time bucket in the tentative portion of the MPS, then *all* materials needed to satisfy that requirement can be ordered and received in time. For example 6-4, the longest stacked lead time for item 7 is $L(7) + L(6) + L(3) = 1 + 1 + 2 = 4$. Therefore, requirements in time buckets 1 through 4 of the MPS for item 7 are firm. For the MPS for item 5, only the first time bucket is firm.

Sometimes the MPS can be increased within the firm portion, and the resulting requirements can still be met. For example, suppose the MPS for item 7 is increased from 10 to 11 in time bucket 4. The reader can verify that this increase can be accommodated by increasing only planned order releases (i.e., without changing any order already released). In problem 6-8, you are asked to determine by how much more the MPS could be increased and accommodated in the same manner. This process is called *trial fitting* [5].

It may be that (say, for marketing reasons) it is mandatory to increase requirements in the firm portion beyond what can be feasibly accommodated. In this case, overtime and subcontracting are two ways of avoiding disappointing a customer. Of course, decreases can always be accommodated more easily, the only effects being that productive resources may be used earlier than they need to be and inventory is held unnecessarily. For this reason, management will often allow the last time buckets in the firm portion of the MPS to be tentative with respect to *decreases* in requirements.

Sometimes increases in requirements can be accommodated when at first it appears impossible to do so. The explosion process is typically computerized and hence is performed automatically according to predetermined decision rules. It may be possible to override the automatic process and thereby satisfy requirements. As an example, suppose 5 units of requirements for item 7 are advanced from week 3 to week 1. The resulting MRP calculations appear in table 6-10. An examination of the calculations reveals that net requirements for item 6 in week 1 cannot be met, because of the one-week lead time between order placement and receipt for item 6. The only way to relieve requirements for item 6 is to alter planned order releases for item 7. Evidently the decision rule being used to plan orders for item 7 is that

Table 6-10 Netting computations for revised MPS for item 7 that illustrate requirements which cannot be met

Period (week) t	P.D.	1	2	3	4	5	6	7	8	9	10	11
Gross requirements (r_t^7)		15	10	5	10	10	10	10	10	10	10	10
Scheduled receipts (x_{t-1}^7)		20										
Projected on hand	0	5	−5	−10	−20	−30	−40	−50	−60	−70	−80	−90
Net requirements			5	5	10	10	10	10	10	10	10	10
Planned order releases (x_t^7)		20			20		20		20		20	
Gross requirements (r_t^6)		20	0	0	20	0	20	0	20	0	20	0
Scheduled receipts (x_{t-1}^6)	6	−14	−14	−14	−34	−34	−54	−54	−74	−74	−94	−94
Projected on hand		14			20		20		20		20	
Net requirements		14										
Planned order releases (x_t^6)		14		20				20		20		

items are always ordered in lot sizes of 20. This decision rule, followed automatically by the computer, can be overriden in this case. In table 6-11, this has been done by specifying that for item 7, orders of 5 and 15 be released in weeks 1 and 2, respectively. This results in requirements for item 6 which can be met. In fact, the planned order releases for item 6 are now equivalent to the original ones in table 6-6, so the remaining explosion will not cause any further difficulty. In order to keep the computer from later changing the planned order releases back to their old values, the values $x_1^7 = 5$ and $x_2^7 = 15$ are designated as *firm planned orders*. A firm planned order is considered to be as unchangeable as an order which has already been released.

The ability to solve the above problem by using firm planned orders depends on the ability to ascertain that the gross requirements for item 6 were a result of planned order releases for item 7. In general, item 6 might be used in more than one "parent" item. When the gross requirements for an item are identified by parent item for each time bucket, the requirements are said to be *pegged*. Pegging of requirements for item 4 in example 6-4 would identify that the gross requirements for item 4 were caused by planned order releases for both items 6 and 7.

Changes in MPS requirements, as well as the occurrence of other events such as order releases and arrival of stock, occur continually. The inventory records (such as those in tables 6-5 through 6-11) must be updated to recognize such changes. This is accomplished by reexploding requirements, from end items down to raw materials. There are two approaches in common use for accomplishing the reexplosion. The first, called *regenerative MRP*, accumulates all change information for a period of time (typically one week), enters the accumulated information, and explodes requirements at the end of each such period. The second approach is known as *net change MRP*. In this case, each transaction is fed to the system as it occurs. Since a transaction can affect only an item, its predecessors, the predecessors of its predecessors, etc., a partial explosion takes place to update the records of only those items affected by the change. Thus under net change MRP, inventory information is kept more current. This is at a cost resulting from more extensive computer requirements needed to handle the program logic and the more frequent updating calculations. Regeneration and net change may be thought of as two extreme philosophies. In practice, some intermediate logic may be used. For example, net changes may be batched and processed daily (say, overnight) rather than instantaneously. Or, inventory status may be updated daily while master production schedules are only changed (regenerated) weekly.

A thorough and readable treatment of MRP concepts is offered by Orlicky [5]. The book is recommended to those interested in a careful exposition of the logical considerations in MRP.

Table 6-11 Netting computations of table 6-10, revised by use of firm planned orders

Period (week) t	P.D.	1	2	3	4	5	6	7	8	9	10	11
Gross requirements (r_t^7)		15	10	5	10	10	10	10	10	10	10	10
Scheduled receipts (x_{t-1}^7)		20										
Projected on hand	0	5	−5	−10	−20	−30	−40	−50	−60	−70	−80	−90
Net requirements			5	5	10	10	10	10	10	10	10	10
Planned order releases (x_t^7)		5	15		20		20		20		20	
Gross requirements (r_t^6)		5	15		20		20		20		20	
Scheduled receipts (x_{t-1}^6)												
Projected on hand	6	1	−14	−14	−34	−34	−54	−54	−74	−74	−94	−94
Net requirements			14		20		20		20		20	
Planned order releases (x_t^6)		14		20		20		20		20		

6-3 APPLICABILITY OF MRP

This section addresses some of the issues related to applicability of the MRP approach. The issues can be generated by first reviewing the assumptions or prerequisites to the use of the approach and then examining ways of ensuring that the assumptions are, in fact, valid. Proceeding to apply MRP when the prerequisites are not met has disastrous consequences. This is because the users of material controlled by the MRP system rely heavily on the fact that the system will deliver material when and where it is needed. Failure of the system has serious repercussions. The consequences are likely to be disruption or discontinuance of production and failure to meet schedules and end-item demands.

The primary prerequisites to using MRP are

1. A master production schedule for all end items being supported by the system
2. A valid bill of material showing all predecessor/successor relationships
3. Attainable lead times between order release and material delivery
4. Predetermined ordering rules (e.g., lot sizes) for all items controlled by the systems

These prerequisites are discussed below. There is an additional requirement for valid inventory records (i.e., file data integrity). This matter is addressed in chapter 9.

Without the master production schedule(s), MRP cannot generate requirements for any item. The MPS must be specified for a planning horizon of sufficient length that component order releases can be planned. However, since the MPS is a reflection of external demands, this implies that demand forecasts must be reliably made for this same planning horizon. We have already seen that it is possible to incorporate safety stock into the MPS to accommodate uncertainty in demands. If management's philosophy is to meet demand as it occurs, this safety stock is generally essential. Of course, the policy may be to meet demand only to a degree. No matter—the MPS is always a production schedule, not a demand schedule.

Some end items are virtually impossible to forecast in their demanded form until an order is received. Any item for which a combination of options exists is of this type. Who can predict how many brand Z automobiles will be ordered with air conditioning, automatic transmission, two doors, and pink upholstery, by a customer who expects delivery in 10 days? The solution to this problem is to produce a MPS for each optional assembly, or *module*. Final assembly of the modules into automobiles can then be deferred until customer orders are a reality. The final assembly schedule is thus distinct from the MPS for each module. Uncertainties in final configuration are again handled by using safety stock. For example, if it has been predicted that 100 automobiles will be demanded in a given time period, the MPSs might call for 55 two-door and 55 four-door modules (plus perhaps 2 or 3 with no doors at all).

Bills of materials (BOM) must exist for every end item for which an MPS exists. If modules (rather than final assemblies) are being scheduled, then a BOM must be documented for each module. This is not a trivial task, as illustrated in the following example.

Example 6-5 A plant assembles telephone sets which have two options with choices for each option. The options are push button or dial and black or beige color. The major subassemblies in each telephone are

1. Cord and receiver (color-dependent)
2. Housing, except front face (color-dependent)
3. Front face (differs between push-button and dial sets)
4. Either dial or push-button set (dial is always clear plastic; push-button set is color-dependent)
5. Electronic assembly (assume identical for all telephones)

The end items in this case are the modules. *Modular bills of material* would have to be set up as in table 6-12. Notice that one of the modules, called the "common" module, consists of those subassemblies which are common to all options. There is a problem with the push-button sets which are used in only one *option combination*—either black push-button or beige push-button. These parts cannot belong to any of the existing modules, and so they have been designated as being in module "X." Such parts are undesirable from an MRP point of view, since an MPS must be created for module X. This requires a forecast of an option combination, which is what was being avoided by going to modular MPSs and BOMs in the first place. The problem can sometimes be remedied by redesign of the part (say, using color-independent push-button sets). If this is not feasible, another approach is to include the parts in another module and to require less than one subassembly per module. For example, suppose that the MPSs for dial and push-button sets are based on a forecast of 40 percent push-button sets, plus or minus 10 percent. Then a sensible solution would be to include black push-button sets in the black module at a rate of 0.4 set per module. (This is like a reject allowance in reverse.) Beige push-button sets would similarly be included in the beige module. Finally, a safety stock of push-button sets would be required to handle the ± 10 percent uncertainty.

Table 6-12 A list of modular bills of material for telephone sets

Module	Major assemblies
Beige	Beige cord/receiver; beige housing
Black	Black cord/receiver; black housing
Dial	Dial face; dial set
Push button	Push-button face
Common	Electronic assembly
X	Black and beige push-button sets

Lead times, indicating the time between order release and order receipt, are essential to the MRP procedure. Lead times for purchased items are arrived at by consensus between vendor and buyer. However, lead times for items made in-house are not so readily obtained. It would seem that they would be easy to obtain since they depend more directly on conditions within the firm. The problem is that since manufacturing lead times are set in-house, the freedom of choice of the lead times adds another dimension to the decision-making problem. Shop lead time for a job is affected by the priority given to that job and by the capacity of the shop to handle its load at any particular point in time. The MRP approach assumes lead times are both known and attainable. As such, MRP is capacity-insensitive. In order for these assumptions to be valid, the requirements for manufacturing shop capacity must be determined in time to make arrangements to provide that capacity.

MRP can be used in a simulation mode to assist in arriving at attainable capacity levels, as outlined in figure 6-6. A tentative master production schedule (or the tentative portion of a larger MPS) is used to explode material requirements. These material requirements are converted (using time standards) to resource requirements. The resources most often of concern are, of course, labor and machine time. The result of this conversion might appear as in figure 6-7. If capacity is insufficient and cannot be increased (using, say, overtime or subcontracting), then revision to the MPS must be made. In the situation shown in figure 6-7, this will be rather simple, since all that is needed is that some requirements be shifted by a time bucket or so.

This is not a book about production planning and control. The reader desiring more information about shop floor priorities, shop scheduling, and production control in the MRP context is referred to Orlicky [5], Wight [9], and most issues of the journal of the American Production and Inventory Control Society (APICS) [11].

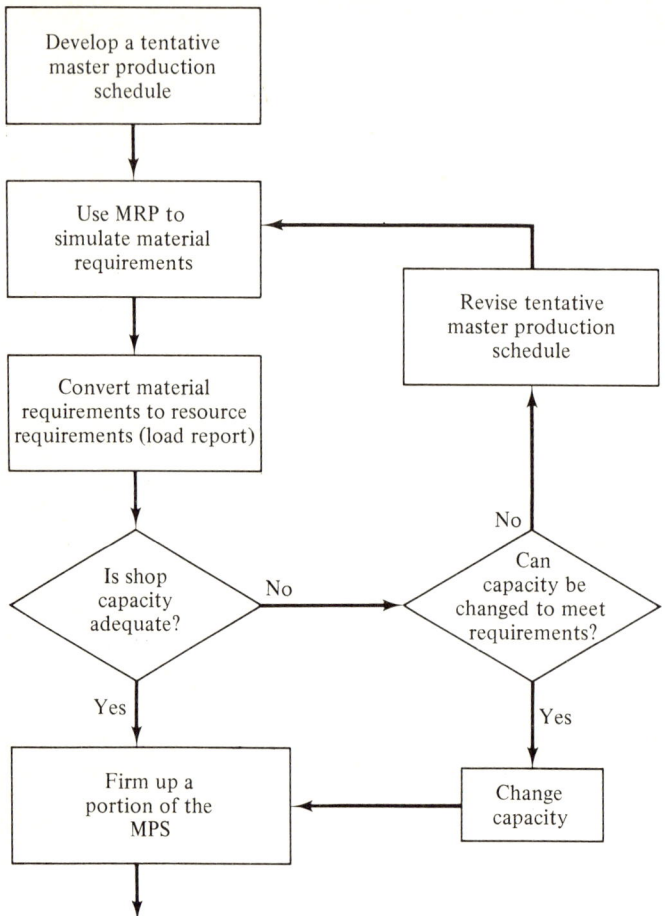

Figure 6-6 Using MRP to assist in planning capacity requirements.

Ordering rules, or lot sizing rules, are assumed available to the (computerized) requirements explosion procedure. This topic is treated in section 6-4.

A final word is in order about the applicability of MRP. It is, like any other mechanism for determining when and how much to order, just a tool; without a considerable amount of judgment, the tool will not be successfully applied. Moreover, MRP is just another model and, like all models, must be tempered to reality. One of the most troublesome assumptions about MRP is that lead times are assumed known. Uncertainty in demand is filtered through the MPS, but MRP is not so insulated from uncertainty in supply. Whether because of slippage of delivery dates or receipt of defective mate-

CHAPTER 6: CONTROLLING MULTIECHELON INVENTORIES **165**

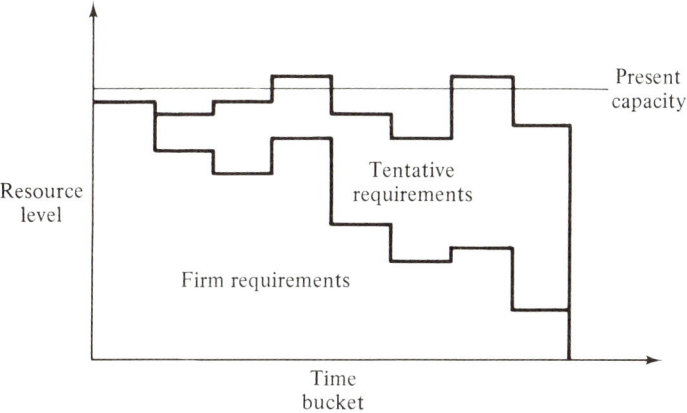

Figure 6-7 A load projection based on firm and tentative capacity requirements.

rial, supply failures require continuing vigilance—and, in some cases, the snake under the MRP rock—safety stocks.

6-4 MULTIECHELON LOT SIZING

In this section, several approaches to determining when and how much to order for each item in a multiechelon inventory network are discussed. The first part of the section exposes a number of alternative myopic procedures, which only consider one echelon at a time. The extension of these procedures to the multiechelon environment is considered in the latter part of the section.

As is the case throughout this book, there is an emphasis on the cost effects of a particular approach. In a manufacturing situation (as most MRP applications are), there may be many other important issues, such as machine capacities, limits on work-in-process inventory levels, package quantities, etc. The reason for advancing the cost-conscious approaches are that (1) they are easily programmed for computers, (2) they provide definite answers, and (3) in lieu of more pressing concerns, they at least do justice to one concern of management—costs. They can be applied with as little or as much manual override as is deemed appropriate.

The problem at hand can be summarized as follows. For an n-period planning horizon, echelon j faces gross requirements r_t^j, $t = 1, 2, \ldots, n$. The initial inventory y_0^j will be assumed to be zero. (In general, any initial stock can be applied toward satisfying, and hence reducing, gross requirements in the earliest time periods.) For simplicity, assume that the ending inventory y_n^j is also zero. (Any value could be specified for y_n^j.) Lead time is ignored here without any loss of generality, since any order x_t^j is assumed to be placed in time to arrive in period t. If $L > 0$, then y_0^j is taken to include any scheduled receipts resulting from previously released orders. Shortages are not permitted to be planned, so $y_t^j \geq 0$ for all j and t.

A simple cost structure is assumed throughout this section, unless otherwise indicated. An ordering (or setup) cost k is incurred every time an order is released. The cost h of holding 1 unit of stock for one time period is assessed on the inventory on hand at the end of the period. The problem is to find x_t^j, $t = 1, 2, \ldots, n$, which economize on the total ordering and holding cost over the n-period planning horizon.

A way of finding an optimal (i.e., minimum-cost) solution to this problem has already been shown in section 4-2. The algorithm presented there was developed to handle a more general situation involving concave costs and incurrence of shortages. That method simplifies in the present case to the following algorithm, referred to as the *Wagner-Whitin algorithm* after its authors [8]. Let c_{im} be the cost associated with releasing an order in period $i + 1$ which will exactly satisfy requirements in periods $i + 1, i + 2, \ldots, m$. Then

$$c_{im} = k + \sum_{t=i+1}^{m-1} \left(\sum_{\tau=t+1}^{m} r_\tau^j \right) \qquad (6\text{-}9)$$

Equation (6-9) is a simplification of equation (4-8). Define f_i as the minimum cost in periods $i + 1, \ldots, n$ if an order is placed in period $i + 1$. Then

$$f_i = \min_{i+1 \leq m \leq n} \{c_{im} + f_m\} \qquad (6\text{-}10)$$

Equation (6-10) is identical to equation (4-10). After c_{im} is calculated for $0 \leq i \leq m \leq n$, the algorithm consists of (starting with $f_n = 0$) calculating $f_{n-1}, f_{n-2}, \ldots, f_0$ in that order. The value of f_0 will be the cost of the optimal ordering schedule.

Example 6-6 Requirements for echelon j for nine periods are 4, 0, 3, 1, 8, 3, 0, 6, 0. The values of k and h are 10 and 1, respectively. The calculations using equations (6-9) and (6-10) are summarized in table 6-13. The value of $m^*(i)$ in the right-hand column is the value of m which yielded the minimum, f_i, in equation (6-10). The value $m(0) = 4$ says that the minimum cost is obtained by ordering in period 1 enough stock to last through period 4. The optimal solution is to order 8 in period 1, 11 in period 5, and 6 in period 8, at a total cost of 42.

The above procedure is guaranteed to find an optimal solution. However, there are several heuristic approaches which are computationally much simpler, although they do not provide such a guarantee. Four of these

Table 6-13 Calculations for the Wagner-Whitin solution of example 6-6. Values of c_{im} appear in the body of the table

i \ m	1	2	3	4	5	6	7	8	9	f_i	$m^*(i)$
0	10	10	16	19	51	66	66	108	108	42	4
1		10	13	15	39	51	51	87	87	38	4
2			10	11	27	36	36	66	66	34	4
3				10	18	24	24	48	48	33	4
4					10	13	13	31	31	23	7
5						10	10	22	22	20	7
6							10	16	16	16	9
7								10	10	10	8 or 9
8									10	10	9

will be reviewed now. Each of these heuristics start with the present period (period 1) and scan each successive period until a stopping criterion is met. Then an order is placed to satisfy requirements up through the stopping period. The procedure is then repeated, beginning with the period beyond the stopping period. Let i be the starting period for any given set of periods to be scanned and $m(i)$ be a candidate stopping period. Also let $m^*(i)$ be the stopping period chosen on the basis of the stopping criterion.

The first heuristic, called *period order quantity*, sets

$$m^*(i) = i - 1 + \sqrt{\frac{2k}{\bar{r}h}} \tag{6-11}$$

where $\bar{r}$ is the average requirements over the planning horizon:

$$\bar{r} = \frac{1}{n} \sum_{t=1}^{n} r_t^j \tag{6-12}$$

The rationale behind this is that the number of periods covered by an order $[m(i) - i + 1]$ should equal the average number which could be covered using an economic order quantity $EOQ = \sqrt{2k\bar{r}/h}$. The time between orders is then simply $EOQ/\bar{r} = \sqrt{2k/(\bar{r}h)}$. For example 6-6, $\bar{r} = 2.78$, so $m^*(i) = i - 1 + \sqrt{7.19} = i + 1.68$. Rounding off, an order should be placed every three periods. However, in this as well as all heuristics, there is no point in ordering in a period t in which $r_t^j = 0$. Thus, order 7 in period 1, 12 in period 4, and 6 in period 8. The total cost of this policy is 55.

A second heuristic (endorsed by some vendors of computerized MRP packages) is called *least unit cost* because it chooses $m(i)$ to minimize

$UC(m, i)$, the cost per unit required during the interval up through the stopping period:

$$UC(m, i) = \frac{k + h \sum_{t=i}^{m(i)} (t - i) r_t^j}{\sum_{t=i}^{m(i)} r_t^j} \qquad (6\text{-}13)$$

The calculations involved in applying the least-unit-cost heuristic to example 6-6 are shown in table 6-14. The solution calls for orders to be placed in periods 1, 4, and 8 for 7, 12, and 6 units, respectively. Total cost of this policy is 55. (It is the same policy arrived at using the period order quantity heuristic.)

A third heuristic approach is known as the *least-total-cost approach* [2]. This approach defines the *economic part-period (EPP) ratio* as the number of part periods (PP) for which the holding cost would equal the ordering cost:

$$h(EPP) = k \qquad EPP = \frac{k}{h} \qquad (6\text{-}14)$$

For example 6-6, $EPP = 10$, which says that the stopping period $m(i)$ is that period for which the number of part-periods of stock held for the order under consideration is most nearly equal to the EPP. Table 6-15 shows the computations involved in applying the least-total-cost algorithm to example 6-6. In this example, the same optimal solution as found using the Wagner-Whitin algorithm was obtained by using this heuristic, although that will not always happen.

Table 6-14 Calculations for the least-unit-cost solution of example 6-6

i	m(i)	Lot size	Total cost	UC(m, i)	m*(i)
1	1	4	10	2.50	
	2	4	10	2.50	
	3	7	16	2.29	3
	4	8	19	2.38	
	5	16	51	3.18	
4	4	1	10	10.00	
	5	9	18	2.00	
	6	12	24	2.00	
	7	12	24	2.00	7
	8	18	48	2.67	
8	8	6	10	1.67	
	9	6	10	1.67	9

Table 6-15 Calculations for the least-total-cost solution of example 6-6

i	m(i)	Lot size	Part-periods (PP)	m*(i)
1	1	4	0	
	2	4	0	
	3	7	6	
	4	8	9	4
	5	16	41	
5	5	8	0	
	6	11	3	
	7	11	3	7
	8	17	21	
8	8	6	0	
	9	6	0	9

The final heuristic lot sizing algorithm to be considered here is called the *Silver-Meal* approach after its authors [6]. Their emphasis is on the cost *per period*. If an order is placed in period i to satisfy demands through period $m(i)$, the cost per period $CPP(m, i)$ is

$$CPP(m, i) = \frac{k + h \sum_{t=i}^{m(i)} (t - i) r_t^j}{m(i) - i + 1} \quad (6\text{-}15)$$

The algorithm dictates that the stopping period $m^*(i)$ is chosen to be the first period for which $CPP(m + 1, i) > CPP(m, i)$. By letting p be the number of periods in an order $[p = m(i) - i + 1]$ and using equation (6-15), this inequality becomes

$$\frac{k + h \sum_{t=i}^{m^*(i)+1} (t - i) r_t^j}{p + 1} > \frac{k + h \sum_{t=i}^{m^*(i)} (t - i) r_t^j}{p}$$

This reduces algebraically to

$$hp[m^*(i) + 1 - i] r_{m^*(i)+1}^j > k + h \sum_{t=i}^{m^*(i)} (t - i) r_t^j$$

which in turn can be expressed as

$$p^2 r_{m^*(i)+1}^j > \frac{k}{h} + \sum_{t=i}^{m^*(i)} (t - i) r_t^j \quad (6\text{-}16)$$

Table 6-16 illustrates the computational procedure as applied to example 6-6. Note that the procedure terminates with $m^*(8) = 9$ even though the

170 PART II: INVENTORY CONTROL MODELS

Table 6-16 Calculations for the Silver-Meal solution of example 6-6

i	$m(i)$	p	$p^2 r^j_{m(i)+1}$	$\dfrac{k}{h} + \sum_{t=i}^{m(i)}(t-i)r^j_t$	$m^*(i)$
1	1	1	0	10	
	2	2	12	10	2
3	3	1	1	10	
	4	2	32	17	4
5	5	1	3	10	
	6	2	0	13	
	7	3	54	13	7
8	8	1	0	0	
	9	2	?	0	9

relationship in equation (6-16) cannot be evaluated. The solution calls for orders to be placed in periods 1, 3, 5, and 8 for quantities of 4, 4, 11, and 6, respectively. The total cost of this policy is 44.

Table 6-17 displays a summary of results for all five algorithms, as applied to example 6-6. It would be naive to draw any conclusion about the relative effectiveness of the various approaches from this sample of one short planning horizon. All that can be said is that only the Wagner-Whitin approach guarantees a minimum-cost solution, albeit at the expense of a heavier computational burden. It is interesting to note that each of the nonoptimal heuristics uses a different cost criterion. Berry [1] compares the Wagner-Whitin, period order quantity, and least total cost (alias part-period balancing) along with the classic EOQ approach for 25 data sets consisting of five values each of the ratio $EOQ/\bar{r} = \sqrt{2k/(\bar{r}h)}$ and the coefficient of variation (ratio of standard deviation to mean) of demands over time. His conclusions focus on the undesirability of using the classic EOQ when the ratio $\sqrt{2k/(\bar{r}h)}$ is not near an integer value or when a highly "lumpy"

Table 6-17 Comparison of results of applying lot size algorithms to example 6-6

Algorithm	Cost criterion	Cost for example 6-6
Wagner-Whitin	Minimum cost	42
Period order quantity	Economic average order interval	55
Least unit cost	Minimum cost per unit	55
Least total cost	Balance ordering and holding costs	42
Silver-Meal	Minimum cost per period	44

demand time pattern exists. (The latter is evidenced to some extent by a high coefficient of variation.) Of course, both the classic *EOQ* and the period order quantity approaches respond only to average demand, and hence should not be expected to compare well in the face of lumpy or erratic demand.

One property which is true of all the methods applied so far is that *an order for an item is never timed to arrive in any period in which there are no requirements for that item*. This property has a profound effect on multiechelon lot sizes, as the following discussion indicates.

It is easy to see that, in considering one item in a multiechelon network by itself, this property makes economic sense, for the cost assumptions used in this section. It is apparent that any order timed to arrive in a period of zero requirements could be deferred by one period, at a savings in holding costs and no increase in ordering costs.

Consideration of each item by itself in determining lot sizes is a form of suboptimization, as shown by the following hypothetical example.

Example 6-7 Suppose a two-echelon network consists of only two items. Item 2 has a MPS calling for 1 unit of product per week for an indefinite number of weeks into the future. The ordering cost and holding cost for item 2 are 8 and 1, respectively. Item 1 supplies item 2 on a one-for-one basis. The ordering cost and holding cost for item 1 are 360 and 20, respectively. Lead times and present stock levels are zero. Plan order releases for the two items by determining lot sizes.

Application of the Wagner-Whitin algorithm to item 2 indicates that an order for 4 units should be placed every four weeks. This becomes the requirements schedule for item 1. Applying the Wagner-Whitin algorithm to item 1 with these requirements yields the result that 8 units of item 1 should be ordered every eight weeks. The total cost per week is 3.5 for item 2 and 67.5 for item 1, or 71 per week for both items.

The solution just derived is *not* optimal. An alternate solution (which itself is not necessarily optimal) is to order 6 units of item 2 every six weeks and the same for item 1. This results in a total cost per week of 3.83 for item 1 and 60 for item 2, which gives 63.83 per week for both items. Thus the cost per week obtained by considering each item separately is at least 11 percent too high.

Application of lot size rules on an item-by-item basis has the effect of suggesting larger and larger lot sizes as one moves from the last (end-item) echelon to the first (purchased raw material) echelon. This phenomenon, which can create diseconomies of the type discovered in example 6-7, is more prevalent in a pure coalescence structure (in which each item has a unique successor item) than in other structures (such as arborescences). This is because the combination of planned order releases of two (or more) successors of an item usually results in requirements occurring in a larger percentage of the time buckets.

The author has shown [4] that under fairly general cost conditions and for the special case of a series structure, there is a minimum-cost solution which has the property that no item is received in any period for which requirements for that item are zero. More precisely, recall that x_t^j is defined as the amount of item j ordered during period t and y_t^j as the inventory of item j held at the end of period t. Also let $c_t^j(x_t^j)$ and $h_t^j(y_t^j)$ be the respective ordering and holding costs. Assume zero lead times. Then the following theorem has been shown to be true.

Theorem 6-1 [4] [10] If for the series network $c_t^j(\cdot)$ and $h_t^j(\cdot)$ are concave on $(0, \infty)$; $c_t^j(\cdot)$ is nonincreasing in t; and $h_t^j(\cdot)$ is nondecreasing in j for $t = 1, 2, \ldots, n$ and $j = 1, 2, \ldots, N$; then there exists a minimum-cost set of order releases for which

$$y_{t-1}^j x_t^j = 0 \qquad t = 1, \ldots, n;\ j = 1, \ldots, N \qquad (6\text{-}17)$$

and

$$x_t^j = 0 \Rightarrow x_t^{j-1} = 0 \qquad j = 2, \ldots, N \qquad (6\text{-}18)$$

A dynamic programming type of recursive algorithm is provided in [4] to find an optimal solution with these properties.

The above conditions are not too restrictive. The concavity assumptions have been discussed previously (see chapter 4). The assumption that h_t^j is nondecreasing in j is frequently true because the capital cost is applied to an ever-increasing item value as it progresses through the assembly process. The assumption that c_t^j is nonincreasing in t is reasonable in the short term (within one year). It also allows for the learning-curve type of efficiency improvement. Although the theorem applies only to a series inventory network, property (6-18) should not be way out of line in more general structures. And there is some justification that the lot size of a predecessor should be at least as large as that of its successor (assuming a one-for-one quantity relationship).

Veinott [7] has shown, under somewhat more harsh cost assumptions, that there exists a minimum-cost set of order releases which has properties analogous to equations (6-17) and (6-18) for any arborescence network. His analog to (6-18) is

$$y_{t-1}^{B(j)} \cdot x_t^j = 0 \qquad t = 2, \ldots, n;\ j = 1, \ldots, N$$

He provides a dynamic programming type of recursive algorithm to obtain an optimal solution with that property.

Any model which finds minimum-cost solutions to general multiechelon inventory network situations is likely to be complex indeed. With the exception of a few special cases, cost-conscious lot sizes will probably be determined on an echelon-by-echelon basis. The only consolation to this situation is that the solutions so obtained at least suboptimize costs.

6-5 SUMMARY

An inventory is said to have multiple echelons whenever any two items bear a supply-demand relationship. Such items are said to belong to separate echelons. In general there may be many echelons. Also, many multiechelon structures are possible, including coalescence (pull together) and arborescence (branch apart) structures.

In multiechelon structures, inventory levels of items several echelons removed from external (retail) demand tend to fluctuate more widely than those of the retail items themselves. This prevalent undesirable characteristic can be reduced by shortening delays such as lead times.

A widely used approach for controlling inventories in coalescence structures is called material requirements planning, or MRP. In MRP, requirements (internal plus external demands) are segmented into time buckets, usually of daily or weekly duration. Then order releases are planned to meet the requirements. Stress is placed on delaying order releases until they are necessary to meet requirements (called the principle of delayed timing). The MRP approach is successfully applied only if there exist valid master schedules of external demands and accurate bills of material which define the coalescence structure.

Lot sizes for items in a multiechelon structure can be chosen by considering one echelon at a time. Several approaches yield results which approximately minimize costs, while requiring far less computational burden than an approach which guarantees a minimum-cost ordering schedule.

REFERENCES

1. Berry, William L.: "Lot Sizing Procedures for Requirement Planning Systems: A Framework for Analysis," *Production and Inventory Management*, vol. 13, no. 2, second quarter, 1972.
2. De Matteis, J. J.: "An Economic Lot Sizing Technique: The Part-Period Algorithm," *IBM Systems Journal*, vol. 7, no. 1, pp. 30-38, 1968.
3. Forrester, Jay W.: "Industrial Dynamics—Understanding the Forces Causing Industrial Fluctuation, Growth, Stability and Decline," *Harvard Business Review*, July-August 1958.
4. Love, S. F.: "A Facilities in Series Inventory Model with Nested Schedules," *Management Science*, vol. 18, no. 5, pp. 327-338, January 1972, pt. I.
5. Orlicky, Joseph: "Material Requirements Planning," McGraw-Hill, New York, 1975, 292 pp.

6. Silver, Edward A., and H. C. Meal: "A Heuristic for Scheduling Lot Size Quantities for the Case of a Deterministic Time-Varying Demand Rate and Discrete Opportunities for Replenishment," *Production and Inventory Management*, vol. 14, no. 2, second quarter, 1973.
7. Veinott, Arthur F., Jr.: "Minimum Concave-Cost Solution of Leontief Substitution Models of Multi-Facility Inventory Systems," *Operations Research*, vol. 17, no. 2, pp. 262–291, March–April 1969.
8. Wagner, Harvey M., and T. M. Whitin: "Dynamic Version of the Economic Lot Size Model," *Management Science*, vol. 5, no. 1, 1958.
9. Wight, Oliver W.: "Production and Inventory Management in the Computer Age," Cahners Publishing, Boston, 1975, 284 pp.
10. Zangwill, Willard I.: "A Deterministic Multi-Product, Multi-Facility Production and Inventory Model," *Operations Research*, vol. 14, no. 3, pp. 486–507, May–June 1966.
11. *Production and Inventory Management*, journal of the American Production and Inventory Control Society, Washington D.C., published quarterly.

EXERCISES

6-1 Describe each of the following situations properly as a multiechelon inventory network.

(a) A flow shop is a job shop in which every job is processed through the same identical sequence of operations. The shop has the capability of processing eight different types of product (jobs).

(b) Suppose, in figure 6-1, that all retail items are stored at the same location prior to shipment.

(c) Raw material is formed into parts which are assembled into subassemblies which are assembled into salable products. Ten percent of a certain part are found defective and are returned to fabrication for reworking, after which they can be used in assembly.

6-2 Repeat example 6-1 with the following sequence of demands for $t = 1$ to 25: 6, 6, 6, 6, 6, 6, 6, 6, 6, 6, 7, 6, 9, 4, 6, 5, 8, 6, 5, 10, 7, 7, 6, 9, 5. How do the results compare with those of example 6-1?

6-3 Repeat example 6-1 with the following modified conditions:

(a) The lead time $L(j)$ equals zero for all j.

(b) In addition to (a), the informational lead time of one period is eliminated, so that the following ordering decision rule can be used:

$$x_t^j = x_t^{j+1} + \tfrac{1}{2}(12 - y_{t-1}^j) \qquad j = 1, 2, 3$$

where x_t^j is rounded up to an integer value as it was in example 6-1.

6-4 Repeat example 6-1, except change the ordering decision rule, equation (6-4), to

$$x_t^j = x_{t-1}^{j+1}$$

6-5 You are given the information in table 6-18 regarding seven items in a multiechelon inventory and the following master production schedules.

Item	1	2	3	4	5	6	7	8	9	10	11
7	3	6	12	8	15	15	15	15	15	15	15
4	6	2	8	8	8	8	8	8	8	8	8

Complete the netting process to plan material requirements for all items.

6-6 Repeat problem 6-5 where item 6 is required to have a safety stock of 7 units.

6-7 Repeat problem 6-5 where 8 percent of item 3 is received in a defective condition and must be returned to the vendor.

6-8 In example 6-4, to what maximum level can the (master) scheduled requirement of 10 units of item 7 in time bucket 4 be increased without having to change any order which has already been released?

6-9 Bicycles can be ordered in three colors (red, green, and blue). Two styles are available (men's and women's). (Ignore wheel size in this problem.) Also, any bike can come with 3-speed or 10-speed gearshift. The major assemblies needed to build a bicycle are frame, gearshift assembly, front-wheel assembly, rear-wheel assembly, and trim kit (handle bar, seat, reflector, pedals, and fenders). The frame and the fenders are color-coded. Also the gearshift assembly consists of gears, cables, and housing. The housing is also color-coded. The seats differ for men's and women's models.

Specify a set of modular bills of materials and explain how you would handle any difficulties associated with parts belonging to more than one module.

6-10 Demand for an item for the next 10 periods is as follows: 6, 3, 0, 5, 8, 0, 1, 2, 7, 9. It costs \$9 to place an order and \$3 per unit held from one period to the next. There is no initial stock, and the stock level at the end of the 10

Table 6-18 Data for problem 6-5

Item i	Successor j	g_{ij}	Lead time	Initial stock level	Planned receipts (period)	Lot size
1	5	2	1	100	—	200
2	5, 7	1, 1	1	6	—	—
3	6	4	1	40	20(1)	—
4	6, customer	1, 1	1	2	60(0)	60
5	7	1	2	14	30(1)	—
6	7	1	2	6	—	20
7	customer	1	1	3	—	—

periods is required to be zero. There is no lead time. Determine the timing and placement of orders and the total cost according to each of the following approaches:
(a) Wagner-Whitin
(b) Period order quantity
(c) Least unit cost
(d) Least total cost
(e) Silver-Meal

PART THREE

INVENTORY CONTROL DATA

CHAPTER
SEVEN
DEMAND FORECASTING

In the preceding chapters we have been concerned with the development of effective models on which to base ordering decisions. The emphasis in these models has been on the rational, or scientific, use of available information to achieve an objective as closely as possible. Thus, the success of model implementation depends on the accessibility of reliable data. Indeed, the best model is only as good as the data used to drive it. Two classes of data are particularly critical to the effective control of inventories via the methods suggested in this book: cost behavior and demand behavior. This is not to say that other information (e.g., lead times and capacities) is not important. Ironically, there seems to be a more persistent lack of agreement on how to ascribe values to costs and potential demands than on how to use the values, once obtained. This and the following chapter will address these issues for demand data and cost data, respectively.

7-1 THE FORECASTING PROBLEM

No one would dispute that a forecast of some type is an absolute prerequisite to planning inventory levels. The question is, What type? There are many kinds of forecasts, depending on their intended use. One hears regularly about forecasts of the economy, prices, interest rates, business conditions, technology, and so on. The subject of this chapter is demand forecasting, for which the following characteristics will be assumed:

1. Forecasts are for demands for single-echelon inventories, i.e., independent demands.
2. The demands are due to a stable, established market, not for new products or obsolete ones. (The last section discusses a departure from this.)
3. The time span covered by the forecast is short (one day to a few months). This span is generally sufficient for planning single-echelon inventory levels for an organization whose location and capacity are already determined.
4. The forecast will be expressed in units of demand for an item or group of items, or in closely associated units (e.g., dollars or packaged quantities).
5. The forecast will be stated as a single value or as a range of values or as both. It can be argued that the only reasonable forecast involves a range of values since there is always forecast error. On the other hand, implementation may be computerized, in which case the associated inventory control algorithm may well be based on a single forecast value. In this case the forecast error itself can be explicitly recognized and included in the control algorithm as a variance.

Approaches to demand forecasting may be classified in a variety of ways. The most widely recognized classification is *statistical versus nonstatistical*, sometimes referred to as quantitative versus qualitative. A statistical approach is one in which numerical data of a specified form are transformed via a model or algorithm to an explicit numerical forecast. Statistical approaches are often characterized as being more objective, more accurate, and/or more complex than nonstatistical approaches. Perhaps the objectivity comparison is the most valid of the three, since the use of a model would generate identical forecasts from identical data. Any statement regarding accuracy should be based on sound empirical evidence. A guess based on experience can be very accurate indeed. As for complexity, compare any questionnaire-based market research study with a simple average of historical data. In the following sections (7-2 through 7-7) statistical approaches are emphasized. They are better suited to incorporation into a computerized inventory control system than are nonstatistical approaches.

Another classification of forecasts is by type of source data, the primary distinction being whether the forecast is *intrinsic* (based solely on prior history of the item in question) or *extrinsic* (based on other related exogenous indicators). Examples of both types are included in this chapter, but, as discussed in section 7-7, the former type holds greater promise as an effective aid to routine control of inventories.

7-2 MODELING DEMAND AS A TIME SERIES

Any statistical approach requires a model which accepts input and generates forecasts. The input data typically include a sequence of previously observed demand values, usually representing demands for equally spaced periods of time. By letting d_t be the demand during the tth time period, the sequence $[d_t]$ will be referred to as a *time series*, or simply a series. A forecast for d_t for a future period t will be denoted by $\hat{d}_t$. Forecasts will be generated at the beginning of a time period (or, equivalently, at the end of the preceding time period). Typically, at the beginning of period k, the model will have available the time series $d_1, d_2, \ldots, d_{k-1}$ (and possibly other data) and will generate $\hat{d}_k$, a forecast for period k.

There are many types of statistical forecasting models which appear on the surface to be widely varying in structure. In order to highlight the underlying unity inherent in these models and to facilitate comparisons among them, a common sequence of five steps will be identified for formulating and using each model. These steps (which form the subsections of this section) are as follows:

1. Observe characteristics of the time series.
2. Build a model (functional form).
3. Estimate the coefficients of the model.
4. Calculate forecast values.
5. Monitor forecast quality.

Although all five of these steps may be performed during the planning (modeling) phase, the last two are also done repetitively during the execution (forecasting) phase.

Observation of Time Series Characteristics

Time series often exhibit recurring patterns. It is desirable to detect these patterns and recognize them in forecast models. After all, the whole purpose of modeling is to explain the behavior of the time series. The patterns commonly recognized are trends and cycles. In figure 7-1 these patterns are illustrated as they might appear with typical random fluctuations present. Figure 7-1 consists of plots of the data in table 7-1. These data will be used to illustrate many of the concepts in this chapter. Trends and cycles and random fluctuations may be referred to as *sources of variation*, or *effects*. In figure 7-1, series B and C exhibit, respectively, a trend effect and a cyclic effect. Trend effects may be linear, as in series B, or nonlinear. Linear trends rarely persist for long periods of time, but in the short range a trend may be sufficiently linear to be treated as such. Some people like to make a distinc-

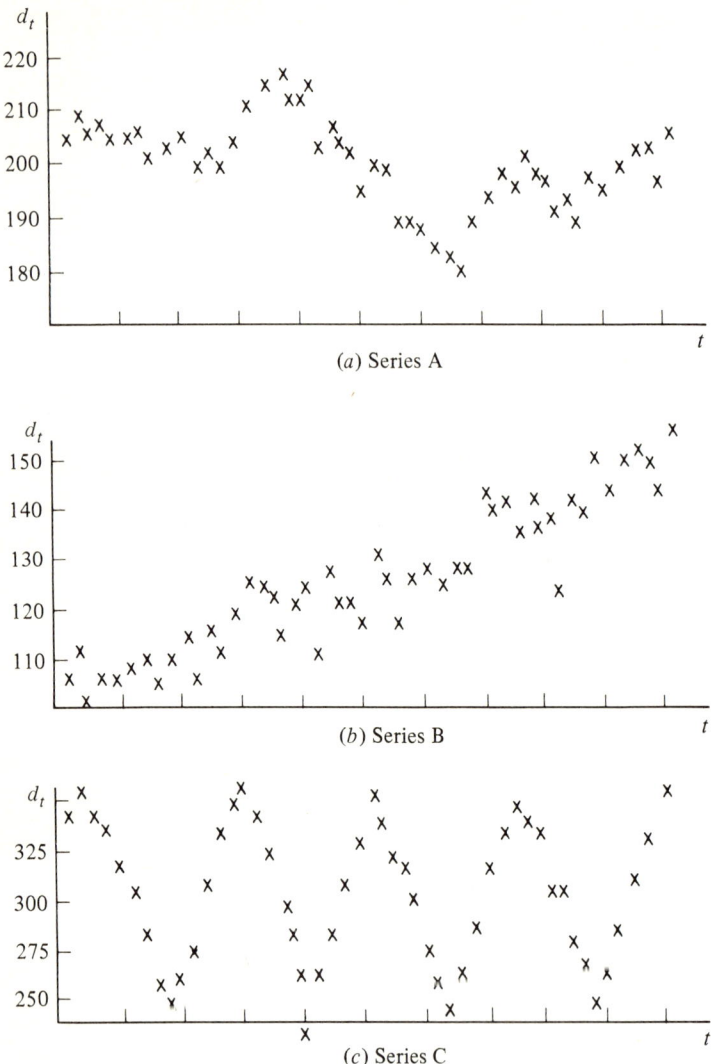

Figure 7-1 Plots of the time series in table 7-1.

tion between a cyclic effect and a seasonal effect. The latter might be deemed less "regular" (i.e., less sinusoidal) or of shorter "period" (time between peaks). In this chapter, all such effects will be termed "cyclic." If the reader insists, he or she may think of a cycle which has an annual period (e.g., as in the sale of snow shovels) as a seasonal effect.

In the absence of any effects other than random ones, a series will be referred to as *stationary*. Series A in figure 7-1 appears to be stationary. In

Table 7-1 Three demand time series

Period	Series A	Series B	Series C	Period	Series A	Series B	Series C
t	d_t	d_t	d_t	t	d_t	d_t	d_t
1	204	105	338	26	199	130	350
2	209	111	353	27	198	126	341
3	205	100	339	28	187	117	322
4	206	105	334	29	187	127	318
5	204	104	319	30	186	128	300
6	204	106	302	31	182	125	273
7	205	108	280	32	180	128	253
8	200	104	253	33	177	128	241
9	201	109	246	34	188	142	262
10	204	113	257	35	193	140	284
11	198	106	274	36	198	141	315
12	201	114	312	37	196	135	332
13	198	110	331	38	201	142	348
14	203	119	349	39	198	137	340
15	211	124	353	40	197	138	331
16	216	123	340	41	189	123	302
17	218	121	324	42	191	142	302
18	212	114	298	43	188	139	275
19	212	120	280	44	196	150	263
20	214	123	260	45	194	143	244
21	201	110	235	46	199	150	258
22	207	127	259	47	203	151	283
23	204	121	277	48	203	149	311
24	201	121	307	49	196	142	327
25	193	117	326	50	204	157	351

the loose sense, a stationary series displays affinity for (i.e., does not permanently drift from) a single mean value. More formally, a series $[d_t]$ is *stationary of order zero* if its probability distribution does not change with time. From this it follows that the mean $E[d_t]$ and variance $\sigma^2_{d_t}$ of d_t are time-invariant.

There are other nonrandom effects such as impulses (sudden surges in demand) and steps (sudden shifts in $E[d_t]$), but these are not continually recurring effects (as are trends and cycles) and are not usually explicitly recognized in the model. Of course, these effects do occur and do affect the quality of the forecast (see the subsection "Monitoring Forecast Quality"). If such effects can be predicted, the advance knowledge can be used to manually overrride the model forecast.

Another important characteristic of a demand time series is the possible existence of dependence among successive series values d_t and d_{t+k}. A barber who sees an abnormally large number of regular customers in a given week is likely to see less than the average number the following week. Thus, demand in a given week affects demand the following week, in the sense that d_t and d_{t+1} are correlated. Since d_t and d_{t+1} are two realizations of the same series, they are said to be "autocorrelated." The *autocorrelation* ρ_j *at lag j* of the series is given by

$$\rho_j \equiv \frac{\text{covariance }(d_t, d_{t-j})}{\text{variance } d_t}$$

$$= \frac{E[(d_t - \mu)(d_{t-j} - \mu)]}{E[(d_t - \mu)^2]} \quad (7\text{-}1)$$

where μ is the mean demand which was referred to above as $E[d_t]$. If ρ_j is positive (negative), then the larger the value of d_{t-j}, the larger (smaller) d_t will tend to be. For the barber, ρ_1 would be negative. Of course, since d_t is perfectly correlated with itself, it is always the case that $\rho_0 = 1$. In general, if it appears that a demand series is significantly autocorrelated ($\rho_j \neq 0$ for some $j \geq 1$), one of the models of section 7-6 may be appropriate.

Model Construction

The second step in the modeling process is the specification of an appropriate functional form. The typical functional form consists of two parts: a random component superimposed on a function representing the basic demand pattern. For example, consider series A in table 7-1. A simple model for this series would be

Model A-1: $\qquad d_t = \alpha_0 + \varepsilon_t \qquad t = 1, 2, \ldots \qquad (7\text{-}2)$

Here, α_0 is a constant representing the mean of the series and ε_t is a random error term with mean 0 and variance σ^2. This model, without the random error component, is plotted in figure 7-2(a). A commonly made assumption is that ε_t is normally distributed. This deserves some scrutiny. For example, demand for antifreeze would be skewed to the right (in the positive direction) because of spurious purchases in response to cold weather snaps.

One of the strongest points about model A-1 is its simplicity. One should always strive to keep a model as simple as possible while still reflecting reality. This is known as the principle of *parsimony*. Consider again series A in table 7-1. This series represents daily sales of newspapers at a busy street corner. These sales average 200 papers. Suppose a survey revealed that, on the average, of the customers who purchase papers on a given day 80 percent will purchase a paper the next day, 10 percent will purchase a paper two days hence, and 10 percent will not purchase one again (at least not for several days). This means that on the average, 20 new

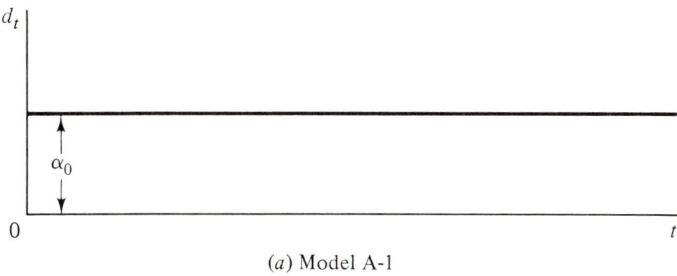

(a) Model A-1

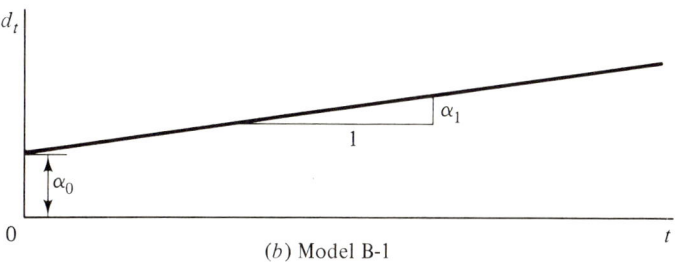

(b) Model B-1

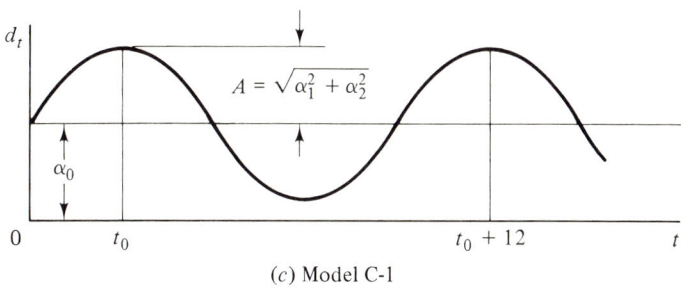

(c) Model C-1

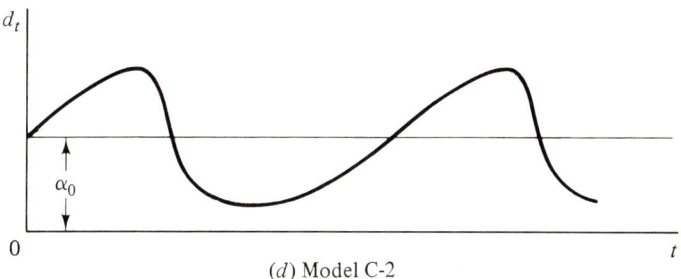

(d) Model C-2

Figure 7-2 Plots of some models for time series A, B, and C.

customers buy a paper each day. In this case, an appropriate model is

Model A-2: $\quad d_t = 0.8d_{t-1} + 0.1d_{t-2} + 20 + \varepsilon_t \quad t = 1, 2, \ldots$ (7-3)

This is an example of an *autoregressive* model, a type discussed in section 7-6.

Now consider series B of table 7-1. A reasonable model is

Model B-1: $\quad\quad\quad d_t = \alpha_0 + \alpha_1 t + \varepsilon_t \quad t = 1, 2, \ldots$ (7-4)

where α_0 and α_1 are parameters whose values must be estimated from the data. This model is not stationary. However, a stationary model can be formulated by taking the first difference w_t of the series:

Model B-2: $\quad w_t = d_t - d_{t-1} = \alpha_1 + \varepsilon_t - \varepsilon_{t-1} \quad t = 1, 2, \ldots$ (7-5)

The stationary model w_t can be analyzed by using the techniques in section 7-6.

Series C of table 7-1 is clearly cyclic in nature. A parsimonious model which will handle cycles is

$$d_t = \alpha_0 + \alpha_1 \sin \omega t + \alpha_2 \cos \omega t + \varepsilon_t \quad t = 1, 2, \ldots$$

If t is in months and the cycle is annual, then $\omega = (2\pi \text{ radians/year})/(12 \text{ months/year})$, so the model becomes

Model C-1:

$$d_t = \alpha_0 + \alpha_1 \sin \frac{2\pi t}{12} + \alpha_2 \cos \frac{2\pi t}{12} + \varepsilon_t \quad t = 1, 2, \ldots \quad (7\text{-}6)$$

where the α_j must be estimated from the data. This model is plotted in figure 7-2(c). The mean demand is α_0. For purposes of understanding the model, the amplitude A (half the difference between maximum and minimum model demand) is given by

$$A = (\alpha_1^2 + \alpha_2^2)^{1/2}$$

The relative magnitude of α_1 and α_2 determine the timing of the maximum and minimum model demands. If t_0 is a time (in months) of the maximum model demand, α_1 and α_2 are given by

$$\alpha_1 = A \sin \frac{2\pi t_0}{12} \quad (7\text{-}7)$$

$$\alpha_2 = A \cos \frac{2\pi t_0}{12} \quad (7\text{-}8)$$

For example, if $t_0 = 3$ (that is, April 1), then $\alpha_1 = A$ and $\alpha_2 = 0$. In this special case, then, the cosine term could be deleted from model C-1 entirely.

The estimation of coefficients in general is discussed in the next subsection, and for sinusoidal models in section 7-5.

Often model C-1 will not adequately describe a cyclical series. For example, in figure 7-1(c), demand seems to build up gradually and then to decrease rather suddenly. The sine wave of model C-1 is too symmetric. This is remedied by including two more terms in the model which add the effect of another cycle with twice the frequency of the original cycle. The model then becomes

Model C-2:
$$d_t = \alpha_0 + \alpha_1 \sin \frac{2\pi t}{12} + \alpha_2 \cos \frac{2\pi t}{12} + \alpha_3 \sin \frac{2\pi t}{6}$$
$$+ \alpha_4 \cos \frac{2\pi t}{6} + \varepsilon_t \qquad t = 1, 2, \ldots \qquad (7\text{-}9)$$

Figure 7-2(d) is a plot of model C-2 with coefficients suitable for series C. The estimation of these coefficients is discussed next.

Coefficient Estimation

After the model has been constructed, it is necessary to estimate the coefficients α_j. This is commonly done by using historical demand values. (It is possible to incorporate subjective opinion into the coefficient estimates. This is not considered here.) If a large quantity of historical data exists, it is customary to use only the most recent data. For example, for model A-1 ($d_t = \alpha_0 + \varepsilon_t$), α_0 could be estimated by a_0:

$$a_0 = \bar{d} \equiv \frac{1}{n} \sum_{k=t-n+1}^{t} d_k \qquad (7\text{-}10)$$

This estimate is called an *n-period moving average*. If for some reason all available historical data are to be used, then $n = t$ in the above estimate. One should beware in this case that for large n, a_0 responds sluggishly to new information.

Estimation based on demand history is usually done in such a way that the resulting model "fits" the historical data closely. Let $\hat{d}_k$ be the value of the model at period k, ignoring the error term ε_k. Define e_k as the difference between the actual demand in period k and this model value:

$$e_k = d_k - \hat{d}_k$$

The coefficients can be given values which minimize the sum of squared errors (*SSE*):

$$SSE \equiv \sum_{k=t-n+1}^{t} (d_k - \hat{d}_k)^2 = \sum_{k=t-n+1}^{t} e_k^2$$

Thus, for model A-1, the coefficient a_0 would be valued so that

$$SSE = \sum_{k=t-n+1}^{t} (d_k - a_0)^2$$

is minimized. We can use differential calculus to obtain the value

$$\frac{dSSE}{da_0} = 0 = -2\left[\sum_{k=t-n+1}^{t} (d_k - a_0)\right]$$

which solves to yield

$$a_0 = \frac{1}{n} \sum_{k=t-n+1}^{t} d_k = \bar{d}$$

which is the moving average, equation (7-10).

Techniques for coefficient estimation for various types of models will be discussed in sections 7-3 to 7-6.

Calculation of Forecast Values

Suppose a model has been developed and the model coefficients have been estimated by using historical data $d_{t-n+1}, \ldots, d_t$. Then the forecast for any future period $t + \tau$ ($\tau = 1, 2, 3, \ldots$) can be obtained by evaluating the expected value of the model at time $t + \tau$. The coefficients α_j are given their estimated values a_j. For example, for model A-1, the forecast demand $\hat{d}_{t+1}$ would be given by

$$\hat{d}_{t+1} = a_0$$

This forecast assumes that $E[\varepsilon_{t+1}] = 0$. Examples of forecast calculations for various models are given in sections 7-3 to 7-6.

Monitoring Forecast Quality

Suppose that a forecast model has been in use for some time, so that there is a history of values for both d_t and $\hat{d}_t$, and hence for $e_t = d_t - \hat{d}_t$. It is then possible to observe how well the model is working. Moreover, no matter how well or for how long the model has worked in the past, the critical issue is whether the model is *still* working. Therefore, assuming that demand information is available up through period t, it is desirable to monitor the behavior of the forecast using data, say, for the most recent n periods.

Two qualities of forecasts of concern are accuracy and precision. A *precise* forecast is one for which the variation in forecast error is small. An *accurate* forecast is one for which the average of the forecast errors is close to zero. Thus an accurate forecast exhibits a lack of bias. A measure of forecast quality which is updated each period will be called a *tracking signal.* Tracking signals designed to monitor precision are based on error variation, while those monitoring accuracy are based on average error.

A straightforward signal for tracking precision is the error variance s_e^2. Thus,

$$TS - 1 = s_e^2 = \sum_{k=t-n+1}^{t} \frac{(e_k - \bar{e})^2}{n-1}$$

where $\bar{e}$ is the average error over the same time span:

$$\bar{e} = \frac{1}{n} \sum_{k=t-n+1}^{t} e_k$$

The signal $TS - 1$ measures precision in the absolute sense. It may be desirable to use a tracking signal which would compare error variation with variation in the demand series itself. Such a signal is

$$TS - 2 = \frac{s_e^2}{s_d^2}$$

where s_d^2 is an estimate of the variance of the demand series itself, given by

$$s_d^2 = \sum_{k=t-n+1}^{t} \frac{(d_k - \bar{d})^2}{n-1}$$

The (unattainable) ideal value for $TS - 2$ is zero. In later sections we will see what values of this and other tracking signals are attainable for various models.

A simple tracking signal for monitoring forecast accuracy is the average error:

$$TS - 3 = \bar{e} = \sum_{k=t-n+1}^{t} \frac{e_k}{n}$$

This signal, like $TS - 1$, is an absolute measure, which makes it difficult to compare two models unless the same demand series data are used. The signal

$$TS - 4 = \frac{\bar{e}}{\bar{d}}$$

which measures the average error as a fraction of the average demand, facilitates model comparison by providing a measure of the relative magnitude of error. Another signal, which indicates the relative bias in the errors, is

$$TS - 5 = \frac{1}{n} \sum_{k=t-n+1}^{t} \frac{e_k}{|e_k|}$$

The value of $TS - 5$ will always range between -1 and $+1$. A zero value for $TS - 5$ suggests a lack of bias; a value near ± 1 warns of a serious bias.

Tracking signals are useful both during the model development and debugging phase and during the execution (use) phase. In the latter case, a dynamic control procedure may be useful in conjunction with the tracking signal. For example, a control chart, analogous to those used in statistical quality control, can be constructed so that if the tracking signal falls outside the control limits, corrective action may be considered. In the case of one of the models in the next section [equation (7-19)], such corrective action is automatically taken, resulting in updating of model coefficients without manual intervention.

7-3 ANALYSIS OF STATIONARY MODELS

Suppose that steps 1 and 2 of the modeling process have led to the conclusion that the demand series can be adequately represented by the stationary model

$$d_t = \alpha_0 + \varepsilon_t$$

The next step is to estimate the coefficient α_0 by a_0. Even for this simple model, there are a variety of ways of doing this. We have already seen (section 7-2) that if a_0 is chosen according to the criterion of minimizing the sum of squared errors

$$\min_{a_0} \left\{ \sum_{k=t-n+1}^{t} (d_k - a_0)^2 \right\}$$

then a_0 turns out to be the average demand for the n most recent periods:

$$a_0 = \bar{d} = \frac{1}{n} \sum_{k=t-n+1}^{t} d_k \qquad (7\text{-}11)$$

Thus the least-squares criterion applied to this stationary model results in the calculation of a_0 as a *moving average*.

An important consideration in any forecasting scheme, whether computerized or not, is computational efficiency. The value of a_0 can be updated each period as new demand series information becomes available. Instead of using equation (7-11), a_0 can be calculated recursively. Let $a_0(t)$ be the value of a_0 calculated by using information available up through period t. Then it can be readily verified by the reader that

$$a_0(t) = a_0(t-1) + \frac{d_t - d_{t-n}}{n} \qquad (7\text{-}12)$$

At the end of any period t, the forecast $\hat{d}_{t+\tau}$ for demand in period $t + \tau$ is given by

$$d_{t+\tau} = a_0(t) \qquad \tau = 1, 2, 3, \ldots \qquad (7\text{-}13)$$

The least-squares criterion used above to estimate α_0 gives equal weight to each of the n most recent demands. A reasonable modification of this criterion would be to give more weight to the more recent demands, in that a larger penalty is assessed for failure of the model to fit the more recent demands. More specifically, a_0 may be given a value which minimizes the weighted sum of squared errors (WSSE):

$$WSSE \equiv \sum_{k=t-n+1}^{t} w_k(d_k - \hat{d}_k)^2 = \sum_{k=t-n+1}^{t} w_k(d_k - a_0)^2 \qquad (7\text{-}14)$$

with $w_t > w_{t-1} > \cdots > w_{t-n+1}$. This is known as the *weighted least-squares criterion*.

A very popular special case of equation (7-14) assigns the weights as

$$w_k = \alpha(1-\alpha)^{t-k} \qquad k = t-n+1, t-n+2, \ldots, t; \; 0 < \alpha < 1$$

where α is a parameter, the selection of whose value will be discussed later. These weights have the property that $w_t > w_{t-1} > \cdots > w_{t-n+1}$.

Thus, in this case, a_0 will be given the value which minimizes the weighted sum of squared errors:

$$WSSE = \sum_{k=t-n+1}^{t} \alpha(1-\alpha)^{t-k}(d_k - a_0)^2$$

This value is obtained by solving the equation

$$\frac{dWSSE}{da_0} = -2 \sum_{k=t-n+1}^{t} \alpha(1-\alpha)^{t-k}(d_k - a_0) = 0$$

which yields

$$a_0(t) = \frac{\sum_{k=t-n+1}^{t} \alpha(1-\alpha)^{t-k} d_k}{\sum_{k=t-n+1}^{t} \alpha(1-\alpha)^{t-k}} = \frac{1}{1-(1-\alpha)^n} \sum_{k=t-n+1}^{t} \alpha(1-\alpha)^{t-k} d_k$$

$$(7\text{-}15)$$

If n is allowed to go to ∞, the expression (7-15) for calculating a_0 becomes

$$a_0(t) = \sum_{-\infty}^{t} \alpha(1-\alpha)^{t-k} d_k \qquad (7\text{-}16)$$

Subtracting $(1 - \alpha)a_0(t - 1)$ from $a_0(t)$ gives

$$a_0(t) - (1 - \alpha)a_0(t - 1) = \alpha d_t$$

Thus $a_0(t)$ can be calculated recursively by

$$a_0(t) = \alpha d_t + (1 - \alpha)a_0(t - 1) \tag{7-17}$$

The forecast using the information available at the end of period t is simply

$$\hat{d}_{t+1} = a_0(t) \tag{7-18}$$

Thus, equation (7-17) can be reexpressed in terms of the forecast values as

$$\hat{d}_{t+1} = \alpha d_t + (1 - \alpha)\hat{d}_t \tag{7-19}$$

This is the operational form of this forecast. The forecast $\hat{d}_{t+1}$ is seen to be a compromise between the most recent demand d_t and the one-period-old forecast $\hat{d}_t$ of d_t. This compromise value $\hat{d}_{t+1}$ is called the *smoothed* value of the demand time series. Moreover, from equations (7-16) and (7-18) we have

$$\hat{d}_{t+1} = \sum_{-\infty}^{t} \alpha(1 - \alpha)^{t-k} d_k$$

Thus the smoothed value depends "exponentially" on the previous demand values, in that the weights associated with successively earlier periods decay exponentially. This gives rise to the name "exponential smoothing" as a label for the process of forecasting by using equation (7-19). More properly, the name is "single-" or "first-order" exponential smoothing.

The parameter α is called the *smoothing constant* and is generally given a value between 0 and 1. The closer α is to zero, the more the demand series is smoothed, that is, the more reliance is placed on earlier history. On the other hand, a value near 1 will cause the forecast to be highly sensitive, responding to recent demand fluctuations. For the model A-1, α is usually given a value between 0.1 and 0.3.

As an example of the application of the moving average and exponential smoothing approaches, consider the data of series A in table 7-1. The computations are shown in table 7-2. For the smoothing procedure α is chosen to be 0.25. For the moving-average technique $n = 7$. The first seven data points are used to initiate the moving-average procedure. The initial estimate $a_0(7)$ of α_0 is taken to be the average of the first seven demands. The error e_t is the difference between d_t and $\hat{d}_t$. In table 7-2 this is calculated using values of $\hat{d}_t$ which have been rounded to the nearest integer.

A possible procedure for assigning a value to α is to find the value of α which minimizes the cumulative squared error

$$\sum_k (d_k - \hat{d}_k)^2$$

Table 7-2 Computational results of applying the least-squares and weighted least-squares criteria to series A

Procedure → Equation →	t	d_t	Moving average $(n = 7)$ (7-12)		Exponential smoothing $(\alpha = 0.25)$ (7-19)	
			$a_0(t) = \hat{d}_{t+1}$	e_t^2	$\hat{d}_{t+1}$	e_t^2
	1	204				
	2	209				
	3	205				
	4	206				
	5	204				
	6	204				
	7	205	205.3 = 205	—	205.3 = 205	—
	8	200	204.7 = 205	25	204.0 = 204	25
	9	201	203.6 = 204	16	203.2 = 203	9
	10	204	203.4 = 203	0	203.4 = 203	1
	11	198		25		25
			See problem 7-1			
	48	203	196.3 = 196	81	198.3 = 198	36
	49	196	197.0 = 197	0	197.7 = 198	4
	50	204	199.3 = 199	49	199.3 = 199	36

over a time frame of recent demand periods. This procedure could lead to a value of α outside the range of 0.1 to 0.3. If the value is greater than 0.3, the demand series may be highly autocorrelated, in which case the appropriate model may be of the type discussed in section 7-6.

The value of α being used in a particular application may become inappropriate at some point in time. For example, suppose that in a single period there is an unusually large demand caused by circumstances which will not recur. The exponential smoothing forecast will "remember" this large demand for several subsequent periods, producing inflated forecasts. A remedy for this situation is to temporarily increase the value of α, causing the exponential smoothing mechanism [equation (7-19)] to "forget" the unusually high demand. In general, the process of changing the value of α in response to such circumstances is called *adaptive control* of the smoothing constant.

It is possible to achieve automatic adaptive control by coupling the quality of the forecast with the modification of α. One possibility is to simply set

$$\alpha = |TS - 5| = \frac{1}{n} \left| \sum_{k=t-n+1}^{t} \frac{e_k}{|e_k|} \right| \qquad (7\text{-}20)$$

Thus when unusual conditions cause a bias in the forecast, α will increase temporarily, as desired. Another criterion for choosing a value for α is introduced in problem 7-2.

7-4 ANALYSIS OF LINEAR TREND MODELS

In section 7-3 the stationary model $d_t = \alpha_0 + \varepsilon_t$ was treated twice. First, the use of the least-squares criterion to estimate α_0 resulted in a moving-average forecast. Second, estimation of α_0 to satisfy the exponentially weighted least-squares criterion led to the first-order exponential smoothing forecast. In this section the same two estimation criteria are applied to the linear trend model $d_t = \alpha_0 + \alpha_1 t + \varepsilon_t$. This results in two forecasting techniques which are called *linear regression* and *second-order exponential smoothing*, respectively. A technique such as one of these two is necessary, because neither the moving-average model nor the first-order smoothing model of the previous section handles trends adequately.

By applying the least-squares criterion, $a_0(t)$ and $a_1(t)$ are to be given values which minimize the sum of squared errors:

$$SSE = \sum_{k=t-n+1}^{t} [d_k - a_0(t) - a_1(t)k]^2$$

The solution being sought in this development is arrived at more easily if the model is reexpressed in such a way that the time origin is shifted to period t. In this case, the term $a_0(t)$ represents the estimate of the coefficient α_0 in the model

$$d_\tau = \alpha_0 + \alpha_1(\tau - t) + \varepsilon_\tau \qquad (7\text{-}21)$$

Thus the origin of the time coordinate for the model shifts each period, so that α_0 is the y intercept of the model, which occurs at time t. This is illustrated in figure 7-3. By using the model in equation (7-21), a forecast for demand in period $t + \tau$ would be given by

$$\hat{d}_{t+\tau} = a_0(t) + \tau a_1(t) \qquad (7\text{-}22)$$

where $a_1(t)$ is the estimate of the slope α_1 made at time t as described below.

The least-squares criterion implies that we seek values of $a_0(t)$ and $a_1(t)$ which minimize

$$SSE = \sum_{j=0}^{n-1} \{d_{t-j} - [a_0(t) - a_1(t)j]\}^2 \qquad (7\text{-}23)$$

where j is interpreted as the age of the data being used.

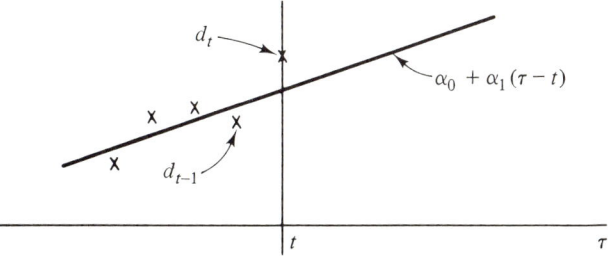

Figure 7-3 Linear trend model with the time origin shifted to the current period t.

Setting the derivatives $\partial SSE/\partial a_0(t)$ and $\partial SSE/\partial a_1(t)$ equal to zero yields the equations

$$a_0(t) = \frac{4n-2}{n(n+1)} \sum_{j=0}^{n-1} d_{t-j} - \frac{6}{n(n+1)} \sum_{j=0}^{n-1} j d_{t-j} \quad (7\text{-}24a)$$

$$a_1(t) = \frac{6}{n(n+1)} \sum_{j=0}^{n-1} d_{t-j} - \frac{12}{n(n-1)(n+1)} \sum_{j=0}^{n-1} j d_{t-j} \quad (7\text{-}24b)$$

The reader is invited to verify these two equations (problem 7-3).

Computationally, it is far easier to convert these two equations to a recursive form in which $a_0(t)$ and $a_1(t)$ are expressed in terms of $a_0(t-1)$, $a_1(t-1)$, d_t, and d_{t-n}. Again left to the reader (problem 7-4) is the algebraic conversion of the above two equations to the following more useful relationships:

$$a_0(t) = \left(\frac{n-5}{n+1}\right) a_0(t-1) + \frac{3(n-1)}{n+1} a_1(t-1)$$
$$+ \frac{2}{n} d_{t-n} + \frac{4n-2}{n(n+1)} d_t \quad (7\text{-}25)$$

$$a_1(t) = \frac{-12}{(n+1)(n-1)} a_0(t-1) + \frac{n+7}{n+1} a_1(t-1)$$
$$+ \frac{6}{n(n-1)} d_{t-n} + \frac{6}{n(n+1)} d_t \quad (7\text{-}26)$$

Thus operationally, the recursive linear regression forecasting process consists of initially calculating values of a_0 and a_1, nonrecursively using n periods of history and equations (7-24a) and (7-24b), and then applying equations (7-25) and (7-26) each period thereafter to obtain the coefficient estimates. Then equation (7-22) is used to make future-period forecasts. The procedure will be illustrated numerically after the corresponding results for the exponentially weighted least-squares criterion are developed.

The weighted least-squares criterion implies that we seek values of $a_0(t)$ and $a_1(t)$ which minimize

$$WSSE = \sum_{j=0}^{\infty} \alpha(1-\alpha)^j \{d_{t-j} - [a_0(t) - a_1(t)j]\}^2 \qquad (7\text{-}27)$$

where j is again interpreted as the age of the data being used.

Setting the derivatives $\partial WSSE/\partial a_0(t)$ and $\partial WSSE/\partial a_1(t)$ equal to zero and solving for $a_0(t)$ and $a_1(t)$ yields (see problem 7-5)

$$a_0(t) = (2-\alpha) \sum_{j=0}^{\infty} \alpha(1-\alpha)^j d_{t-j} - \alpha \sum_{j=0}^{\infty} j\alpha(1-\alpha)^j d_{t-j} \qquad (7\text{-}28)$$

$$a_1(t) = \alpha \sum_{j=0}^{\infty} \alpha(1-\alpha)^j d_{t-j} - \frac{\alpha^2}{1-\alpha} \sum_{j=0}^{\infty} j\alpha(1-\alpha)^j d_{t-j} \qquad (7\text{-}29)$$

In this form, the equations for calculating $a_0(t)$ and $a_1(t)$ are cumbersome, to say the least. As for previous models considered, computational effort can be greatly reduced if equations (7-28) and (7-29) can be converted to a recursive form in which $a_0(t)$ and $a_1(t)$ can be calculated in terms of $a_0(t-1)$, $a_1(t-1)$, and d_t. In problem 7-6 the reader is asked to verify that the appropriate equations are

$$a_0(t) = (1-\alpha)^2[a_0(t-1) + a_1(t-1)] + (2-\alpha)\alpha d_t \qquad (7\text{-}30)$$

$$a_1(t) = -\alpha^2 a_0(t-1) + (1-\alpha^2)a_1(t-1) + \alpha^2 d_t \qquad (7\text{-}31)$$

It is interesting to observe the behavior of the estimates $a_0(t)$ and $a_1(t)$ for the extreme cases $\alpha = 0$ and $\alpha = 1$. For $\alpha = 0$, equations (7-30) and (7-31) become

$$a_0(t) = a_0(t-1) + a_1(t-1)$$

and

$$a_1(t) = a_1(t-1)$$

Thus the forecast is completely insensitive to any new demand information when $\alpha = 0$. For $\alpha = 1$, equations (7-30) and (7-31) imply that

$$a_0(t) = d_t \qquad \text{and} \qquad a_1(t) = d_t - d_{t-1}$$

Thus for $\alpha = 1$, the forecast depends only on the most recent demand information. It should be apparent that α should be given an intermediate value.

A further simplification of equations (7-30) and (7-31) follows immediately from the fact that, by equation (7-22),

$$\hat{d}_t = a_0(t-1) + a_1(t-1)$$

Thus equations (7-30) and (7-31) become

$$a_0(t) = (1 - \alpha)^2 \hat{d}_t + (2 - \alpha)\alpha d_t \qquad (7\text{-}32)$$

$$a_1(t) = a_1(t - 1) + \alpha^2 (d_t - \hat{d}_t) \qquad (7\text{-}33)$$

Thus, operationally, the *second-order exponential smoothing* process consists of using equations (7-32) and (7-33) each period (t) to obtain estimates of the coefficients $a_0(t)$ and $a_1(t)$. Then forecasts for future periods are obtained by using equation (7-22). The process is initiated by choosing initial estimates $a_0(0)$ and $a_1(0)$.

As an example of the use of the two linear trend models developed in this section, the procedures are applied to series B, the data for which appear in table 7-1. The first seven data points are used to initiate the linear regression procedure for which n is chosen to be 7. For the double exponential smoothing procedure, α is chosen to be 0.25. Calculation of the regression model coefficients for $t = 7$ is done by using linear regression [equations (7-24)]. These coefficients are $a_0(7) = 105.89$ and $a_1(7) = 0.11$, as shown in table 7-3. It is important to calculate these values accurately, since any deviation from the correct values will cause the recursive use of equations

Table 7-3 Computational results of applying the least-squares and weighted least-squares criteria to series B

Procedure → Equation →	Linear regression ($n = 7$)				Double exponential smoothing ($\alpha = 0.25$)			
	(7-25)	(7-26)	(7-22)	(7-34)	(7-32)	(7-33)	(7-22)	(7-34)
t	d_t	$a_0(t)$	$a_1(t)$	$\hat{d}_{t+1}$	e_t^2	$a_0(t)$	$a_1(t)$	$\hat{d}_{t+1}$	e_t^2
1	105								
2	111								
3	100								
4	105								
5	104								
6	106								
7	108	105.89	0.11	106	—	107	1.00	108	—
8	104	105.00	−0.14	104	4	106.25	0.75	107	16
9	109	108.25	1.04	109	25	107.88	0.88	109	4
10	113	110.43	1.14	111	16	110.75	1.13	112	16
11	106	109.39	0.75	110	25	109.38	0.75	110	36
12	114				16				16
				See problem 7-7					
48	149					150.69	1.44	152	9
49	142					147.63	0.81	148	100
50	157					151.94	1.38	153	81

(7-25) and (7-26) to yield coefficients $a_0(t)$ and $a_1(t)$ which diverge from the correct values as t increases. This difficulty can also be guarded against by periodically (say, every 10 time periods or so) reinitializing the coefficients $a_0(t)$ and $a_1(t)$ using ordinary linear regression [equations (7-24)]. No such difficulty occurs with the double exponential smoothing procedure, which was initialized with the "rough" estimates $a_0(7) = 107$ and $a_1(7) = 1$, as shown in table 7-3. The squared error resulting from each forecast is calculated as

$$e_t^2 = (d_t - \hat{d}_t)^2 \tag{7-34}$$

where $\hat{d}_t$ is the forecast made in the preceding period. The computations are shown in table 7-3. As was the case in table 7-2, these squared errors are calculated on the basis of rounded-off values of $\hat{d}_t$.

7-5 ANALYSIS OF CYCLIC MODELS

One of the most prevalent effects in demand series $[d_t]$ for any type of item is the cyclic effect. If t is measured in hours, days, or months, then it is common to have to contend with a daily, weekly, or annual cycle, respectively. In spite of this prevalence, there does not seem to be much unification of thought regarding how to model the series. Perhaps this is because it is difficult to specify a simple functional form to describe the cyclic phenomena.

In this section two major modeling approaches will be developed. The first approach accounts for the cyclic effect using a *base series* which, on the short term, is considered to be invariant and to which a modification is made each period in order to generate a forecast. The second approach employs the notion of a *Fourier*, or *sinusoidal, series* to reflect the cyclic effect. These techniques are by no means the only reasonable ones. For example, the models of section 7-6 can be extended to handle cycles, at the cost of a considerable amount of complexity.

Another approach that is always possible is to simply ignore the fact that cyclic effects are present. If the length of each period t is short in comparison to the length of the cycle, this is probably the most sensible alternative. For example, if weekly forecasts are made of a demand series with an annual cycle, a trend model may be adequate.

Base Series Models

All base series models decompose demand into two components (not counting random error). One component is called the *base series* $[b_t]$, which explicitly reflects the cyclic variation in demand. The other component modifies the base series to account for effects which are causing demand to consistently differ from the base series. This modification is usually either *multiplicative* or *additive*. To be specific, assume that monthly forecasts are made of a demand having a 12-month cycle. Then the base series is a set of 12 numbers which reflect what is felt to be the typical demand for each month of the cycle. These 12 numbers usually are based on historical data and are assumed to have values which are determined before they are needed for a forecast. The way in which these values are assigned is discussed later. For now, assume for simplicity that the values are fixed, so that $b_{t+12} = b_t$, $t = 1, 2, \ldots$. Then the multiplicative base series model is

$$d_t = b_t r_t + \varepsilon_t \tag{7-35}$$

where r_t is a ratio which is updated each period. During the cycle in which the base series is established, called the *initial cycle*, $r_t = 1$. Thereafter, r_t responds to any persistent change in demand in subsequent cycles. For example, if the *average* demand during the second cycle is, say, 1.2 times that of the initial cycle, then r_t should approach 1.2 during the second cycle.

An alternative to the multiplicative model is the additive base series model given by

$$d_t = b_t + s_t + \varepsilon_t \tag{7-36}$$

where s_t is a term which, like r_t, is updated each period. In this case, s_t has value zero during the initial cycle. Again, if the average demand during the second cycle is, say, 1.2 times that of the initial cycle, then s_t should approach

$$(0.2)\left(\tfrac{1}{12} \sum_{t=1}^{12} b_t\right)$$

Depending on the particular demand series, a choice is made between models (7-35) and (7-36). For example, if the demand series represents a share of a cyclic (seasonal) market, then the multiplicative model would apply. Then r_t would reflect either a change in the total market or a change in the share of the market. If a series has a cyclic and a noncyclic component, the additive model may be preferred. For example, a product such as spark plugs satisfies a new-engine (cyclic) as well as a replacement (noncyclic) market. In this case, s_t reflects the changes in the noncyclic demand.

Of course, the multiplicative and additive effects could be combined into one model.

The base series $[b_t]$ is established during one cycle (the initial cycle) and is based on history from previous cycles. If only limited historical data are available, one might set

$$b_t = d_{t-12} \qquad t \text{ in the initial cycle} \tag{7-37}$$

This suffers the shortcoming of reflecting random variation in the base series. One remedy, for a series with a stable history, would be to let b_t be a

200 PART III: INVENTORY CONTROL DATA

three-period moving average:

$$b_t = \tfrac{1}{3}(d_{t-12} + d_{t-24} + d_{t-36}) \qquad t \text{ in the initial cycle} \qquad (7\text{-}38)$$

or some variant thereof. Another method is mentioned in problem 7-8.

Periodically the base series itself should be updated. This might be done once every several cycles or even as often as once every cycle. Thus an equation such as (7-37) or (7-38) might be used every kth cycle.

The values of r_t or s_t are updated every period. To avoid oversensitivity to random fluctuations in demand, the values of r_t or s_t usually are smoothed by using one of the approaches of section 7-4. Forecasts for period $t + 1$ are calculated by

$$\hat{d}_{t+1} = r_t b_{t+1} \qquad (7\text{-}39)$$

for the multiplicative model, and by

$$\hat{d}_{t+1} = b_{t+1} + s_t \qquad (7\text{-}40)$$

for the additive model.

As an example, a base series model is applied to series C, the data for which appear in table 7-1. The multiplicative model, equation (7-35), is used. The calculations appear in table 7-4. The base series for time periods 1 to 12 is assumed known from prior demand history. Beginning with $t = 13$, the base series is updated every cycle by the equation

$$b_t = \tfrac{1}{3}d_{t-12} + \tfrac{2}{3}b_{t-12} \qquad (7\text{-}41)$$

The value of r_t is obtained by exponential smoothing, using a variant of equation (7-17):

$$r_t = \alpha \frac{d_t}{b_t} + (1 - \alpha)r_{t-1} \qquad (7\text{-}42)$$

where α is arbitrarily chosen to be 0.2 for this example.

Fourier Series Models

A Fourier series model accounts for cyclic variation by representing the demand series as a sum of sinusoidal terms of one or more frequencies. Two examples of such models have already been encountered as models C-1 and C-2 in section 7-2. The reader is encouraged to review that development as necessary. In this subsection the estimation of model coefficients (step 3) and the making of forecasts (step 4) will be the primary topics of discussion.

Consider the model C-1 [equation (7-6)]:

$$d_t = \alpha_0 + \alpha_1 \sin \frac{2\pi t}{12} + \alpha_2 \cos \frac{2\pi t}{12} + \varepsilon_t \qquad t = 1, 2, \ldots \qquad (7\text{-}6)$$

Table 7-4 Computational results of applying a multiplicative base series model to series C

Equation	(7-41)	(7-42)	(7-39)	(7-34)
t	d_t	b_t	r_t	$\hat{d}_{t+1}$	e_t^2
1	338	333	1.00	345	—
2	353	345	1.01	348	64
3	339	341	1.01	344	81
4	334	334	1.01	322	100
5	319	319	1.01	306	9
6	302	303	1.00	278	16
7	280	278	1.01	281	4
8	253	258	1.00	245	784
9	246	245	1.00	255	1
10	257	255	1.00	278	4
11	274	278	1.00	311	16
12	312	311	1.00	335	1
13	331	334.7	1.00	348	16
14	349	347.7	1.00	340	1
15	353	340.3	1.01	337	169
16	340	334.0	1.01		9
		See problem 7-9			
48	311	311.6	1.00	331	1
49	327	331.3	1.00	349	16
50	351	348.5	1.00	—	4

In section 7-2, a geometric interpretation was given to this model. If t_0 is the time of the maximum model demand and the amplitude of the model is A, then

$$\alpha_1 = A \sin \frac{2\pi t_0}{12} \tag{7-7}$$

$$\alpha_2 = A \cos \frac{2\pi t_0}{12} \tag{7-8}$$

Of course, α_0 is the average demand. This suggests that the estimates a_0, a_1, a_2 can be obtained readily by using the historical data for one cycle to graphically estimate α_0, t_0, and A and using equations (7-7) and (7-8) to obtain the estimates a_1 and a_2 of α_1 and α_2. However, the approach taken here, as in previous sections, is to derive coefficient estimates by using the least-squares criterion. Thus we seek values for $a_0(t)$, $a_1(t)$, and $a_2(t)$ which minimize the sum of squared errors:

$$SSE = \sum_{k=t-n+1}^{t} \left\{ d_k - \left[a_0(t) + a_1(t) \sin \frac{2\pi k}{12} + a_2(t) \cos \frac{2\pi k}{12} \right] \right\}^2 \tag{7-43}$$

202 PART III: INVENTORY CONTROL DATA

Setting first derivatives equal to zero and solving yields the following equations (see problem 7-11), provided that the data cover an integral number of cycles, i.e., that n is a multiple of 12:

$$a_0(t) = \frac{1}{n} \sum_{k=t-n+1}^{t} d_k \tag{7-44}$$

$$a_1(t) = \frac{2}{n} \sum_{k=t-n+1}^{t} d_k \sin \frac{2\pi k}{12} \tag{7-45}$$

$$a_2(t) = \frac{2}{n} \sum_{k=t-n+1}^{t} d_k \cos \frac{2\pi k}{12} \tag{7-46}$$

As with previous models, the possibility of recursive calculation reduces the computational burden associated with estimating model coefficients. It can be algebraically verified that equations (7-44) to (7-46) can be converted to the recursive form:

$$a_0(t) = a_0(t-1) + \frac{d_t - d_{t-n}}{n} \tag{7-47}$$

$$a_1(t) = a_1(t-1) + \frac{2}{n} \left(\sin \frac{2\pi t}{12} \right) (d_t - d_{t-n}) \tag{7-48}$$

$$a_2(t) = a_2(t-1) + \frac{2}{n} \left(\cos \frac{2\pi t}{12} \right) (d_t - d_{t-n}) \tag{7-49}$$

Forecasts for future periods are then given by

$$\hat{d}_{t+\tau} = a_0(t) + a_1(t) \sin \frac{2\pi(t+\tau)}{12} + a_2(t) \cos \frac{2\pi(t+\tau)}{12} \tag{7-50}$$

Table 7-5 shows the results of applying this approach to demand series C. The computations are extensive enough to warrant the use of a computer. Natural extensions of the Fourier series approach render the computer even more necessary. Possible extensions include (1) the addition of more sinusoidal terms in the model (as in model C-2), (2) the addition of a trend term in the model, and (3) the use of the exponentially weighted least-squares criterion instead of the ordinary least-squares criterion.

7-6 MODELS RECOGNIZING DEMAND SERIES AUTOCORRELATION

In section 7-2 the possible existence of autocorrelation among demand series values was discussed. Model A-2 for series A, which recognized such autocorrelation, was developed. The reader may wish to review these two items

Table 7-5 Computational results of applying Fourier series forecasting model C-1 to series C

Equation →	(7-47)	(7-48)	(7-49)	(7-50)	(7-34)
t d_t	$a_0(t)$	$a_1(t)$	$a_2(t)$	$\hat{d}_{t+1}$	e_t^2
1 338					
2 353					
3 339					
4 334					
5 319					
6 302					
7 280					
8 253					
9 246					
10 257					
11 274					
12 312	300	50	4	328	—
13 331	299.42	49.42	2.99	344	9
14 349	299.08	48.84	2.66	348	25
15 353	300.25	51.17	2.66	343	25
	See problem 7-12				
48 311	298.50	45.51	6.53	327	25
49 327	298.08	45.09	5.80	340	0
50 351	298.33	45.52	6.05	344	121

before proceeding with this section. In this section, two classes of models for dealing with autocorrelated series will be treated. These are known as *autoregressive* and *moving-average* models, not to be confused with the moving-average forecast based on the stationary, *non*autocorrelated series in section 7-3.

A series is *autoregressive of order p, AR(p)*, if it is described by the model

$$d_t = \alpha_0 + \alpha_1 d_{t-1} + \alpha_2 d_{t-2} + \cdots + \alpha_p d_{t-p} + \varepsilon_t \tag{7-51}$$

Model A-2, hypothesized for the daily street corner sales of newspapers, is an example of an $AR(2)$ model:

Model A-2: $\qquad d_t = 0.8 d_{t-1} + 0.1 d_{t-2} + 20 + \varepsilon_t \tag{7-3}$

Of course, this model should not be used without question for forecasting, because it is not based on the data. The usual procedure is to estimate the coefficients from the data (step 3) and use the resulting model for forecasting (step 4).

The estimation of coefficients α_k, $k = 0, 1, \ldots$, for autocorrelated series models is intimately associated with the autocorrelations ρ_j ($j = 0, 1, \ldots$). Recall from equation (7-1) that the autocorrelation at lag j is given by

$$\rho_j = \frac{E[(d_t - \mu)(d_{t-j} - \mu)]}{E[(d_t - \mu)^2]} \qquad j = 0, 1, 2, \ldots \qquad (7\text{-}1)$$

where μ is the mean of the demand time series. To simplify the development of the relationship between ρ_j and α_k, assume that $\mu = \alpha_0 = 0$. This in no way affects the probabilistic behavior of the process, so the results apply in general. For $\mu = 0$ we have

$$\rho_j = \frac{E[(d_t)(d_{t-j})]}{E[d_t^2]} \qquad j = 0, 1, \ldots \qquad (7\text{-}51a)$$

Now

$$E[(d_t)(d_{t-j})] = E\left[\left(\sum_{k=1}^{p} d_k d_{t-k} + \varepsilon_t\right)(d_{t-j})\right]$$

$$= \sum_{k=1}^{p} \alpha_k E[d_{t-k} \cdot d_{t-j}]$$

since $E[\varepsilon_t] = 0$. Thus

$$\rho_j = \frac{\sum_{k=1}^{p} \alpha_k E[d_{t-k} d_{t-j}]}{E[d_t^2]}$$

$$= \frac{\sum_{k=1}^{p} \alpha_k E[d_{t-k} d_{t-j}]}{E[d_{t-j}^2]}$$

So

$$\rho_j = \sum_{k=1}^{p} d_k \rho_{k-j} \qquad j \geq 1, \text{ where } \rho_0 = 1 \qquad (7\text{-}52)$$

The set of equations (7-52) is called the *Yule-Walker* equations. Of course, in a practical situation, the ρ_j are not known and must be estimated by the sample autocorrelations r_j, $j = 1, 2, \ldots$. If demand history is available for periods $1, 2, \ldots, t$, then $t - j$ pairs (d_t, d_{t-j}) are available for estimating r_j according to the equation

$$r_j = \frac{\frac{t-1}{t-j-1} \sum_{i=j+1}^{t} (d_i - \bar{d})(d_{i-j} - \bar{d})}{\sum_{i=1}^{t} (d_i - \bar{d})^2} \qquad (7\text{-}53)$$

where $\bar{d}$ is the average demand $= (\sum_{i=1}^{t} d_i)/t$. If the demand series is really an autoregressive process, then the values of ρ_j decay exponentially as j

increases. This is used as a test of the appropriateness of the autoregressive model: if the r_j appear to (roughly) decay exponentially, the model of equation (7-51) is considered a reasonable one to entertain. Usually t is large in relation to j, so equation (7-53) is often simplified to

$$r_j = \frac{\sum_{i=j+1}^{t}(d_i - \bar{d})(d_{i-j} - \bar{d})}{\sum_{i=1}^{t}(d_i - \bar{d})^2} \quad (7\text{-}54)$$

In practice, then, equation (7-54) is used to obtain the r_j, $j = 1, \ldots, p - 1$, which are substituted for ρ_j in equation (7-52). This results in p linear equations and p unknowns, $a_1, \ldots, a_p$. (The coefficients α_k have been replaced in equation (7-52) by their estimated a_k.) Solution then leaves only the coefficient α_0 without an estimate. This is easily remedied since, from equation (7-51),

$$E(d_t) = E(\alpha_0 + \alpha_1 d_{t-1} + \alpha_2 d_{t-2} + \varepsilon_t)$$
$$= \alpha_0 + \alpha_1 E(d_{t-1}) + \alpha_2 E(d_{t-2}) + E(\varepsilon_t)$$
$$= \alpha_0 + \alpha_1 E(d_t) + \alpha_2 E(d_t) + 0$$

Thus

$$\alpha_0 = E(d_t)(1 - \alpha_1 - \alpha_2)$$

Replacing parameters by their estimates yields

$$a_0 = \bar{d}(1 - a_1 - a_2) \quad (7\text{-}55)$$

The procedure is now illustrated for the example involving the sale of newspapers on a street corner. The sample autocorrelations are given by applying equation (7-54) to series A. The reader is asked to verify (problem 7-13) that the resulting r_j values are given by

j	0	1	2	3	4	5	6	7	8
r_j	1.00	0.834	0.725	0.583	0.444	0.276	0.181	0.126	0.112

Notice that the values of r_j decay exponentially as j increases. This supports the appropriateness of the autoregressive model, equation (7-51). The Yule-Walker equations (7-52), with a_k replacing α_k, become

$$0.834 = 1.00 a_1 + 0.834 a_2$$
$$0.725 = 0.834 a_1 + 1.00 a_2$$

These solve to yield $a_1 = 0.755$ and $a_2 = 0.095$. Substitution into equation (7-55) then yields $a_0 = 29.9$. Thus the model generated from the data is

$$d_t = 0.755 d_{t-1} + 0.095 d_{t-2} + 29.9 + \varepsilon_t \qquad (7\text{-}56)$$

This compares well with the hypothetical model expressed by equation (7-3). The forecast for demand in period $t + 1$ is then given by

$$\hat{d}_{t+1} = 0.755 d_t + 0.095 d_{t-1} + 29.9 \qquad (7\text{-}57)$$

The results of applying this forecasting approach to the series A data appear in table 7-6. A very favorable (low) average squared error results, indicating that the added burden of developing the autoregressive model (instead of using a simple moving average or exponential smoothing) may have been worth the effort. Of course, in the example used here, the same data used to develop the model are also employed to "implement" it. Although in practice one does not benefit from such "foresight," one does expect that if the demand series really is autocorrelated so that an autoregressive model applies, then it should pay to use such a model.

The other class of models treated in this section for handling autocorrelated series is called the "moving-average" class. A series is *moving average of order q, $MA(q)$*, if it is well modeled by

$$d_t = \alpha_0 + \alpha_1 \varepsilon_{t-1} + \alpha_2 \varepsilon_{t-2} + \cdots + \alpha_q \varepsilon_{t-q} + \varepsilon_t \qquad t = 1, 2, \ldots \quad (7\text{-}58)$$

Consider again the example in section 7-2 dealing with the barber's weekly demands for haircuts. Suppose the barber cuts an average of 100 heads per week. These demands are largely a matter of *when, not if*, since most of the barber's customers are regular. Thus, in a given week, if an abnormally large number of customers demand haircuts, the following week's demand will be less by approximately the same amount. Thus a reasonable model would be that for an $MA(1)$ process with $\alpha_1 = -1$:

$$d_t = 100 - \varepsilon_{t-1}$$

In order to forecast with this model, it should be verified with actual data.

Like $AR(p)$ models, the coefficients α_k, $k = 0, 1, \ldots, q$, of $MA(q)$ models are estimated by relating them to the sample autocorrelations r_j. The relationship is easily derived, but not always readily used. Recall from equation (7-51a) that, assuming that $\mu = \alpha_0 = 0$,

$$\rho_j = \frac{E[(d_t)(d_{t-j})]}{E(d_t^2)} \qquad (7\text{-}59)$$

Now the numerator of this expression equals

$$E[(\varepsilon_t + \alpha_1 \varepsilon_{t-1} + \cdots + \alpha_q \varepsilon_{t-q})(\varepsilon_{t-j} + \alpha_1 \varepsilon_{t-j-1} + \cdots + \alpha_q \varepsilon_{t-j-q})] \qquad 1 \le j \le q$$

CHAPTER 7: DEMAND FORECASTING

Table 7-6 Computational results of applying an autoregressive forecasting model to the data of series A

Equation →	(7-57)	(7-34)
t $\quad$ d_t	$\hat{d}_{t+1}$	e_t^2
1 $\quad$ 204	—	—
2 $\quad$ 209	207	—
3 $\quad$ 205	205	4
4 $\quad$ 206	205	1
5 $\quad$ 204	203	1
6 $\quad$ 204	203	1
7 $\quad$ 205	204	4
8 $\quad$ 200	200	16
9 $\quad$ 201	201	1
10 $\quad$ 204	203	9
See problem 7-14		
48 $\quad$ 203	202	1
49 $\quad$ 196	197	36
50 $\quad$ 204	203	49

But this, in turn, is equivalent to

$$E[\alpha_j \varepsilon_{t-j}^2 + \alpha_1 \alpha_{j+1} \varepsilon_{t-j-1}^2 + \cdots + \alpha_{q-j} \alpha_q^2 \varepsilon_{t-q}]$$

plus error cross-product terms which have zero mean since the ε_t are independent. Thus the numerator becomes

$$\varepsilon^2(\alpha_j + \alpha_1 \alpha_{j+1} + \cdots + \alpha_{q-j} \alpha_q) \qquad 1 \leq j \leq q$$

By similar reasoning, the denominator in equation (7-59) equals

$$\varepsilon^2(1 + \alpha_1 + \cdots + \alpha_q)$$

Therefore the autocorrelations are given by

$$\rho_j = \begin{cases} \dfrac{\alpha_j + \alpha_1 \alpha_{j+1} + \cdots + \alpha_{q-j} \alpha_q}{1 + \alpha_1^2 + \cdots + \alpha_q^2} & 1 \leq j \leq q \\ 0 & j > 1 \end{cases} \qquad (7\text{-}60)$$

In practice, r_j is substituted for ρ_j and a_j for α_j in equation (7-60) and the a_j are solved for. This solution is not necessarily straightforward, since it involves a nonlinear relationship. One important feature of equation (7-60) is that it indicates that the autocorrelations have zero value for $j > q$. Thus if the r_j calculated from the data have approximately zero value for $j > q$, the use of the $MA(q)$ model is supported.

For $q = 1$, equation (7-60) implies that

$$r_1 = \frac{a_1}{1 + a_1^2}$$

so that

$$a_1 = \frac{1}{2r_1} \pm \left[\frac{1}{(2r_1)^2} - 1\right]\left(\frac{1}{2}\right) \quad (7\text{-}61)$$

Generally the moving-average forecasting procedure involves (assuming $q = 1$ is appropriate) estimating α_0 by $a_0 = \bar{d}$, estimating α_1 by a_1 from equation (7-61), and forecasting demand using the equation

$$\hat{d}_{t+1} = a_0 + a_1(d_t - \hat{d}_t) \quad (7\text{-}62)$$

Many extensions of forecasting procedures recognizing demand autocorrelations are possible, but they are beyond the scope of this text. Two good references—[1] and [5]—are available to the interested reader.

7-7 EXTRINSIC FORECASTING

All the forecasting approaches treated so far in this chapter have had as a thread of commonality the fact that the models recognized only demand history as a basis for the forecast. Thus, the approaches have been *intrinsic*, taking the general form

$$d_t = f(\text{demand history})$$

The most common criticism of such models is that they appear to evade the question, What causes d_t to take on the value it does? Actually, the question is not entirely ignored, but is given the answer "demand history." The next comment by the skeptic usually refers to the fact that there must be other determinants of demand behavior which are ignored by the intrinsic model. Thus an *extrinsic* model of the form

$$d_t = f(\text{indicators})$$

should be entertained. An "indicator" is any variable which might have a cause-effect relationship with demand. Actually, the cause-effect phenomenon is both unnecessary and difficult to justify theoretically. The relationship usually sought between an indicator and the demand is correlation. Of course, all indicators need not be exogenous; demand history may still be included as an (endogenous) indicator.

Before an investigation is launched into extrinsic forecasting, a word of warning is in order. Keep in mind that demand forecasts of the type discussed in this chapter must be made repeatedly, for each of possibly thousands of items, and frequently by a computer. Thus it is imperative that the following properties of extrinsic data not be ignored. Each indicator time series should be:

1. Relevant (thought to affect demands)
2. Timely (available in time to be useful)
3. Accessible (consistently available to the forecaster)
4. Reliable (accurate and consistently calculated)
5. Cheap

In a firm in which there is adequate control over data quality, historical demand data are more likely to possess these properties than most other indicators. For exogenous indicators, the existence of such properties is not automatic. Perhaps this is one reason why extrinsic approaches are considered more appropriate for forecasting total company or division sales, rather than short-term detailed item demands.

Indicators may be classified by their degree of generality as follows:

General economic indicators: Include gross national product (GNP), unemployment, personal income, interest rates, money supply, and census figures.
General business indicators: Include inventories, production, prices, backorders, profits, and capital investment figures.
Specific business indicators: Examples are construction contracts, housing starts, new-car purchases, and agricultural statistics.

Determination of relevant indicators for particular demand series is no trivial process. It involves statistical expertise coupled with experience and judgment. Research results will shed additional light on the subject. For example, a study of the use of GNP as a sales indicator [6] revealed that it is more reliable for certain consumer durables, including truck trailers, copper, and roller bearings, than for nondurables such as bread products, shoes, or agricultural chemicals.

Examples for particular products can be revealing. Furniture sales have been shown [7] to be related to housing starts, level of disposable income, and prior period sales. A can company uses income levels, number of drinking establishments per capita, and population age distribution as indicators of demand for beer cans. A major drug producer is reported [7] to have correlated the sales of pharmaceuticals with disposable income!

Timeliness was listed above as a desirable objective of an indicator. An indicator is referred to as *leading, coincident,* or *lagging* depending on whether the indicator precedes, parallels, or follows in time the demand it is being used to forecast. For example, the average work week and new orders for durable goods are two leading business indicators, while the inverse of the unemployment rate and expenditures for new plant and equipment are, respectively, a coincident and a lagging indicator. Leading indicators are ready to use, in that they are potentially available before they are needed in making a forecast. The shortcoming of a lagging (or even a coincident) indicator is that it is not so available. This necessitates a double forecast—first the indicator must be forecast ahead to the point in time at which it will relate to the demand in question, then the demand itself is forecast based on the forecast of the indicator.

The last three qualities which a good indicator should possess are availability, reliability, and low cost. The forecasts must be able to identify and use a data source whose data meet these qualities. Sources may be broadly classified as providing information of three types: raw data, statistically analyzed data, and raw data together with the computer facilities and data files needed to allow users to do their own analysis.

Raw data sources are myriad. First, there are the periodic publications of various government agencies such as those listed in table 7-7. Other sources are industry and trade associations (such as the American Iron and Steel Institute or the National Lumber Manufacturers' Association); financial and securities publications (e.g., the *Wall Street Journal* and *Barron's*); and business news publications such as *Business Week* or *Fortune* magazines.

Results of the statistical analysis of data by specialists are sometimes made public. For example, the University of Pennsylvania's Wharton School maintains a computerized econometric model of the economy which consists of several hundred equations relating various business and economic variables. Output takes the form of predictions regarding all kinds of economic conditions (labor, inventories, capacity to supply, etc.). Several other models are similarly maintained.

General Electric Company maintains a data base which allows users, operating on GE's time-sharing computer system, to build their own forecasting models. The system, called "management analysis projection" (MAP), is a prototype of several similar systems, a brief account of which appears in [8].

7-8 COMPARISON OF FORECASTING APPROACHES

As pointed out in section 7-1, forecasts may be classified as statistical or nonstatistical, and the former category subclassified into intrinsic and extrinsic statistical approaches. The chapter has stressed statistical approaches

Table 7-7 A few government publications containing raw data suitable for extrinsic forecasting

Publication title (frequency)	Publishing organization	Description of contents
Statistical Abstract of the United States (annual)	U.S. Bureau of the Census Social and Economic Statistics Administration U.S. Department of Commerce	Over 1000 charts and tables of industrial, political, social, and economic statistics
Survey of Current Business (monthly)	Bureau of Economic Analysis Social and Economic Statistics Administration U.S. Department of Commerce	General business indicators; current business statistics; income and employment statistics
Business Conditions Digest (monthly)	Bureau of Economic Analysis Social and Economic Statistics Administration U.S. Department of Commerce	Several hundred economic time series; classification of indicators as leading, coincident, or lagging
Economic Indicators (monthly)	U.S. Council of Economic Advisors to the President	Numerous series related to income, employment, production, business activity, prices, and money markets

because they are considered to be more appropriate for routine (and possibly computerized) short-term demand forecasting. Formal nonstatistical approaches (e.g., the delphi method) are not particularly suited for this application because (1) it takes too long to develop a forecast for each item and (2) the cost per forecast is prohibitive. For these reasons, they are applied more successfully to predicting long-range trends, forecasts by division or product line, and new-product forecasting. This is not meant to imply that *informal* nonstatistical approaches do not meaningfully apply to item demand forecasting. The exercise of judgment of an experienced human being who is familiar with stock movements results in highly effective forecasts which are implicit in his or her ordering decisions. Too, any nonroutine impending event which would affect demands can be recognized only by human foresight.

Conceptually, any forecasting approach could be evaluated on a two-dimensional cost plane. The "controllable" costs could be accumulated to contribute to the first dimension. These are the costs associated with making the forecasts, including costs of model development and maintenance, data acquisition, computation, and other procedural costs. The second dimension reflects the "resultant" costs, which include costs resulting from forecast imperfection, such as holding and shortage costs, expediting, lost sales, etc. A plot of alternatives for a particular firm might appear as in figure 7-4. However, any attempt to infer general preferences for particular approaches from such a plot is rendered futile because of the unique characteristics of any individual firm. Cost surrogates are often used in place of costs. Thus forecast inaccuracy may become a substitute for resultant costs, while computer data processing time is used in lieu of controllable costs.

A thorough comparison of nonstatistical, intrinsic, and extrinsic approaches has been made by Chambers, Mullick, and Smith [3]. A small portion of their evaluation has been extracted and interpreted to form figure 7-5. It is recommended that the interested reader consult the original publication for details.

Groff [4] has compared several precisely defined (intrinsic) models empirically on the basis of mean absolute error. Based on simulation, using over 60 actual demand series, the forecasting errors of the best-of-ten Box-Jenkins models were either approximately equal to or greater than the errors of corresponding exponentially smoothed models! (Some analysis of seasonal models was also performed.)

A unique universal ranking of the utility of forecasting approaches is not meaningful. For inventory control purposes, the approaches chosen should be adaptive and computationally feasible (e.g., recursive calculation) and should yield tolerable forecast errors. Beyond that lie a host of circumstances which collectively will help to define preferences for particular approaches. The next section elaborates on considerations of this type.

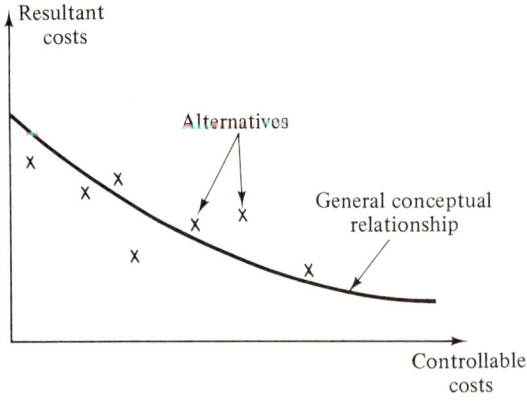

Figure 7-4 Conceptual cost comparison of alternative forecasting approaches.

CHAPTER 7: DEMAND FORECASTING **213**

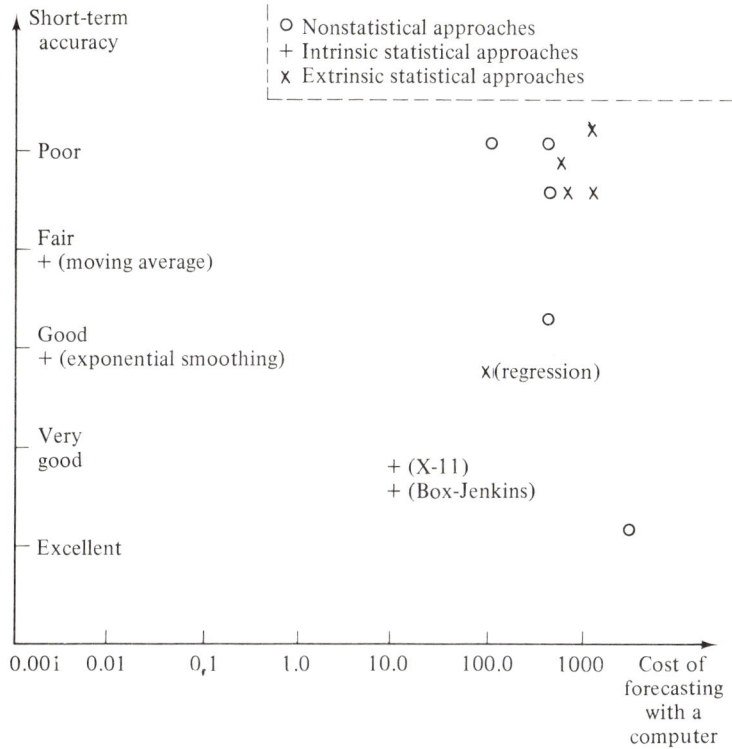

Figure 7-5 Cost surrogate comparison of alternative forecasting approaches (interpretively extracted from [3]).

7-9 FORECASTING IN THE INVENTORY CONTROL CONTEXT

The preceding sections of this chapter have exposed a number of techniques potentially useful in providing forecast information for inventory control purposes. The degree to which the potential is realized depends heavily on the manner in which forecast information is translated into control decisions. The heart of the translation problem involves a reconciliation of differences between what is normally produced by the forecasting system and what is required by the ordering system. If the ordering decisions are computerized, this translation can be performed automatically. In this case, a well-defined translation process must be designed and programmed. In this section are discussed several of the most common aspects of the translation problem.

A major concern in any control system is data integrity. For lack of the right numbers, the same computer that makes the techniques of the preceding sections feasible can, with equal objectivity and efficiency, render them useless. The data errors which confound the forecasting approach may be thought of as being of three types. There will always be data errors which occur sporadically and which, when not detected and corrected, will result in larger forecast errors and poorer ordering decisions. The only remedy is system design flexibility to enable manual after-the-fact changes, coupled with vigilant effort (e.g., double checking) in making correct data entries.

The second type of error is generated externally and may or may not be avoidable by careful systems design. For example, suppose it is known that demand d_t in a certain period t is going to be abnormally large (e.g., demand for cranberry sauce during Thanksgiving week). If this phenomenon is ignored, two errors result. First, of course, any forecast model will fail miserably at forecasting the unusual demand. Second, the abnormal demand will enter the historical series data and will incorrectly inflate forecasts for subsequent periods. Thus system capability for segregating unusual demands must exist. Of course, if the abnormal demand is not predictable (e.g., if a competitor temporarily cuts prices), then the forecast error in the period of abnormal demand is unavoidable. Of course, the abnormal demand can still be erased from series history.

The third type of error is one of misinterpretation of facts, and it should be designed out of the system. For example, suppose "demands" are recorded in the system when the customer's order is filled. Consider how each of the following events would distort demand history:

1. An item is out of stock, so the customer cancels the order.
2. An item is out of stock, so the order is held for three periods after which it is filled.
3. The wrong item is shipped to the customer who returns it in exchange for the correct item.

In each case, the actual demand may be misrepresented. The remedy here is a simple admonition: Make sure that it is *real* demands (in timing and quantity) which are recorded as such. Data integrity is discussed at greater length in chapter 9.

There has been an emphasis in this chapter on making forecasts $\hat{d}_{t+\tau}$. Of equal importance is knowledge of the forecast error. Recall that many of the inventory control models in chapters 3 and 4 implicitly involved the establishment of a buffer stock to accommodate random fluctuations in demand. These buffer stocks frequently are set at levels which will satisfy maximum reasonable demand. For example, suppose it is desired to satisfy 95 percent of the demand in a future period, $t + \tau$. The forecast error $e_k = \hat{d}_k - d_k$ is a random variable having probability distribution function $F_e(z) = P[e_k \le z]$. Thus the appropriate buffer stock will be the value of z for which $F_e(z) = 0.95$. The forecasting problem is one of maintaining an estimate of $F_e(z)$ each period along with the forecast $\hat{d}_t$. This may be done by forming a histogram of forecast errors which is updated each period. Sometimes it is assumed that $F_e(z)$ obeys a specified functional form, in which case standard tables may be used to establish buffer stock values. For example, if e_k is assumed to be normally distributed with zero mean, then the buffer stock needed to satisfy 95 percent of the demand in a given period would be $1.645 s_e$, where s_e^2 is the calculated error variance:

$$s_e^2 = \sum_{k=t-n+1}^{t} \frac{e_k^2}{n-1}$$

for n sufficiently large (say, $n \ge 30$) to assume that $s_e^2 = \sigma_e^2$, the true error variance.

The forecasts developed in this chapter have been for period demands. There is frequently a need for a forecast of demand over a number of periods. For example, if a fixed-order cycle inventory control system (chapter 4) is used, a forecast of demand over a lead time L is required, where $L = 1 +$ delivery lag. Thus if decisions are made weekly and the delivery lag is one week, then a two-period $(L = 2)$ forecast is needed.

In general, just as for single-period forecasts, the problem becomes one of forecasting the mean demand and the variance of the forecast error over L periods. L need not be an integer, but for simplicity it is assumed to be here. Let $D(L)$ be the cumulative demand during the next L periods $t + 1, \ldots, t + L$. Define $e(k)$ as the error associated with the forecast $\hat{d}_{t+k}$ of demand in period $t + k$, using information available through the current period t. Let $\hat{D}(L)$ be a forecast of $D(L)$, using information available through the current period t. Finally, let $E(L)$ be the error associated with $\hat{D}(L)$. Then

$$\hat{D}(L) = \sum_{k=1}^{L} \hat{d}_{t+k} \tag{7-63}$$

and

$$E(L) = \hat{D}(L) - D(L) \tag{7-64}$$

Since the forecasts $\hat{d}_{t+k}$, $k = 1, 2, \ldots, L$, are not independent, it is difficult to express the variance $\sigma_E^2(L)$ of $E(L)$ in a convenient functional form. Instead, it is recommended that $\sigma_E^2(L)$ be estimated empirically by maintaining an updated sample variance $S_E^2(L)$, calculated each period from the most recent observations of $E(L)$.

All the techniques of this chapter are suited for items for which there exists a "stable" market. By stable market is meant that demand for the item has occurred for a number of prior time periods sufficient to establish an historical series pattern, and will continue to follow the same pattern in the foreseeable future. In other words, the past can be extrapolated into the future. There are many kinds of inventoriable items for which the market is not "stable." Any item which is likely to become obsolete is an example, as is any new item for which a market has not been developed. For such items a life cycle may be developed to aid in forecasting during the period of unstable market. A "life cycle" will be defined to be a projected cumulative demand forecast for the "life" (period of unstable demand) of the item. Some representative life cycles are shown in figure 7-6. Item (a) has a fairly certain total demand but uncertain life (e.g., due to weather). Item (b) has a predictable life but an unpredictable total demand. Item (c) is an example of a new item. The shape of the curve reflects a catch-on introductory period, a period of rapid sales when many first-time purchases are made, and finally a stable market which includes new and replacement purchases. Item (d) is a contract to provide fuel for a fleet of trucks for one year. It is definite in both cumulative demand and timing, and hence does not need to be forecast at all. If the "life" is long in relation to forecast periods [as it would be for item (c)], the conventional methods of this chapter may be employed. Generally, one would use life cycles when they provide more information about future demand than would a conventional forecast based on historical data.

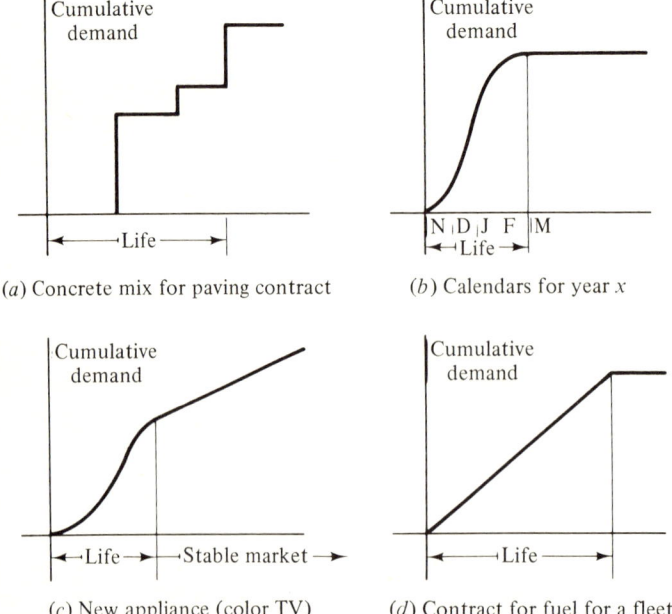

Figure 7-6 Some representative life cycles.

Another feature common to all the forecasting approaches in this chapter is that they apply to single items, or, more properly, to stock-keeping units. A *stock-keeping unit* (SKU) is an inventoriable item which cannot be further subdivided as to size, color, material, brand, etc. Thus, a spark plug is not an SKU, but a Champion J8J spark plug is. Sometimes it may be impossible to forecast SKUs but feasible to forecast a related collection of SKUs which may be called an *aggregated item*. For example, SKUs may represent a *variation* (such as color) within an aggregated item. Or, they may represent an *option*, such as an extra protective coating. Of course, an option is just a special case of a variation. If the methods of this chapter are used to forecast an aggregated item, the problem of disaggregating the forecast remains. This is usually done on a "share of the total demand" basis. It is generally easier to forecast each SKU separately, although this may lead to an unnecessarily high investment in inventory. The choice depends on the willingness of the customer to accept a substitute (i.e., a variation) for the item originally demanded. Some of these concepts were explored in chapter 5.

There is no one approach to forecasting demands which should be preferred by all firms. Moreover, there is no one approach to forecasting demands which should be preferred by one firm for all items. The choice is many-faceted, the primary determinants being pattern of item demand history, relative level of item demand activity, and the likelihood that historical item demand behavior will repeat itself.

7-10 SUMMARY

Demand forecasting provides some of the data needed to drive the models developed in the preceding chapters of this book. Forecasts are classified as statistical (based on numerical data) or nonstatistical. Also, forecasts may be identified as intrinsic (based solely on demand history) or extrinsic (based on other indicators). Most intrinsic forecasts are statistical.

A stepwise intrinsic statistical forecasting procedure involves the following:

1. Observing the characteristics of the demand time series.
2. Building an appropriate model.
3. Estimating coefficients of the model.
4. Forecasting.

Common forms of model include stationary, linear-trend, and cyclic models. Cyclic models include both additive and multiplicative base series models, and sinusoidal (Fourier) models.

Coefficients can be estimated by choosing those coefficients which minimize the sum of squared deviations between actual observed demands and corresponding model estimates. This leads to either the moving-average stationary model or the standard linear-regression trend model. If the squared deviations are exponentially weighted, the models become first- and second-order exponential smoothing models for the stationary and linear-trend cases, respectively.

Models recognizing correlations between successive time series values may result in a potentially more accurate forecast model. Two such models, called moving-average and autoregressive models, differ in the number of time periods (finite and infinite, respectively) over which correlations are recognized. Because these models involve a heavier computational burden and a more intricate analysis, they should be used for items for which forecast accuracy is the most critical.

Extrinsic forecasts are based on indicators which may be leading, coincident, or lagging, depending on whether the indicator occurs before, during, or after the demand correlated with it. Leading indicators are the most useful for forecasting.

Perhaps the single most important caveat which can be offered is that one must strive to forecast real demands, not pseudo demands such as orders or sales.

REFERENCES

1. Box, George E. P., and Gwilym M. Jenkins: "Time Series Analysis Forecasting and Control," Holden-Day, San Francisco, 1970.
2. Carman, Hoy F.: "Improving Sales Forecasts for Appliances," *Journal of Marketing Research*, vol. 9, p. 214, May 1972.
3. Chambers, John C.; S. K. Mullick; and D. D. Smith: "How to Choose the Right Forecasting Technique," *Harvard Business Review*, vol. 49, no. 4, p. 45, July–August 1971.
4. Groff, Gene K.: "Empirical Comparison of Models for Short Range Forecasting," *Management Science*, vol. 20, no. 1, pp. 22–31, September 1973.
5. Nelson, Charles R.: "Applied Time Series for Managerial Forecasting," Holden-Day, San Francisco, 1973.
6. Osborne, Harlow: "Characteristics of Sales Forecasts Based on Gross National Product," *Financial Analysts Journal*, vol. 26, no. 5, p. 39, September–October 1970.
7. Parker, George G. C., and Edilberto L. Segura: "How to Get a Better Forecast," *Harvard Business Review*, vol. 49, no. 2, p. 99, March–April 1971.
8. "G.E.'s 'Management Analysis Projection,'" *Sales Management*, vol. 107, no. 14, pp. 31–33, December 27, 1971.

EXERCISES

7-1 For table 7-2:

(*a*) Complete the first few missing rows to gain an understanding of the mechanics of the forecasting models.

(b) Complete the remainder of the table, verifying the entries in the text for the last three time periods. You may wish to use a computer program to do this.

(c) Calculate and compare the mean square errors for each forecast procedure.

7-2 Determine the value of α for which the weighted average age of the data used in the single exponential smoothing model [equation (7-16)] is equal to that in the moving-average model [equation (7-11)].

7-3 Show by using calculus that equations (7-24a) and (7-24b) yield the minimum value of SSE in equation (7-23).

7-4 You are asked here to show that equations (7-25) and (7-26) are algebraically equivalent to equations (7-24a) and (7-24b). This can be done by first using (7-24a) and (7-24b) to obtain expressions for $a_0(t-1)$ and $a_1(t-1)$, substituting these into the right-hand sides of equations (7-25) and (7-26), and showing that the left-hand sides of (7-25) and (7-26) are obtained.

7-5 Using calculus, show that equations (7-28) and (7-29) yield the minimum value of $WSSE$ in equation (7-27). Some results regarding summation of series are helpful here. For $0 \le \beta \le 1$,

$$\sum_{j=0}^{\infty} \beta^j = \frac{1}{1-\beta} \qquad \sum_{j=0}^{\infty} j\beta^j = \frac{\beta}{(1-\beta)^2} \qquad \sum_{j=0}^{\infty} j^2 \beta^j = \frac{\beta(1+\beta)}{(1-\beta)^3}$$

7-6 You are asked to show that equations (7-30) and (7-31) are algebraically equivalent to equations (7-28) and (7-29). This can be done in a manner analogous to that suggested in problem 7-4.

7-7 (a)–(c) Repeat problem 7-1(a) to (c) for table 7-3.

(d) Verify that the coefficients for the linear regression $a_0(50)$ and $a_1(50)$ are identical to those which would be obtained using ordinary linear regression [equations (7-24)].

7-8 It has been suggested by some that instead of using equation (7-38) to update the base series b_t, you use the equation

$$b_t = \tfrac{1}{3}(d_{t-11} + d_{t-12} + d_{t-13})$$

What is wrong with this approach?

7-9 (a)–(c) Repeat problem 7-1(a) to (c) for table 7-4. In (c), no comparison can be made until one of problems 7-10(c) and 7-12(c) is also completed.

7-10 (a) Prepare a table similar to table 7-4 in which you apply an additive rather than a multiplicative cyclic model to the series C data from table 7-1. Use equation (7-41) together with

$$s_t = 0.2(d_t - b_t) + 0.8 s_{t-1} \qquad s_1 = 0$$

Complete the first few rows to gain an understanding of the mechanics of this model.

(b) Complete the calculations for the entire table.

(c) Calculate the mean square error and compare with the similar result in problem 7-9(c).

7-11 Show, using calculus, that equations (7-44) to (7-46) yield values of $a_0(t)$, $a_1(t)$, and $a_2(t)$ which minimize SSE in equation (7-43).

7-12 (a)–(c) Repeat problem 7-1 for table 7-5. Computer calculations are recommended. In (c), compare the result with that for problems 7-9(c) and 7-10(c).

7-13 Apply equation (7-54) to the data of series A (table 7-1) to calculate the autocorrelation coefficients r_j. You may have access to a computerized routine which will calculate these r_j for you, as a check.

7-14 (a)–(c) Repeat problem 7-1(a) to (c) for table 7-6. For (c), compare the result with that obtained in problem 7-1(c).

CHAPTER
EIGHT
COST ESTIMATION

Just as demand forecasts are essential to the development and implementation of any ordering decision model, cost estimates are likewise a necessity. The goal here is the same in both cases—to obtain as reliable a set of data as possible at reasonable expense. Several features of cost data give them a different nature from demand data:

1. Cost data are generally updated less frequently than demand forecasts, because costs are not expected to fluctuate as erratically as demands.
2. Many well-defined schemes are recognized for generating and maintaining demand information expressly for inventory control purposes. Such is not the case for cost data. Most cost data are developed by accountants whose purposes traditionally center on providing an accurate portrayal of the financial position of the firm. Fortunately there is a trend toward increased recognition of the managerial accounting discipline which, unlike financial accounting, serves primarily to provide data to directly assist in managerial decision making.
3. There is relatively little doubt about what data are sought for demand forecasts. Such is not the case with cost data, as will be seen below.
4. Compared with demand forecasting literature, there is a dearth of published material available on the subject of cost estimation.

For inventory control purposes, the central goal of cost estimation is to determine the incremental inventory-related costs. An *incremental* cost is one which is affected by the decision(s) being made. A cost may easily be inventory-related but not incremental. For example, if ample warehouse space is available for all stored material, then the storage cost is not incremental. A more troublesome example is depreciation. Taken by itself, depreciation is not a cost, but an expense in the sense that it is recognized as a deduction from income. Hence, depreciation may appear not to be an incremental cost. (The tax effect of depreciation is a cost, though.) However, depreciation *reflects* the true cost of investment in a building. If the quantity of stock held affects the size of the building erected to hold it, then depreciation may indeed be an incremental cost. It depends on the time frame of construction decisions compared with that of inventory control decisions. On the short term, inventory quantities do not affect building size; in the long term, they do.

The four major categories of costs which have appeared repeatedly in the models in this book are material costs, holding costs, shortage costs, and ordering costs. In this order, estimation of these costs is discussed in the following sections.

8-1 MATERIAL COSTS

Estimation of material costs plays a central role in all inventory modeling. Many of the models in this book have required an explicit value for the cost of material. Even those models which have not, however, still rely on material costs indirectly. Material cost is needed in order to evaluate capital costs which are part of holding costs. Also, if sales are lost, the resulting lost contribution depends on the cost of material (see shortage costs, section 8-3).

Of the four cost categories, material costs receive the most attention from the accountants. In this section, the common accounting conventions for material costs are reviewed, and the problems and pitfalls associated with the blind use of accounting figures for inventory control purposes are discussed. The data in table 8-1 will be used to illustrate the accounting conventions.

Accountants distinguish between two methods of record keeping for inventories, called the *periodic* and *perpetual* methods. For our purposes, the difference between the two is the timing of the recognition of stock issues. The perpetual method recognizes issues as they occur, while the periodic method defers recognition of issues to the end of some period of time. (Accountants refer to the fact that a physical inventory is usually taken at the end of the period under the periodic method, but this is of no concern to us. The important thing is that issues are recognized at this time.) There need be *no* relation between periodic versus perpetual accounting methods and periodic and continuous review for inventory control. The ordering decision

Table 8-1 A set of representative inventory transactions for one item

Date	Received Quantity	Received Price	Issued Quantity	Balance Quantity
December 31				0
March 10	40	$3.00		40
May 6	40	2.50		80
July 26			50	30
December 23	40	3.20		70
December 31			35	35

maker might keep continuous records on quantities while the accountant uses the periodic method for quantities, costs, or both. In table 8-1, under the periodic method, the two year-end balances of 0 and 35 units would be the only balances recognized.

When an issue is recognized, a cost transfer is also recognized. The value of the cost transfer depends on the accounting convention used for this purpose: three common conventions are first in–first out (FIFO), last in–first out (LIFO), and moving average. These are best illustrated numerically. Table 8-2 displays the calculations for each of the three cost conventions under both periodic and perpetual issue recognition. Notice that only under the FIFO method are identical ending inventory values obtained for both periodic and perpetual issue recognition. There are five different values for the ending inventory on hand, ranging from $101.50 to $112.00, depending on the accounting conventions used.

All the calculations in table 8-2 have in common the fact that costs of acquisition were used to value inventory on hand. Several other such methods, each one weighing the same acquisition costs differently, are also in use but seem to be less widespread, and will not be discussed here. However, some approaches used by accountants alter the values of stock on hand by considering more than the acquisition costs. One approach is to value inventories at *market*, or replacement, cost. Some bounds may be placed on this valuation; e.g., if the market value exceeds the net realizable value (selling price), the net realizable value is used instead. A variant of this approach is to value inventories at *lower of cost or market*, i.e., at acquisition cost or replacement cost, whichever is less. This variant has traditionally been used in the interest of being conservative in assigning a value to stock on hand.

Another approach, called the *retail* inventory method, is used by retail or merchandising concerns. It consists of maintaining the ratio of cost of stock held to its (retail) sale price. Then the value of goods on hand at any

Table 8-2 Accounting computations for the transactions of table 8-1, under three costing conventions

	Periodic					
	Transaction			Balance		
Date	Quantity	Price	$	Quantity	Price	$
FIFO						
12/31				0		0
3/10	+40	3.00	120.00			
5/6	+40	2.50	100.00			
7/26						
12/23	+40	3.20	128.00			
12/31	{−40 −40 −5	3.00 2.50 3.20}	−236.00	35	3.20	112.00
LIFO						
12/31				0		0
3/10	+40	3.00	120.00			
5/6	+40	2.50	100.00			
7/26						
12/23	+40	3.20	128.00			
12/31	{−40 −40 −5	3.20 2.50 3.00}	−243.00	35	3.00	105.00
Moving average						
12/31				0		0
3/10	+40	3.00	120.00			
5/6	+40	2.50	100.00			
7/26						
12/23	+40	3.20	128.00			
12/31	−85	2.90	246.50	35	2.90	101.50

Table 8-2 (continued)

Date	Perpetual					
	Transaction			Balance		
	Quantity	Price	$	Quantity	Price	$
FIFO						
12/31				0		0
3/10	+40	3.00	120.00	40	3.00	120.00
5/6	+40	2.50	100.00	{40	3.00	120.00
				\40	2.50	100.00
7/26	{−40	3.00	−120.00			
	\−10	2.50	25.00	30	2.50	75.00
12/23	+40	3.20	128.00	{30	2.50	75.00
				\40	3.20	128.00
12/31	{−30	2.50	75.00			
	\−5	3.20	16.00	35	3.20	112.00
LIFO						
12/31				0		0
3/10	+40	3.00	120.00	40	3.00	120.00
5/6	+40	2.50	100.00	{40	3.00	120.00
				\40	2.50	100.00
7/26	{−40	2.50	100.00			
	\−10	3.00	30.00	30	3.00	90.00
12/23	+40	3.20	128.00	{30	3.00	90.00
				\40	3.20	128.00
12/31	−35	3.20	128.00	{30	3.00	90.00
				\ 5	3.20	16.00
						106.00
Moving average						
12/31				0		0
3/10	+40	3.00	120.00	40	3.00	120.00
5/6	+40	2.50	100.00	80	2.75	220.00
7/26	−50	2.75	137.50	30	2.75	82.50
12/23	+40	3.20	128.00	70	3.01	210.50
12/31	−35	3.01	−105.35	35	3.01	105.35

time is its retail value times the ratio. The retail value is obtained by subtracting sales from goods available for sale, as illustrated in table 8-3. A little reflection on the calculations in table 8-3 reveals that the retail method is just another way of forming a weighted average of acquisition costs.

The accounting procedures covered so far were discussed in the context of purchased goods, or merchandise. Before the implications of these procedures for inventory decision making are assessed, additional concepts which arise when manufacturing inventories are held will be exposed. Differences in inventory values arising out of changes in accounting conventions are likely to be much greater for manufacturing inventories than for merchandise.

The value of a manufacturing inventory item is generally taken to include all the cost of getting the item into its existing state. This cost includes three ingredients: material, labor, and overhead. At each manufacturing step, the "value added" to the item is the cost of additional material, labor, and overhead incurred at that step. Manufacturing inventories are typically broken into three classes: raw materials, work in process, and finished goods. Raw material values need not include labor and overhead; the other two classes typically do. When the finished goods are ultimately sold, the purchase cost plus all the value added is subtracted from sales revenue as cost of goods sold.

The details of the various ways of associating labor and overhead with an item are covered in any standard book on cost accounting. A few comments about the basic concepts will suffice here. Applying costs to units of product inevitably involves some form of averaging, in which a cost incurred in some period of time is divided by the number of units produced to determine a cost per unit. Accountants distinguish between *job order costing* and *process costing*. In the former, products are valued on an individual unit or batch basis by applying labor and overhead costs to each unit or batch. In process costing (applicable, say, to chemical production, petroleum, or

Table 8-3 Valuation of inventory using the retail method

	At cost	At retail
Beginning inventory	5000	8,000
Purchases	2000	4,000
Goods available for sale	7000	12,000
Deduct sales	3791.67†	6,500
Ending inventory	3208.33†	5,500

† Cost = $\frac{7}{12}$ retail

lumber milling), labor, overhead, and even material costs are applied based on averages over a much longer period of time (say, one quarter). In either case, though, some costs must be *applied* to the product using an average. Most overhead costs are applied this way, since such costs (supervision, utilities, maintenance, etc.) cannot be precisely identified with a unit of output. Some *base* must be used to determine the actual amount of such costs to be applied. Common bases include direct labor hours and machine hours. Thus maintenance costs may be applied to each unit of product at the rate of x/y dollars per machine-hour required to make the product, where x is the total maintenance cost incurred during the y hours that the machine was used.

Frequently *standard* costs rather than actual costs are applied to units of products. This is especially true of material costs and direct labor costs. The standard is, of course, tied to reality in that it reflects what actual costs were in the past (historical standards) or what they could be under "good manufacturing practice." Any deviation between actual and standard cost is called a *variance*. Standards can be expressed in terms of both quantity and price. For example, the standard material cost per unit of a molded part may be $\$w \cdot z$, which results from the consumption of z units of raw material (plastic) at $\$w$ per unit. This dual form of cost standard can enhance the level of control over the molding process, since the material cost variance can be split into a price variance and a quantity variance. The production department is then accountable for the quantity variance, while purchasing must answer for the price variance. The labor cost analogs to price and quantity material cost standards are called *labor rate* and *labor efficiency* standards. An example of a labor rate variance would be the incurrence of extra labor costs because of overtime, an extra shift, or subcontracting.

So much for material cost accounting in a nutshell. Of concern are the implications of the use of accounting system data for estimating material costs for inventory control purposes. The main difficulty involved in using accounting data is neither that accountants are failing to record all the costs nor that they are recording costs which do not occur. The problem is simply that they are grouping costs in packages which must be unbundled and regrouped for purposes of inventory control. Some costs which are included in the accounting material cost package should be excluded from the inventory control material cost package, and vice versa. A list of some of these costs appears below. The number of such costs in any particular system requiring such attention can, of course, vary. Each accounting system is unique and must be considered individually.

It would be fortuitous, indeed, if an accounting system matched the inventory decision makers' needs exactly. This statement is *not* an indictment of accounting practices. First, the accountant is serving an extremely wide range of users. Moreover, the inventory planner needs costs grouped into some rather unique packages; in fact, the packages may change depending on the particular inventory planning purpose, as seen in some instances below.

Acquisition costs Added to the basic purchase price of ordered goods are certain acquisition costs, some positive and some negative. The positive costs of acquiring goods may be broken into order processing costs and shipping costs. Both relate more to the ordering costs and are therefore discussed in section 8-3. From the standpoint of inventory planning, the portion of the acquisition cost which varies with the quantity ordered should be considered as part of the material cost. Thus if the per-unit portion of the shipping cost is, say, x per pound and the price per pound is y FOB shipping point, then $(x + y)$ is the cost of material. This is important primarily in the determination of the capital investment for holding cost purposes.

The negative acquisition costs take the form of discounted prices. Such discounts may be quantity-based or payment-based. The quantity discount may be order-specific (apply to one particular order) or vendor-specific (apply if the total amount of material ordered from a vendor during some period of time, e.g., a year is sufficiently large). In either case, as long as the discount is nontrivial and is regularly received, the discounted price should be used in determining material cost—again, primarily for capital cost purposes. If the discount is based on payment characteristics (e.g., prompt payment or cash payment), the same criteria can apply.

Quality-related costs Suppose incoming material is routinely inspected (using either sampling or 100 percent). If rejects are returned to the vendor (and replaced by new ones) or are reworked, any cost borne by the company can be considered to be part of the material cost. If rejected material is scrapped or salvaged and additional units must be ordered, the cost of scrapping (less the salvage value), if significant, can be added to the cost of material.

Applied costs As alluded to earlier in this section, labor and overhead costs are applied to material as it flows through process stages (echelons). Even in the incoming inspection activity just mentioned, the inspection labor and overhead costs (test equipment, power, lights) are added to the value of the material. The specifics involved with cost application fill cost accounting books. For our purposes, the accounting distinction between direct and full costing is useful. *Direct* (or *variable*) *costing* assigns only variable costs (costs "directly related" to output) to inventory at each level. "Fixed" costs such as supervision and depreciation are charged on a period-by-period basis. On the other hand, under *full* (absorption) *costing*, all the fixed costs are also applied to each unit of product. For inventory management, what is needed is some form of incremental costing (a form of direct costing), under which all costs which vary as a result of inventory ordering decisions would be applied to the product. This can include costs which the accountant considers fixed, as well as "variable costs."

In a multiechelon environment, the incremental applied costs associated with an echelon are the costs incurred directly as a result of the maintenance of that echelon's inventory level. The chain of events whose costs must be included consists of those processes or activities which take place immediately prior to the replenishment of the echelon being supplied, but not prior to the supplying of the preceding echelon. Thus material costs at echelon j are the sum of material costs at echelon $j-1$ plus labor and overhead required to get material from echelon $j-1$ to echelon j. (Also, it is easy to forget that applied overhead includes the fringe benefits accruing as a result of direct labor.)

Any cost which is not already uniquely associated with an echelon must be *allocated*. For example, if both parts and assemblies are stored in a common warehouse (and, of course, if the size of the warehouse depends on the inventory control decisions being made), then certain warehousing costs must be allocated. What is a holding cost for echelon $j-1$ becomes part of the material cost for stock supplying echelon j.

8-2 HOLDING COSTS

The second category of costs consists of the holding, or carrying, costs. Realistic estimation of these costs again requires that only *incremental* costs be considered. In the case of holding costs, incremental costs are those which vary directly with the amount of stock held. These were introduced in chapter 1 along with other inventory costs. In this section, holding costs will be subdivided into four categories. Capital costs, which form the first category, represent the loss of opportunity to invest funds tied up in inventory. Storage costs are those incurred as a result of the need to house inventories in a physical facility. Service costs include assessments directly against stock held and costs of "processing" inventories while in storage. Finally, risk costs are those based on losses of a casualty nature which occur because inventories are held.

Table 8-4 gives a fairly complete breakdown of costs in each category. Most are self-explanatory, but a few remarks are offered to clarify what some of these costs are intended to include. Many variations of the outline shown are possible. It is intended only as a means of recognizing the predominant holding costs. Owned buildings may, in fact, be separate warehouse structures or a portion of a larger building. Utilities are primarily lighting,

Table 8-4 Categorized holding cost components

I. Capital costs
II. Storage costs
    A. Land
    B. Building
        1. Owned
            a. Depreciation
            b. Property taxes
            c. Insurance
            d. Utilities
        2. Leased
        3. Rented
III. Service costs
    A. Assessments
        1. Inventory taxes
        2. Insurance
    B. Processing
        1. Materials handling
        2. Physical inventory
IV. Risk costs
    A. Obsolescence
    B. Shrinkage
        1. Pilferage
        2. Disappearance
        3. Damage
        4. Spoilage
        5. Devaluation of selling price

temperature, and humidity control, which can be significant if refrigeration is required. Utilities may be paid for under a lease arrangement as well as for owned facilities. Leased and rental facilities are to be distinguished. A leased facility suggests control of an entire building, while rental of facilities is taken to imply control only of space within a building. Taxes and insurance are each segregated into two components: costs directly assessed against inventory held and costs related to facilities housing the inventory. Property taxes apply to land as well as buildings. Physical inventory costs are those related to periodic counting of all stock on hand as part of an accounting or auditing procedure. Shrinkage involves both loss of quantity (e.g., pilferage) and loss of value, as a result of damage, spoilage, and the like. Obsolescence costs also take the form of a reduction in value, but they differ in cause. Causes of obsolescence, unlike shrinkage, are either external to the firm (e.g., competitive market changes or style changes) or internal, but intentional (e.g., engineering changes which eliminate the need for parts).

Two studies have reported results of analyses of holding costs in the above four categories. One [4], a survey of six large manufacturers of packaged goods, compared holding costs derived analytically with cost figures being assumed by each firm. The second [3], a case study of a single company, relates the numerical details and estimation procedures used in an in-depth determination of carrying costs. Both papers express holding costs as a percentage of value of the inventory. Some interesting conclusions regarding the magnitudes of costs follow.

1. In all cases, capital costs were by far the most significant component of holding costs. As a percentage of holding costs, capital costs ranged from 49 to over 96 percent. The lowest figure was from the case study in which an after-tax rate of return was used, even though other costs appear to be before income taxes.
2. Costs were very roughly of equal magnitude in each of the other three categories.
3. Total holding costs ranged from 14 to 43 percent of inventory value (average: 29 percent).
4. In the survey study, holding costs used by the companies bore little resemblance to those calculated by the analyst, except that they were uniformly lower, about one-half of the calculated values on the average.
5. Wide variation among individual companies pointed to the need for each firm to determine its own holding cost percentage.

Of every bit as much importance as the numerical comparisons are the estimating procedures used. The case study [4] provides some examples of specific estimation approaches used for particular costs. For example, the costs related to owned buildings (depreciation, property taxes, and insurance) are estimated by *allocating* total building costs, on the basis of square footage occupied by the inventory in question, as a fraction of total building square footage. Utility costs were also obtained by allocation, except that a preliminary estimation of the fraction of fuel and electricity bills resulting from heating and lighting only was made. This was because stock in storage required no other energy use. Taxes on inventory were allocated on the basis of declared net asset value: total actual personal property tax times the ratio of value of inventory to value of all assets subject to the tax. Obsolescence costs were obtained from writeoffs by plant disposal authorities; stock quantity loss was based on differences between book quantity values and physical inventory counts.

Of interest also is that the case study analyst relied on sources other than accounting data. Utility costs were obtained with the help of plant engineering. Public assessments were used to help determine property tax costs. The cost of capital resulted from manufacturers' estimates. The need to rely on such varied sources for cost data is likely to arise whenever the cost estimation problem is addressed.

The relative numerical magnitude of the capital cost suggests that the greatest amount of attention should be paid to its estimation. Ironically, cost of capital is a controversial subject. Resolution of differences of opinion regarding this cost is, to put it mildly, difficult. The source of the difficulty stems from lack of a consensus in answering the question, If the capital invested to produce or purchase inventory had remained available for investment elsewhere, what return on investment (ROI) could have been expected from the alternative investment? Answers to this question are generally based on

1. The source and cost of funds to finance the investment
2. Available alternative investments and prospective returns
3. The risk involved in all possible investments
4. The duration of each investment
5. The need to ration capital among investments

Not only does the answer vary widely from firm to firm, but it does so over time within the same firm, necessitating a continual reappraisal of what value should be assumed for the cost of capital.

About as simplistic a view of the problem as is possible follows. Suppose capital is obtained at a cost (interest or dividends, say) of i dollars per dollar borrowed per year. There is an opportunity to invest operating capital in a venture which is expected to earn r dollars per unit invested per unit time. The inventory lot size is Q, which has not been determined. The demand rate is fairly constant, so that $cQ/2$ dollars represents the average investment in inventory.

If $r \leq i$, you have no interest in investing in the venture, but prefer to pay back the funds obtained to finance the inventory investment. After all, paying back a loan is analogous to investing in an investment which earns the loan rate. Thus the capital cost may be taken to be $icQ/2$ or icQ, depending on whether available funds are free to be used for other purposes between purchases (or production) or for successive lot sizes. If $r > i$, you prefer to invest available funds in the venture, so that the cost of capital is $rcQ/2$ or rcQ. In either case, the capital cost is an opportunity cost resulting from failure to make an alternative investment.

Any constraint applied to the above situation may change the effective capital cost. For example, if the bank insists that the loan be paid back as soon as possible (perhaps because the bank does not like the risk involved in the alternative venture), then the basis of the cost of capital reverts back to the bank rate i. Most firms seem to select a capital cost somewhere between i and $r\,(>i)$.

The capital cost is typically applied solely to the material cost, although it could be argued that other components of the holding cost represent investments also. If your inventory happens to be jeeps and you must rent land on which to park your inventory, the capital invested in the land is just as real as that invested in the jeeps. Flora [2] has developed a model in which the taxes on profits and the profit rate are used to develop a revised holding cost and hence a revised EOQ.

8-3 SHORTAGE COSTS

The third category of costs for which estimates are desired is shortage costs. This category presents the most formidable estimation problems because many of the costs are resultant (i.e., uncontrollable) costs. In this respect, the cost consequences of failure to deliver on time are like the cost consequences of failure to deliver items of the expected quality—an adverse, volatile, and potentially hostile situation develops, whose exact consequences are unpredictable. This is unfortunate since shortage costs are significant in magnitude. The penalty cost p could easily be 10 times the holding cost h.

The difficulty of estimating shortage costs was alluded to in section 2-3, where a back-door solution to the problem was introduced. This approach called for the specification (by management) of a service level for each inventory item. From the service level a shortage cost was imputed; that is, the shortage cost value obtained was the one which would, in effect, yield the same service level as specified, provided that the cost model used was correct. Thus the imputation of shortage costs suffers because it is subjective, and it is model-specific. Moreover, indiscriminate use of service levels can have a detrimental effect, as the following simple example demonstrates. Suppose a customer orders 10 items, each of which the supplier controls by using a service level of 0.99. Then the probability that the customer gets what was ordered when it is expected is $(0.99)^{10} = 0.9$. This is the probability of having a satisfied customer, and it is *this* level of satisfaction that should be compared with the cost of holding higher inventories (safety stocks).

The actual shortage cost consists of one or more cost components from a conglomerate of possible cost effects. Which components apply in a given case depends on both management policy and "customer" (demander) behavior. Table 8-5 outlines the common cost effects on the basis of four different scenarios. In the first two scenarios, action is taken to avert the impending shortage, while in the second two scenarios no remedial action is taken, so that the shortage is allowed to happen. Of course, remedial action could be taken and the shortage (albeit perhaps a less severe one) could still occur, in

Table 8-5 Cost effects of an impending shortage

Scenario	Primary effect	Cost effects
Remedial action—purchased item	Emergency purchase	Premium material price Loss of purchase quantity discount Extra ordering Rush shipment
	Use of substitute item	Higher cost per unit Adaptation costs Depletion of substitute item
Remedial action—manufactured item	Overtime	Premium labor rate Shift premium
	Subcontracting	Higher manufacturing cost
	Emergency hiring	Inefficient labor Risk of inferior-quality work Extra training expense
	Substitute item	Adaptation Higher unit cost
No remedial action—external demand	Lost sale	Lost contribution
	Lost customer	Additional contribution
	Additional lost customers	Additional contribution Goodwill loss
	Backlogged demand	Special delivery when item arrives Contract penalty Lawsuit Extra paperwork
No remedial action—internal demand	Production downtime	Idle labor Idle equipment (Eventually, see remedial action, manufactured item)
	Failure to meet schedule	(Eventually, see external demand cost effects)
	Unsafe conditions	Damages

which case the cost effects would come from those associated with more than one scenario.

In the first scenario, remedial action is taken to avoid a shortage of a normally purchased item. This could involve a special purchase or substitution of another item. Each action would incur costs such as those shown in the right-hand column. For example, the premium material price would occur if the item were purchased from a source not usually relied upon, such as a competitor. Loss of discount would occur because the emergency purchase either is a rush order or is for a small quantity. Other costs include the cost of placing the extra order and the cost of hurried shipment—special delivery, air freight, or the like.

Remedial action taken in the case of a manufactured item includes overtime (or possibly an increase in second-shift activity), subcontracting, emergency hiring, or substitution of another item.

If the shortage is allowed to occur, the cost effects (table 8-5) depend on whether the demand not being satisfied is external or internal to the supplying organization. Disappointment of a customer (external demander) can lead to loss of the immediate sale, as well as loss of additional sales to the same customer or to other customers. This may cost no more than the contribution (unit revenue less variable unit cost) for each unit of lost sales. The supplier's reputation may be damaged. Even if the sale is not lost, the supplier may be vulnerable to penalties or legal action, depending on the circumstances.

Unsatisfied internal demand is costly on a variety of fronts. Idle labor and equipment can be considered a cost if these resources are being used to capacity, so that idleness at one point in time implies the need for additional capacity later. Unsafe conditions could occur if the item is, say, a critical maintenance item (lubricant, coolant, etc.). One important consequence of failure to supply an item internally is that the resulting disruption can create a domino effect on a chain of succeeding echelons, until finally external customers are affected. Thus all the cost effects in table 8-5 are potentially realized when productive facilities are deprived of material necessary to their functioning. This is why in a manufacturing environment there is such strong emphasis on supplying the needed material on time—no matter what the cost may be.

The difficulties in estimating shortage costs are seen to lie partly in the fact that there is a choice of which costs will actually be incurred, and that if the choice is to pass the shortage on to the customer, then the customer controls the costs incurred. A second problem may be that shortages are inherently a random phenomenon, rather than a planned or controlled event. Thus realism calls for estimation of probabilities of occurrence of shortages, as well as of the resulting costs. Most models which recognize this randomness ask for (or compute) an expected shortage cost. Finally, since shortages are not "supposed to occur," the accounts tend to treat the associated costs as "variations from standard." Regular, separate ledger accounts are hard to find for such "unusual" events. Here, more than anywhere, there is a need for accounting information to reflect *why* a cost (variance) occurred, as well as when and in what dollar amount. Without the answer to this question, shortage cost estimation may still have to begin with "gu."

8-4 ORDERING COSTS

The last category of costs to be estimated is the ordering costs. These costs differ widely depending on whether the items being ordered are purchased or made in-house. Table 8-6 identifies the common ordering costs under each

Table 8-6 Ordering cost categorization

Method of procurement	Occasion	Ordering costs
Purchase	Order approval	Paperwork
	Order placement	Postage, phone charges
		Paperwork
	Shipment	Freight
		Postage
		Demurrage
		Pickup
	Receipt of order	Identification and count verification
		Materials handling
		Paperwork
	Incoming inspection	Labor
		Paperwork
	Billing	Paperwork
Manufacture	Material receipt	Materials handling
		Paperwork
	Setup	Labor
		Material
		Overhead
	Run-in	Labor
		Material
		Overhead
	Shutdown	Labor
		Material
		Overhead
		Paperwork

of these circumstances. Most of the ordering costs, especially for purchase orders, speak for themselves. Notice that costs of processing paperwork crop up at almost every phase of the purchase order cycle. One of the big advantages claimed by vendors of computerized inventory control systems is a reduction in paperwork costs by reducing both the paper processing time and the sheer quantity of paper handled. Shipping costs which count as ordering costs are those which are fixed with respect to shipment quantity and occur every time something is shipped. For example, when a freight car must be left on a siding while it is unloaded, a demurrage charge is customarily made to cover "rental" and handling of the freight car. If orders usually fill only a fraction of a car, this charge is fixed with respect to the quantity ordered. If there are typically many carloads per order, the demurrage charge is properly part of the material cost rather than the ordering cost, since the charge is incremental with the quantity of material ordered. Similar reasoning applies to other shipping costs. To cite another example, pickup costs are ordering costs if, say, a single van is sent to pick up an order regardless of the order size.

Sometimes the distinction between fixed and variable ordering costs is refined by defining a *header* cost as a fixed ordering cost and a *line* cost as the cost per line item ordered. Both these costs are fixed with respect to the quantity ordered and hence are part of the ordering cost, as in chapter 5.

For manufacturing (shop) orders, the most commonly recognized ordering cost is labor associated with the time required to set up a production process (e.g., machine). Table 8-6 is intended to emphasize the fact that many other costs are incurred because a batch is run. There are labor, material, and overhead costs associated with not only the setup of a batch but also the run-in (early portion of the batch) and shutdown. A material cost at setup occurs if a "pipeline" must be filled with material before the batch can be run, as in a paper press or sewing machine. An overhead cost at setup could be cost of energy to heat up the process (furnace, soldering iron). If capacity on a machine is critical, the machine downtime may be considered an overhead cost. Run-in costs include material costs such as early rejects, labor costs such as those resulting from the learning curve phenomenon, and overhead costs such as supervision for items produced early in the batch. Shutdown costs such as disassembly of fixtures, lubrication, and clean-up have material, labor, and overhead components.

Since most ordering costs are associated with the occurrence of tangible events, estimation is not as difficult as for the other cost categories. Occasionally, however, it may not be possible to directly estimate an ordering cost. For example, a supplier may state a material cost which implicitly contains an ordering cost. The *implicit ordering cost* in the price structure "$0.89 for the first 5 units and $0.10 per unit thereafter" is clearly $0.39. The implicit setup cost in the next example is not quite so obvious.

Example 8-1 Seven batches of a product have recently been produced. The operator has recorded the time spent on each batch on the work log. The resulting data appear in table 8-7. The operator's time costs $10 per hour, including wages and fringe benefits. What is the implicit setup cost?

The data are plotted in figure 8-1. A linear relationship between time and batch size is recognized by fitting a line $y_i = a_0 + a_1 x_i$ through the data. (Of course, a_1 is the slope and a_0 is the y intercept.) Here, a_0 is an implicit setup cost, and a_1 is an implicit cost per piece produced. The

Table 8-7 Production data for example 8-1

Batch, i	1	2	3	4	5	6	7
Batch size x_i	14	20	23	10	6	31	19
Time (minutes)	55	74	81	45	34	110	76
Cost ($), y_i	9.17	12.33	13.53	7.52	5.68	18.33	12.67

238 PART III: INVENTORY CONTROL DATA

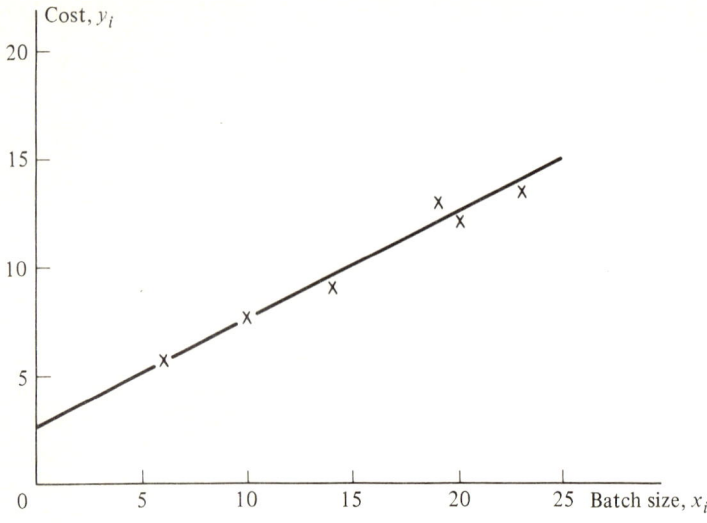

Figure 8-1 Linear regression of the data in table 8-7.

line in figure 8-1 was fitted graphically; linear regression can be used to obtain a more scientific estimate of the setup cost. For example 8-1, it turns out (see problem 8-1) that the y intercept is $2.50, which is the setup cost estimate sought.

In concluding this chapter, the following general framework for all cost estimation activities is offered. For each cost of interest:

1. Identify the cost as an incremental cost. Sometimes the biggest problem in cost estimation is identifying which costs are incremented, and therefore must be estimated. Tables 8-4, 8-5, and 8-6 are designed to aid in identifying these costs. In any event, a cost is incremental if it is affected by the basic inventory control decisions—when and how much to order. Much depends on the time scale involved. In the short run, very few costs are really incremental; in the long run, all are.
2. Devise a means of estimating the incremental costs. For this purpose, accounting data are the most likely source. More often than not (especially in manufacturing concerns), alternative sources of cost information will prove as useful. These sources are both internal and external to the firm. Internal sources include purchasing, production planning and control, warehouse records, and marketing, to name a few. External sources might be vendors, cooperative competitors, published literature, conference contacts, and government indices. Sampling may be used if time is of the essence. In seeking accounting information, approach the

right *kind* of accountant. The accounting profession recognizes two accounting disciplines. The *financial* accountant is concerned with preparation of financial statements and opinions regarding the profitability and worth of the company. She or he may be of help in inventory valuation (material costs). The other type of accountant is called a *managerial*, or cost, accountant. Her or his primary responsibility is the preparation of information which will assist management in making decisions. This person is most likely to be able to provide desired cost estimates.
3. Establish a system for recurring cost estimation. Estimation will be a less formidable task if steps are taken to facilitate future estimating. Costs can be recorded over time and monitored for trends, unusual deviations, and checks that they are still incremental. Some of the techniques for time series documentation and forecasting developed for demands in chapter 7 can be applied to cost data as well. Costs can be forecast to predict future effects of present decisions. An inventory cost data base, whether computerized or not, provides a framework for cost data maintenance and a valuable supplement to the information kept by accountants.

8-5 SUMMARY

The subject of cost estimation has been addressed for each of the four main categories of inventory-related costs: material, holding, shortage, and ordering costs. Material costs are doubly important because they affect the holding cost category as well. Material costs include certain quality-related and overhead costs as well as the costs of acquisition. Accounting data are especially appropriate for use in estimating material costs. Since accountants differ in methods of timing and costing of issues, as well as in valuation bases (such as cost or market), care must be taken in interpreting these data.

Holding costs consist of capital costs, service costs, storage costs, and risk costs. Capital costs are often found to be the most significant of these elements. The cost of capital used depends on several factors such as financing costs, rates of return on other investments, as well as the risk and duration of investments.

Shortage costs are especially difficult to measure because they are highly probabilistic in nature and are partially beyond the control of the firm. Also, the firm must decide how to balance controllable remedial costs such as overtime and emergency purchases against resultant costs such as lost sales and downtime.

Ordering costs are fairly straightforward to estimate. Such costs are those which occur as a result of ordering, but do not vary with the quantity ordered.

240 PART III: INVENTORY CONTROL DATA

In general, successful cost estimating requires that only incremental costs be recognized, and that nonaccounting as well as accounting data sources be used.

REFERENCES

1. Carter, Albert G.: "Computing Inventory R.O.I.," *Management Accounting*, pp. 43–45, July 1973.
2. Flora, J. W.: "Tax Rates, Profits and the Inventory Carrying Charge Rate," *Production and Inventory Management*, vol. 13, no. 2, pp. 35–40, second quarter, 1972.
3. Hall, Thomas W.: "Inventory Carrying Costs: A Case Study," *Management Accounting*, pp. 37–39, January 1974.
4. Lambert, Douglas M., and B. J. La Londe: "Inventory Carrying Costs," *Management Accounting*, pp. 31–35, August 1967.
5. Magee, John F.: "Guides to Inventory Policy—1: Functions and Lot Sizes," *Harvard Business Review*, January–February 1956. See the section on inventory costs.
6. Simons, Harry: "Intermediate Accounting," South-Western, Cincinnati, 1972. See chapters 8 through 10.

EXERCISES

8-1 Use linear regression to derive an implicit ordering cost for the data of example 8-1. That is, determine the value of a_0 which minimizes the value of

$$\sum_{j=1}^{7} [y_j - (a_0 + a_1 x_j)]^2$$

8-2 Identify all setup costs associated with a spray-painting booth in which a batch is a production run of items which all receive three coats of the same color finish.

8-3 The direct labor dollar cost per unit of an item assembled and put into inventory has varied over the past 10 months as follows: 13, 15, 14, 12, 14, 13, 16, 12, 11, 13. Use first-order exponential smoothing to estimate a current value for this component of the material cost for this item. Use $\alpha = 0.25$. Refer to equation (7-19).

8-4 A supplier offers a 10 percent discount off the cost of $14 per unit ordered, for all units ordered in excess of 20. The shipping cost is $10 per shipment ordered, plus $1 per unit shipped. What are the unit ordering cost and unit material cost if 25 units are customarily ordered? *Hint:* Section 3-2 may be of assistance.

PART
FOUR

INVENTORY CONTROL SYSTEMS

CHAPTER
NINE

THE INVENTORY CONTROL SYSTEM

The final chapter of this book addresses matters related to the design of an inventory control system. At the very least, this involves a synthesis of the concepts developed in earlier chapters. There is more to system design, however, than a pure aggregation of techniques. Additional considerations are an absolute requirement for a truly workable system. Consider what has been covered in all the preceding chapters. Leaving aside the introductory material, chapters 3 through 6 were devoted to inventory control *procedures*, chapter 7 to forecasting *procedures* and demand *data*, and chapter 8 to cost *data*. The first section of this chapter, correspondingly, develops systems concepts pertaining to procedures, while the second section addresses system data concepts. It will be seen that in both these sections the concepts transcend those which were covered earlier. For example, in section 9-1, procedures are identified as being of four types: planning, execution, system maintenance, and external reporting. The choices of ordering decision models and forecasting models discussed in chapters 3 through 7 are planning procedures. Forecast updating is an execution procedure. Cost estimation is taken here to be a system maintenance procedure. But in each of the four categories, additional procedures are essential to the operation of a successful system.

In section 9-2 it will be seen that data of the type discussed in chapters 7 and 8 cannot be considered in isolation, but must be structured in such a way that the procedures in section 9-1 can be performed efficiently. The typical inventory control system processes thousands of data elements in a very short time. Hence care must be taken just to make sure that the right data are in the right place at the right time.

A third section addresses the problem of maintaining system integrity. Assurance that the system is "telling the truth" is as elusive as it is critical. The costly consequences of failure to achieve this assurance warrant the attention given to this topic.

9-1 INVENTORY CONTROL SYSTEM PROCEDURES

Procedures are the action portion of the inventory control system, involving some transformation of data. In this section it is assumed that data are always available in a form appropriate for performing the procedures. This is so that the procedures themselves can be the object in focus. Problems associated with data are discussed in section 9-2. As mentioned above, procedures are divided into four groups. This is done on the basis of the level of decision making involved. At the lowest level, the routine activities which affect inventory levels occur. These activities include receiving and issuing of stock and ordering. Procedures for performing these activities are called *execution* procedures. The other three categories of procedures govern higher levels of decision making. These are described below. A final subsection is concerned with the computerization of various procedures and the automation of decision making.

Planning Procedures

"Planning procedures" are defined here as those procedures for deciding how each inventory item will be controlled. This involves two determinations: choice of an ordering decision model and choice of a forecasting model. In most inventories, the best choice of these models is not the same for all items in the inventory. This is due to the *Pareto effect*: "In a many-item inventory, relatively few items require a high degree of control, while the majority of items require a low degree of control."

This effect is named after Vilfredo Pareto, a nineteenth-century economist who, while studying the distribution of wealth among the population, observed that a high fraction (90 percent) of wealth accrued to a low fraction (10 percent) of the population. This same phenomenon occurs in all walks of life. Figuratively speaking, 90 percent of the people in the world occupy 10 percent of the land area; 90 percent of the corn-producing acres in the United States are in 10 percent of the states; and so on. For inventory control purposes, 90 percent of the value of exercising strict control may reside in 10 percent of the items. Traditionally, this value has been measured on the basis of dollar volume, or dollar sales. That is, it has been felt that the highest level of control should be applied to that 10 percent of all items in the inventory which account for 90 percent of the dollar sales. This has given rise to the *ABC classification*. All items are ranked according to their dollar sales (highest first). Then the items comprising, say, 80 percent of the dollar sales are A-class items; the items comprising the next 15 percent of sales are classed as B items; the remaining items are C items. If the Pareto effect applies to the inventory involved, then, say, 20 percent of the items would be in class A, 30 percent in class B, and 50 percent in class C. Then the highest level of control effort would be applied to the A items.

Blind application of ABC control techniques on the basis of the Pareto effect would be as foolhardy as the blind use of a single control technique for all items.

There is nothing sacred about the ABC classification. More likely than not, more categories will be appropriate. Figure 9-1 and table 9-1 illustrate a hypothetical five-class control procedure. Table 9-1 also demonstrates that more than one procedure can be stratified on the basis of the ABC(DE) classification. Both ordering decision models and forecasting models are allowed to differ by class. The values given are intended to be only representative; relative values are more important than absolute ones. Suggested approaches are also intended to depict only relative differences. The approaches for A items are too costly for use with other classes. B-category

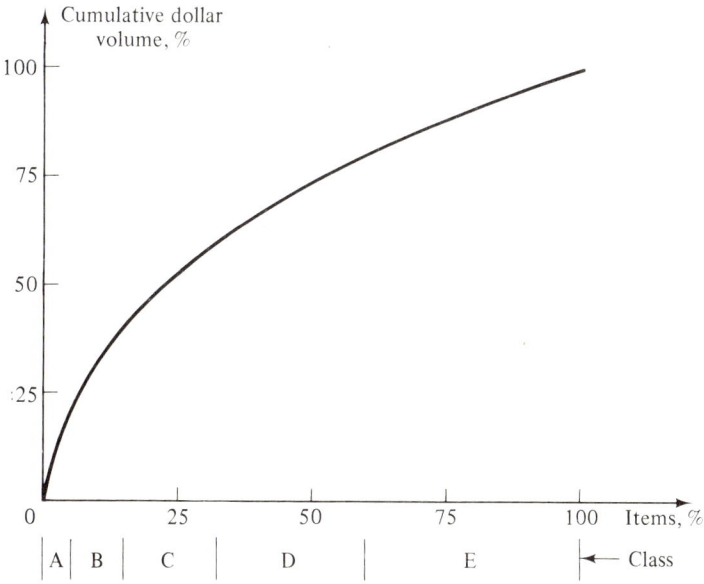

Figure 9-1 A hypothetical five-class stratification of inventory items based on dollar volume. Illustrates the Pareto effect.

Table 9-1 Stratification of hypothetical inventory control and forecasting approaches based on Pareto distribution of demand activity

Demand $-volume category	A	B	C	D	E
$ demand per item per year (relative)	$>10^3$	10^2-10^3	$10-10^2$	$1-10$	$0-1$
Suggested inventory control approaches	Continuous review. Consider each item individually	Periodic review. Possibly coordinated replenishment	Maintain an order-up-to level. Coordinate with higher-demand items	Maintain a stock level of 1 or 2	Do not stock
Suggested forecasting approaches	Box-Jenkins models; deliberate manual review	Smoothing and averaging models	Simple averages	None (possibly a forecast of time between orders)	None

items require reasonable control procedures with low cost per order and per forecast update. Items in class C have demand volume sufficient to warrant maintaining an inventory level which consists mainly of a buffer stock. These items barely warrant a conventional forecast. D-category items are demanded only occasionally. Stock levels of one or a few units are maintained (depending on the typical order size). Replenishment is made whenever demand occurs. Conventional forecasts are meaningless for such "lumpy" demand. Class E items are not stocked, so forecasts are of no value. Other applications of the Pareto effect include frequency of physical inventory (cycle counting) and degree of stockroom security.

Dollar volume is not the only meaningful classification basis. A D item may have very low sales but extremely high dollar value per unit. Also, in a manufacturing environment, low dollar volume does not mean that no control should be applied. For lack of a cheap part, a production line may be shut down. In this case, low dollar volume means that quantities may be kept on hand which will satisfy demand for a long period of time; however, vigilance against shortages is still required.

To complete the planning procedures, the parameters of the models selected for ordering and forecasting must be determined. Thus if a periodic review (s, S) policy is indicated for an item, the values of s and S must be specified. If exponential smoothing is used to forecast an item, the value of α has to be selected. The bulk of chapters 3 through 7 was devoted to the derivation of such parameter values on the basis of costs and demand history.

Execution Procedures

"Execution procedures" are defined as those procedures which (1) carry out plans which were developed as a result of the planning procedures above and (2) record stockroom transactions. These two are closely related. The stockroom transactions involve receiving and issuing, while the execution of planning procedures includes order placement and forecast updating. Order placement generates stock on order which later will be matched with receipts. Receipts will be compared with issues to determine stock on hand. Issues will be balanced against demand to ascertain what shortages exist. Demands will be used to update the forecast, which in turn will provide input to the order placement process. Thus the execution procedures are linked, the bonds being the use of common information. This information is discussed in section 9-2.

System Maintenance Procedures

System maintenance procedures involve *adjustments* to the system caused by unique changes in the properties of the inventory. This is distinct from execution procedures, which dealt with routine transactions. Adjustments include (1) addition or deletion of items from the inventory control system, (2) adjustments to cost data, and (3) adjustments to inventory quantity levels. The latter adjustments occur as a result of physical count and discovery of discrepancies between actual stock levels and those recorded in the system.

Addition or deletion of items included in the system occurs promptly out of the necessity to control the items. Adjustment of quantity levels also occurs regularly, because of accounting inventory valuation requirements. However, the cost data tend to get updated very infrequently.

External Reporting Procedures

The fourth type of procedure is external reporting, which conveys information about system performance to its evaluators. These procedures can be for financial purposes (such as the accounting report on inventory valuation just mentioned), but are usually oriented toward management evaluation. Such auxiliary reports, not needed for direct, day-to-day control of inventories, are often overlooked in system design. Some typical management reports (just to name a few) are as follows:

1. *Vendor performance:* on-time deliveries, proper quantities, adequate quality
2. *Buyer performance:* avoidance of shortages, attainment of favorable prices, appropriate order quantities
3. *Service level:* percentage of demand for an item satisfied on time, one week late, two weeks late, etc.
4. *Slow-moving stock:* list of items lacking demand, together with their inventory levels and suggestions for downgrading to a lower class, return to vendor, dumping, etc.
5. Inventory as a percentage of sales or inventory "turns per year" (which is sales divided by average inventory level)

Like any report designed to enhance management evaluation, these reports should provide meaningful comparisons—vendor against vendor, performance of one division versus another, performance of a firm versus its competitors, performance over time, actual performance versus "optimal" performance.

There are endless possibilities for such reports. The most important implication of such reports for system design is that the data needed to generate the reports must be systematically accumulated over time.

Table 9-2 summarizes the principal inventory control procedures together with a hypothetical range of frequencies of performance of each

Table 9-2 Typical inventory control procedures and representative frequencies of performance

Procedure category	Procedure	Frequency (times per year)
Planning	Ordering decision rule selection	2–4
	Forecast model selection	2–4
	Decision rule parameter determination	2–4
	Forecast model parameter determination	2–4
Execution	Order placement and recording	52–365
	Forecast updating	12–52
	Stock transaction recording	52–∞
	Physical inventory	1–4
	Cycle counting	12–365
System maintenance	Addition/deletion of items	52–365
	Adjustments to cost data	4–12
	Adjustments to quantity data	1–365
External reporting	Managerial report generation	12–365
	Financial report generation	4–12

procedure. The frequencies depend on the particular application and on the degree of computerization of the system, which is the topic of the next subsection.

Computerization of Procedures

Most multi-item inventories today are controlled by procedures which are, to some extent, computerized. It is generally accepted that computerization realizes benefits on several fronts. These benefits can include

Faster data processing
More accurate data processing
Reduction in paperwork
Labor savings
More informed decision making

Of course, the benefits are not cost-free. In addition to the tangible costs associated with acquiring, staffing, and maintaining a computer facility, there is the price of discipline. A computerized system is more demanding of managerial talent and diligence than a manual one. Like the proverbial girl with the curl in the middle of her forehead, a computerized system can, when good, be very very good, but will, if bad, be horrid. The system being computerized must be workable; a computerized nonsystem cannot be.

Conceptually, any of the procedures in table 9-2 can be computerized. However, since the computer best handles procedures with high levels of computation and low levels of judgment, it is not surprising that such procedures promise the most value per unit of computerization expense. Now, it happens that the procedures which occur most frequently tend to be those which involve the most computation and the least judgment. Hence the execution procedures, along with the maintenance procedure of addition and deletion of items, are most likely to involve heavy use of computerized information. Indeed, stock transaction recording is the first candidate for computerization. It becomes harder to justify computerization of the less frequently performed procedures. For instance, should order placement be computerized? Again, it is the computational and not the judgmental aspects of a procedure which should be computerized. Thus orders for nuts and bolts might be computerized, while those for costlier items would not. Often, a computer will be programmed to *suggest* orders to a purchaser who applies personal judgment to approve or disapprove the suggestion.

Even if all procedures are not computerized, all items should be. Even if complete manual control of an item is called for, the computer makes an excellent record keeper for stock levels, transaction history, and inventory valuation. Also, it is simpler to administer a uniform policy of transaction recording to all items, rather than wrestling with two classes of items.

Today's computerized inventory control systems have maximized the value of the benefits listed above by making feasible instant transaction recording. Such transaction-oriented systems rely on terminals or other communication devices placed at the points where the transactions occur—receiving dock, inspection area, stockroom, point of sale. Users can interact with the system, requesting information for decision making or updating the stored data. Batch transaction processing remains either an alternative to the terminal-based system or a supplement to it for the less frequent procedures, such as cost updating and quantity adjustments resulting from a physical inventory.

9-2 INVENTORY CONTROL SYSTEM DATA

The procedures identified in section 9-1 all involve processing of data. In that section, data were assumed to be available as needed. This section explores problems associated with ensuring that the proper data are available in a timely manner for each procedure to be performed. This will be done in the context of a computerized system; however, the ideas apply to manual systems as well. For example, a computerized procedure may be referred to as a *program*, e.g., a transaction processing program. Similarly, data files will appear as if they are residing in a computer storage device such as a disk or magnetic tape. Since most control systems for many-item inventories are at least partially computerized, this is an appropriate format.

As was pointed out earlier, the transaction processing procedure is the prime candidate for computerization, and if anything is computerized, it usually is. (There are always exceptions. Conceivably, a computer could be used to determine ordering policy parameters for items which were manually controlled.) For this reason, the data requirements for transaction processing will be discussed first.

The simplest data structure consists of a single *file* which contains all the necessary data. This file is composed of a sequence of records. Each *record* pertains to a single item, or stock-keeping unit, and is subdivided into a string of *fields*. Each field contains a data element. The file will be called simply the *inventory file* (sometimes referred to as the *item master file*).

A representative set of fields contained in each record of an inventory file appears in table 9-3. Although the meanings of most of the data elements listed there are apparent, a few interpretive comments are in order. Record numbers are for file processing purposes. Group codes link items which have something (usually a vendor) in common. Value classification codes are of the ABC type. Order policy codes might be used to designate such options as periodic review, reorder point, optional replenishment, manual order only, etc. Safety factors are values which are multiplied by the standard errors of forecast to obtain safety stocks. Forecast policy codes could include exponential smoothing (or any other forecast models from chapter 7) or no forecast. The smoothing constant fields apply if exponential smoothing is chosen as the forecast policy code. Average demands would be moving averages over recent history. Demand history might consist of several fields containing demands for each of several recent time periods. The forecast value would be for the current or an upcoming period of time. The quantity on reserve is that quantity earmarked for specific demands.

It should be clear that there is a high degree of flexibility regarding what fields should or should not be included in the inventory records. The fields in table 9-3 are merely suggested as typical ones. Many data elements have been excluded to keep the exposition as straightforward as possible. Order quantity restrictions, such as upper and lower limits or requirements that orders be an integer multiple of a given quantity, are examples of such elements.

The right-hand side of table 9-3 displays interactions of each data field with each of several programs (procedures) taken from table 9-2. Fields altered as a result of a program are shown with "O" (output) interactions, while fields used only as sources of data are displayed as having "I" (input) interactions. Technically speaking, some fields are input to a program, altered, and then output again. Most fields affected by the transaction recording program are of this type. In these cases, the input relationship is

Table 9-3 Representative fields in each record of an inventory file and their interaction with several programs

Field	Description	Ordering decision rule parameter determination	Stock transaction recording	Order placement and recording
RN	Record number			
IN	Item number	I	I	I
ID	Item description	I		I
GC	Group code	I		I
VC	Value classification code	I		I
OP	Order policy code	I		I
RP	Reorder point	O		I
RQ	Reorder quantity	O		I
RL	Reorder level	O		I
HC	Holding cost	I		
OC	Ordering cost	I		
MC	Material cost	I		
SC	Shortage cost	I		
RT	Review time	I		I
LT	Lead time	I		I
SF	Safety factor	I		
SS	Safety stock	O		I
FP	Forecast policy code			
AL	Smoothing constant			
AD	Average demand		O	
DH	Demand history		O	
SD	Standard deviation—demand		O	
SE	Standard error of forecast			
FV	Forecast value			I
OH	On hand		O	I
OO	On order		O	O
OR	On reserve		O	
CI	Cumulative issues		O	
CR	Cumulative receipts		O	
CP	Cumulative adjustments positive		O	
CN	Cumulative adjustments negative		O	

suppressed. Keep in mind that these are inputs to and outputs from the inventory files, not from the user interface.

Note that except for identification of the item number, the only inputs to the stock transaction recording program are data related to stock status or activity measures of the item. Stock transaction recording involves essentially no judgment—just updating of the files. (Recall that this is what rendered transaction recording an ideal candidate for computerization.) The logic involved in transaction recording is, however, not as trivial as this might imply. If only the *normal* events affecting inventory levels occurred, namely receipts from vendors and issues to satisfy demands, transaction recording would be trivial. However, successful inventory control systems are designed to accommodate *nonnormal* events since these do occur in the real world. Otherwise, the system would be inadequate in the face of such "messy" transactions as returns to stock of unused material, returns to vendor of defective material, breakage, pilferage, return of stock by dissatisfied customers, etc. Table 9-4 is designed to illustrate a logical approach to recognizing the effects of the many varied transactions on the fields of an inventory record. The symbols + and − designate increases and decreases, respectively, to the values contained in the fields. Notice that all entries under the four "cumulative" fields are positive. The cumulative issues and receipts are a measure of activity level for the item, which may be used to classify the item (ABC) or to determine implications for materials han-

Table 9-4 Effects of inventory transaction recording on fields of the inventory file records

Transaction	Fields affected (cf. table 9-3)							
	OH	OO	OR	CI	CR	CP	CN	DH
Receipt of ordered material	+	−			+			
Receipt of unordered material	+				+			
Issue of unreserved material	−			+				+
Issue of reserved material	−		−	+				
No-history issue	−			+				
Order placement or increase		+						
Order cancellation or reduction		−						
Reservation of material			+					
Cancellation of reservation			−					
Returned goods—nondefective	+				+			−
Returned goods—defective, replace	−				+			
Returned goods—defective, for credit								−
Return to supplier for reworking	−	+		+				
Positive error correction	+					+		
Negative error correction	−						+	

dling capacity requirements. The cumulative adjustments measure system accuracy and shrinkage. The "reservation of material" transaction can cause the amount of stock on reserve to exceed stock on hand, which implies a backorder situation. The "no history issue" can be used to record (1) satisfaction of an unusual demand which should not be allowed to inflate forecasts, (2) return to vendor of good merchandise for credit, or (3) disposal of material from stock. No two transactions listed in table 9-4 have the same effect on the fields. Even so, some transactions affecting stock levels may still not be covered by any of the listed transactions. See problem 9-2.

The inventory control system described so far consists of a single file together with several programs which use that file as a data base, both receiving and depositing information into the file. Many systems in use require more than a single file; in fact, dozens of files can be involved [6]. Individual programs, then, commonly use several files. The following example demonstrates a hypothetical *open-order file*, which is a likely second file to add to a (computerized) system.

Once authorization to make a purchase is obtained, a purchaser decides on a vendor on the basis of price, delivery, and quality of material. An order is placed, lead time elapses, and the order is received—maybe on time, maybe late, and maybe not at all. Also, the material received might or might not conform in type or quantity to that specified in the purchase order. The importance to effective inventory control of monitoring open orders is clear. However, the information shown in the inventory file above is completely inadequate for use in order monitoring and followup. The only information contained there is the total on-order quantity for each item. Data of the type shown as fields in table 9-5 would be more appropriate for open-order control. A record would be created in the open-order file every time an order is placed and would remain there until the order is closed, i.e., until all items included in the order have been satisfactorily received and accounts payable information is complete. The records in the open-order file are not in a meaningful order, and therefore they must be either linked (using pointers which point, say, to the next existing record for the same item) or sorted on one or more of the fields. Table 9-6 displays some of the many uses to which information in an open-order file can be put, depending on the order in which the information is disseminated.

It is seen that when an order is placed, or when material is received, the program which records the transaction must have access to both the inventory file and the open-order file. This is typical of the many-file systems alluded to above. Commonly, many files must be accessed by each program. Moreover, if the inventory control system is interactive, implying that the system is capable of almost instantaneous response to a wide variety of user requests, it is likely that most of the files related to the system will have to be readily accessible most of the time.

Table 9-5 Representative fields in each record of an open-order file and their interaction with order-related events

Description of field	Placement of order	Modification of order	Receipt of material	Closing of order
Purchaser I.D. code	X			
Order serial number	X			
Date order placed	X			
Vendor I.D. code	X			
Item ordered	X			
Quantity ordered	X	X		
Price per unit	X	X		
Delivery date (promised)	X	X		
"Deliver-to" code (department)	X			
Date actually received			X	
Quantity actually received			X	
Receipt document number			X	
Amount charged			X	
Closing flag				X

Table 9-6 Uses of sorted open-order file data

Primary sort	Secondary sort	Applications
Vendor	Date order placed	Writing of the order document
Purchaser	Vendor	Vendor relations; eligibility for quantity discounts
Item number	Delivery date	Material control; expediting, followup on delinquent delivery
Vendor	Date received minus promise date (if nonzero)	Exception reporting
	Quantity ordered minus quantity received (if nonzero)	Input to vendor performance rating
Date received	Vendor	Input to accounts payable
Vendor	Date promised	Closing of purchase order
Purchaser	Item	Input to purchaser performance analysis
Delivery date	Vendor	Writing of "expected receipts" list for receiving planning purposes

There is an economic limit to the number of files which a (computerized) system will support. This limit represents a balance between the value of rapid system responses and the cost of supporting the file accessibility. Certainly the determination of the size, composition, and accessibility of the files involved in an inventory control system is a matter of careful design, as is the specification of all the programs which will access those files. The discussion in this chapter, meant only to develop a level of appreciation, barely scratches the surface of these design considerations. The reader is referred to [5] and [6] for deeper insights into these topics. Of particular value there to those interested would be the implication for file and program requirements of systems for controlling a multiechelon inventory such as that of a manufacturing concern. These systems involve production planning and scheduling concepts beyond the scope of this book. However, the sections on material requirements planning relate to the discussion of that topic in chapter 6.

9-3 INVENTORY CONTROL SYSTEM INTEGRITY

For any system to be effective, the following questions should both be answered in the affirmative: (1) Are the proper data available with which to make good decisions? (2) Are good decisions being made? For our purposes, these two questions are asking whether there exists integrity in the data and in the procedures embodied in an inventory control system. These questions, then, comprise an audit of the system described in the first two sections of this chapter. They are considered separately in the subsections below.

Data Integrity

Inventory control system data integrity can be ensured by design and operational efforts. Design effort is intended to prevent erroneous information from entering or existing in the system. Operational effort is expected to make sure that true information continues to exist in the system by detection and correction of errors. There is an analogy between design versus operational and the preventive versus corrective efforts of any quality assurance program.

Occasionally, the existence of faulty data will manifest itself. Such symptoms as a negative balance where negative balances are impossible (e.g., quantity on reserve) or an unreasonably large or small value point to the need for some file maintenance. Similarly, unreasonable derived quantities such as order quantities or forecasts suggest that the fundamental data from which the quantities were derived are incorrect. Correction is usually straightforward. A well-designed system will catch some logically detectable errors at point of input, refusing acceptance of such data into the system. "Unreasonable" values can be made logically detectable by programming in acceptable value ranges for computer comparison.

More often than not, a data error will go undetected until either an undesirable consequence (e.g., a surprise shortage) occurs or it is accidentally uncovered as a result of some sort of audit procedure. Thus the biggest operational effort in most firms is a formal, periodic check of system data values against values verified by other means.

The *physical inventory* is the classical count-based check on inventory quantities. Traditionally, the physical inventory was taken primarily for dollar valuation purposes, all counts being in dollars. This is, of course, of minimal benefit for inventory control purposes. Fortunately, thanks to computer technology, physical inventories usually include the association of a stock-keeping unit with each count.

Ironically, the physical inventory itself is an error-prone procedure. Normally, the counting is done by persons other than those who usually handle the inventory. This helps to ensure an unbiased count, but can cause miscounts resulting from the inclusion of defective items, consignment goods, and the like. The inventory is frequently taken under "plant shutdown" procedures, with resulting time pressure and fatigue from working long and late. Double counts, each blind to the other, with third-party verification is the best remedy under the circumstances.

The alternative of *cycle counting* is increasingly being accepted in lieu of physical inventory taking, at least for some classes of stock. Under this procedure, a small fraction of items are counted, say, daily or weekly. By the time the fiscal period has elapsed, all items under cycle counting have been counted at least once, and some many times. Since cycle counting is a sampling procedure, often it is felt that each item should be sampled in proportion to its "importance." Importance is measured, say, by unit cost, value of stock on hand, or value demanded per unit time.

There is economic appeal for the use of an *event-based* variant of cycle counting. Under this approach, an item is counted when some event occurs. For example, an item might be counted whenever an issue is made. This would have the advantage that active items are counted more often (perhaps too often). A major advantage to event-based counting is that counts can be made when stock levels are low, thereby saving counting effort. Counting prior to a scheduled receipt is an example. Since the computer can be used to specify which items should be counted, another possibility would be to count those items for which a shortage (based on recent demand level and stock on hand) is imminent [problem 9-4(*b*)].

Another variation on the cycle-counting theme is to "count" stock locations (i.e., identify items and item counts in a fixed storage area) rather than items. This has the advantage of finding items which have been "lost" by the system. Storage location misinformation is just as serious as quantity errors.

Other vulnerable data generation points are at receiving and issuing. Vigilance is required to ensure that stock received is accounted for, especially since vendor packing lists are not divinely inspired. Issuing frequently involves picking material from a larger quantity (e.g., pallet load). Not uncommonly, several partial pallets of an item will exist in stock at the same time and in different storage locations. Of course, this makes inventory counting more difficult and error-prone. Anderson [1] cites a case study in which data accuracy problems of the type mentioned here were detected and corrected.

Even if all transactions are correctly recorded, errors will occur in proportion to the delay in time between transaction occurrence and recording. The trend toward interactive, immediate-response (terminal-based) systems is no doubt due in part to the resulting reduction of stale information in the inventory control system.

Procedural Integrity

As was the case with data integrity, procedural integrity is ensured both by design (prevention) and by operation (correction). In this case, procedural design is intended to minimize the occasion for error, while corrective measures are supposed to detect the control procedures that are generating error. The most important idea to keep in mind in designing integrity-assurance measures is that procedural integrity is primarily a *people* problem. It is the human being on whom integrity depends. Thus the design which ensures procedural integrity is the design which minimizes opportunity for error or fraud. The operational assurance of integrity takes the form of human performance appraisal.

It turns out that if a system is designed with procedural integrity in mind, then performance appraisal is also enhanced. Such a system will have built-in checks and balances which in the short run result in rapid correction of mistakes. Then, in the long run, the record of mistake corrections provides the basis for performance appraisal.

Consider figure 9-2. Depicted there is a hypothetical set of decision makers (rows) for the ordering-receiving cycle of an inventory control system. The objects being controlled by these people (information, material, and funds) are shown (columns) as they might flow during the cycle. The reader is encouraged to become thoroughly familiar with figure 9-2 before proceeding. The comparisons indicated there are the keys to procedural integrity. These are described below.

Comparison C1, made by the inventory controller, compares the purchase requisition made by him or her with the purchase order prepared by the

CHAPTER 9: THE INVENTORY CONTROL SYSTEM **259**

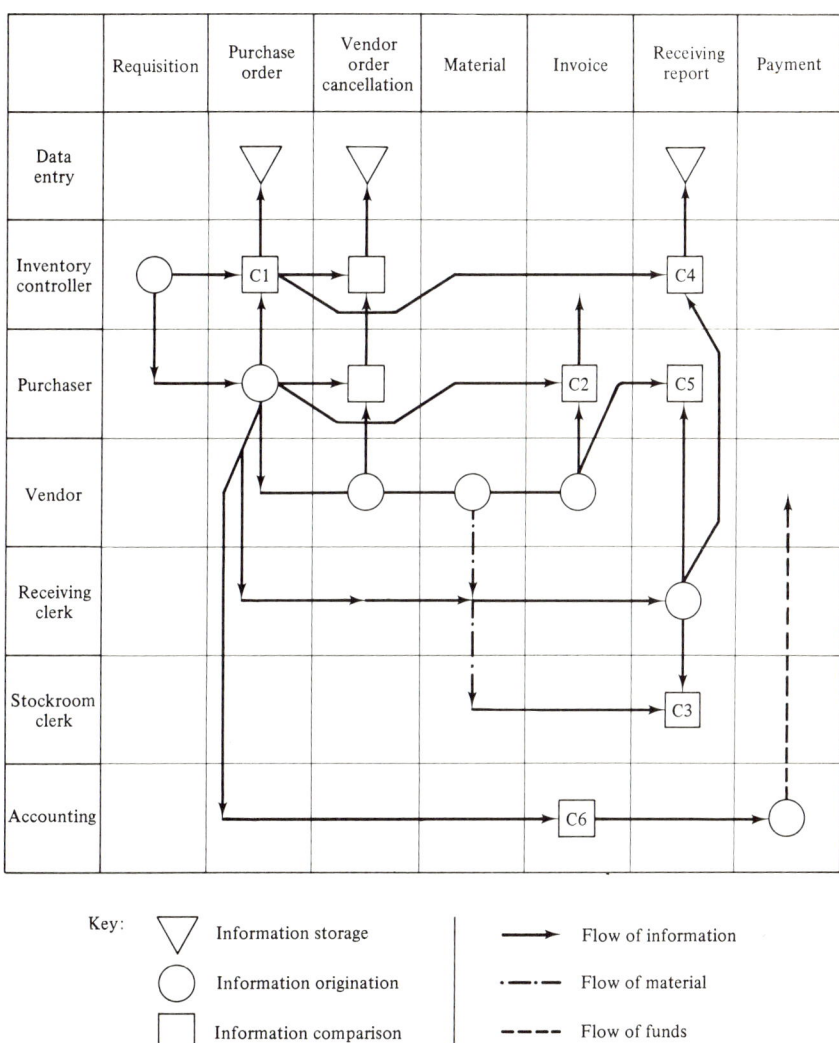

Figure 9-2 System of checks to assure procedural integrity for stock ordering and receipt.

purchaser. Price or quantity discrepancies can be ironed out immediately. In the long term, a record of such differences can contribute to a purchaser performance appraisal.

Comparison C2 is a check made by the purchaser that the basic terms (price and delivery) specified in the purchase order agree with what was shipped, as indicated on the invoice. Discrepancies can be transmitted to the inventory controller who otherwise has no need to see the invoice. Records of C2 are an important ingredient in vendor performance appraisal.

Comparison C3 is a check on the accuracy of the count generated by the receiving clerk. The copy of the purchase order sent to the receiving clerk indicates vendor, receipt date, and items, but no quantities, in order to ensure an independent count.

Comparison C4 is a quantity check made by the inventory controller prior to the updating of inventory system records.

Comparison C5 is another quantity check to ensure that what was paid for was received.

Comparison C6 is an overall audit of the reasonableness of the invoice prior to payment. Long-term quantity discounts are verified and applied to the invoice quantity.

Scrutiny of the above hypothetical system will reveal that most checks have been made more than once. This redundancy not only screens out error but also keeps people honest. This is because responsibility for the redundant checks is segregated into various functions around the firm. This segregation of duty has long been recognized by accountants as a key contributor to what they refer to as *internal control*. Internal control is, for our purposes, synonymous with procedural integrity. Further information relating to internal control may be found in [2] and [3].

Up to this point, the discussion in this subsection has concerned integrity of procedures for ordering and receiving stock. The remaining procedures involve storing and issuing stock. The main procedural integrity consideration in storage is assurance of stock security. Handling and storage systems both should be designed to minimize pilferage and damage to stock. This can involve control of environment (temperature, humidity), proper training of stock handlers, and, most importantly, limitation of access to storage areas. One of the advantages claimed by the manufacturers of automatic storage and retrieval systems is that the "warehouse without people" is an enhancement of stock security.

Integrity of stock-issuing procedures is approached in the same manner as it was for ordering and receiving procedures. The reader is asked to try this in problem 9-5.

In summary, inventory control system design has been depicted as a three-sided challenge: Decide what procedures are included; structure the data system to support the procedures; ensure the integrity of the system. If equal effort is expended on each of those three, the system just might work.

9-4 SUMMARY

Without a system, all the modeling and data discussed in earlier chapters would be of limited value for controlling multi-item inventories. Systems are viewed as consisting of a framework of procedures which are driven by data.

Procedures are identified as being of four types:

1. Planning procedures include determination of ordering policies and forecasting approaches to be used for each item. The Pareto effect suggests that such procedures should be chosen depending on the relative importance of close control of the item.
2. Execution procedures primarily involve order processing and stockroom transactions.
3. System maintenance procedures include cost updating.
4. External reporting procedures provide management with information for making control decisions.

Inventory control data are discussed as if the system is computerized. Most systems for controlling a large number of items fit this condition. Data are logically structured into files consisting of records which themselves contain fields. For example, an inventory status file may contain one record of data for each item. The files are accessed by programs, or computerized procedures.

System integrity implies both data integrity and procedural integrity. Data are kept accurate by preventive measures such as system checks for data reasonableness, and by corrective measures such as physical inventories and cycle counting. Procedural integrity involves the use of checks and balances designed primarily to prevent or correct introduction of human errors into the system.

REFERENCES

1. Anderson, Alan D.: "Inventory Record Accuracy," *Proceedings of the Twentieth Annual Conference of the American Production and Inventory Control Society*, Cleveland, November 1977, pp. 1-20.
2. Committee on Auditing Procedure: "Auditing Standards and Procedures," American Institute of Certified Public Accountants, New York, 1963, p. 27.
3. Stettler, Howard F.: "Systems Based Independent Audits," Prentice-Hall, Englewood Cliffs, N.J., 1974, 784 pp.

4. Zimmerman, Gary W.: "The ABC's of Vilfredo Pareto," *Production and Inventory Management*, vol. 16, no. 3, pp. 1–9, third quarter, 1975.
5. "The Production Information and Control System," IBM Corp., White Plains, N.Y., 1968, 150 pp. Request form no. GE 20-0280-2.
6. "Communications Oriented Production Information and Control System," IBM Corp., White Plains, N.Y., 1972. To obtain eight volumes, request Bill of Forms no. GBOF-4115. See chapter 5 (vol. 4).

EXERCISES

9-1 Prepare a table which looks like table 9-3 and shows the input-output interactions between the fields of the inventory file and each of the programs (procedures) listed below:
   (*a*) Forecast model parameter determination
   (*b*) Addition of new items to the inventory
   (*c*) Forecast updating
   (*d*) Vendor performance reporting

9-2 For each of the following transactions, either tell which transaction in table 9-4 can be considered its equivalent or add another row to table 9-4 showing the effect of the transaction on each field.
   (*a*) Receipt of goods on consignment
   (*b*) Issue of owned goods on consignment
   (*c*) Issue of nonowned goods on consignment
   (*d*) Issue of material from stock to an incoming inspection area
   (*e*) Receipt of stock back from incoming inspection area
   (*f*) Receipt of information indicating that a shipment from a vendor, previously thought to contain 100 units, contains only 97 units

9-3 During the taking of a physical inventory, which fields of the inventory record (table 9-3) would be affected?

9-4 Suppose you have in use an inventory file and an open-order file containing the fields shown in tables 9-3 and 9-5. Devise a scheme (procedure) which could use this information to
   (*a*) Generate a list of items for which shortages exist.
   (*b*) Generate a list of items for which shortages do not exist but are imminent.
   (*c*) Produce a list of items to be cycle-counted.

9-5 Prepare a matrix analogous to figure 9-2 which shows checks and balances that help to ensure procedural integrity for the *issuing* of stock.

APPENDIX A

CUMULATIVE DISTRIBUTION FUNCTION OF THE STANDARD NORMAL PROBABILITY DENSITY

$$\Phi(z) = \int_{-\infty}^{z} \frac{1}{\sqrt{2\pi}} e^{-u^2/2} \, du$$

Note: All table entries are decimal fractions; for example, $\Phi(0.00) = 0.5000$

z	0.00	0.01	0.02	0.03	0.04	0.05	0.06	0.07	0.08	0.09
0.0	5000	5040	5080	5120	5160	5199	5239	5279	5319	5359
0.1	5398	5438	5478	5517	5557	5596	5636	5675	5714	5753
0.2	5793	5832	5871	5910	5948	5987	6026	6064	6103	6141
0.3	6179	6217	6255	6293	6331	6368	6406	6443	6480	6517
0.4	6554	6591	6628	6664	6700	6736	6772	6808	6844	6879
0.5	6915	6950	6985	7019	7054	7088	7123	7157	7190	7224
0.6	7257	7291	7324	7357	7389	7422	7454	7486	7517	7549
0.7	7580	7611	7642	7673	7704	7734	7764	7794	7823	7852
0.8	7991	7910	7939	7967	7995	8023	8051	8078	8106	8133
0.9	8159	8186	8212	8238	8264	8289	8315	8340	8365	8389
1.0	8413	8438	8461	8485	8508	8531	8554	8577	8599	8621
1.1	8643	8665	8696	8708	8729	8749	8770	8790	8810	8830
1.2	8849	8860	8888	8907	8925	8944	8962	8980	8997	9015
1.3	9032	9049	9066	9082	9099	9115	9131	9147	9162	9177
1.4	9192	9207	9222	9236	9251	9265	9279	9292	9306	9319
1.5	9332	9345	9357	9370	9382	9394	9406	9418	9429	9441
1.6	9452	9463	9474	9484	9495	9505	9515	9525	9535	9545
1.7	9554	9564	9573	9582	9591	9599	9608	9616	9625	9633
1.8	9641	9649	9656	9664	9671	9678	9686	9693	9699	9706
1.9	9713	9719	9726	9732	9738	9744	9750	9756	9761	9767
2.0	9772	9778	9783	9788	9793	9798	9803	9808	9812	9817
2.1	9821	9826	9830	9834	9838	9842	9846	9850	9854	9857
2.2	9861	9864	9868	9871	9875	9878	9881	9884	9887	9890
2.3	9893	9896	9898	9901	9904	9906	9909	9911	9913	9916
2.4	9918	9920	9922	9925	9927	9929	9931	9932	9934	9936
2.5	9938	9940	9941	9943	9945	9946	9948	9949	9951	9952
2.6	9953	9955	9956	9957	9959	9960	9961	9962	9963	9964
2.7	9965	9966	9967	9968	9969	9970	9971	9972	9973	9974
2.8	9974	9975	9976	9977	9977	9978	9979	9979	9980	9981
2.9	9981	9982	9982	9983	9984	9984	9985	9985	9986	9986
3.0	9987	9987	9987	9988	9988	9989	9989	9989	9990	9990
3.1	9990	9991	9991	9991	9992	9992	9992	9992	9993	9993
3.2	9993	9993	9994	9994	9994	9994	9994	9995	9995	9995
3.3	9995	9995	9995	9996	9996	9996	9996	9996	9996	9997
3.4	9997	9997	9997	9997	9997	9997	9997	9997	9997	9998

APPENDIX B

UNIT NORMAL-LOSS INTEGRALS

$$I(\gamma) = \int_{\gamma}^{\infty} (u - \gamma) \frac{1}{\sqrt{2\pi}} e^{-u^2/2} \, du$$

Note: All table entries are decimal fractions; for example, $I(0.00) = 0.3989$
For values of $\gamma < 0$, $I(\gamma) = I(-\gamma) - \gamma$
For example, $I(-2) = 0.0085 + 2 = 2.0085$

γ	0.00	0.01	0.02	0.03	0.04	0.05	0.06	0.07	0.08	0.09
0.0	3989	3940	3890	3841	3793	3744	3697	3649	3602	3556
0.1	3509	3464	3418	3373	3328	3284	3240	3197	3154	3111
0.2	3069	3027	2986	2944	2904	2863	2826	2784	2745	2706
0.3	2668	2630	2592	2555	2518	2481	2445	2409	2374	2339
0.4	2304	2270	2236	2203	2169	2137	2104	2072	2040	2009
0.5	1978	1947	1917	1887	1857	1828	1800	1771	1742	1714
0.6	1687	1659	1632	1606	1580	1554	1528	1503	1478	1453
0.7	1429	1405	1381	1358	1334	1312	1289	1267	1245	1223
0.8	1202	1181	1160	1140	1120	1100	1080	1061	1042	1023
0.9	1004	0986	0968	0950	0933	0916	0899	0882	0865	0849
1.0	0833	0817	0802	0787	0772	0757	0742	0728	0714	0700
1.1	0686	0673	0660	0646	0634	0621	0609	0596	0584	0573
1.2	0561	0550	0538	0527	0577	0506	0495	0485	0475	0465
1.3	0455	0466	0436	0472	0418	0409	0400	0392	0383	0375
1.4	0367	0359	0351	0343	0336	0328	0321	0314	0307	0300
1.5	0293	0286	0280	0274	0267	0261	0255	0249	0244	0238
1.6	0232	0227	0222	0216	0211	0206	0201	0197	0192	0187
1.7	0183	0178	0174	0170	0166	0162	0158	0154	0150	0146
1.8	0143	0139	0136	0132	0129	0126	0123	0119	0116	0113
1.9	0111	0108	0105	0102	0100	0097	0094	0092	0090	0087
2.0	0085	0083	0080	0078	0076	0074	0072	0070	0068	0066
2.1	0065	0063	0061	0060	0058	0056	0055	0053	0052	0050
2.2	0049	0048	0046	0045	0044	0042	0041	0040	0039	0038
2.3	0037	0036	0035	0034	0033	0032	0031	0030	0029	0028
2.4	0027	0026	0026	0025	0024	0023	0023	0022	0021	0021
2.5	0020	0019	0019	0018	0018	0017	0017	0016	0016	0015
2.6	0015	0014	0014	0013	0013	0012	0012	0012	0011	0011
2.7	0011	0010	0010	0010	0009	0009	0009	0008	0008	0008
2.8	0008	0007	0007	0007	0007	0006	0006	0006	0006	0006
2.9	0005	0005	0005	0005	0005	0005	0004	0004	0004	0004

INDEX

INDEX

ABC classification, 245
Accounting disciplines, 221
Algorithms:
   dynamic programming, 78-80, 172
   heuristic lot sizing: least total cost, 168
      least unit cost, 167, 168
      period order quantity, 167
      Silver-Meal, 168
   transportation, 85-88
   Wagner-Whitin, 166-171
Allocation, 125
American Institute of Certified Public Accountants, 261
American Iron and Steel Institute, 210
American Production and Inventory Control Society, 163, 174
Anderson, Alan D., 258, 261
Apostol, Tom M., 65
Autocorrelation (*see* Time series)
Automatic storage and retrieval system, 260
Average residual stock, 133

Backlogging (*see* Demands)
Backordering (*see* Demands, backlogged)
Barrett, D. A., 10

Barron's, 210
Base series models (*see* Time series)
Base stock policy (*see* Ordering policies)
Bazaraa, M. S., 66
Berry, William L., 170, 174
Bill of material, 161, 162
   modular, 161, 162
BOM (bill of material), 161, 162
Box, George E. P., 218
Box-Jenkins models (*see* Time series)
Breakpoints (cost), 48
Buffer stock, 5, 91
   and forecast error, 214, 215
   (*See also* Safety stock)
Business Week, 210

Can-order policy (*see* Ordering policies)
Capital costs (*see* Costs)
Carman, Hoy F., 218
Carter, Albert G., 240
Chambers, John C., 212, 218
Christmas tree problem, 95
Coefficient of variation, 170
Concave functions, 72
Constraints, inventory level, 125-129
Contribution, 26, 57, 92
Convex costs, 82-89
Convex functions, 73

267

Correlation:
  of demands, 17
  (*See also* Time series, autocorrelation in)
Cost modeling, 24-28
Cost surrogate, 22
Costs:
  attainable, 49
  capital, 6, 231-233
  characteristics of data, 221
  controllable, 13
  convex, 82-89
  estimation of, 221-240
  expected, 93, 102
  versus expenses, 222
  holding, 6
    assessment of, 26
    capital, 6, 231-233
    concave, 172
    convex, 83, 88
    enumerated, 229, 230
    estimation of, 229-233
    marginal, 93
    modeling of, 25, 26
    quadratic, 37
  imputed, 24
  incremental, 92, 221, 238
  marginal, 83
  material, 7
    enumerated, 228
    estimation of, 222-229
    modeling of, 27
    multiple-item, 124-134
    quantity-dependent, 48-52
    time-dependent, 53
  minimization of: first example, 28-32
    general text approach, 24
  ordering, 7
    concave, 75, 172
    convex, 75
    enumerated, 236
    estimation of, 235-238
    header versus line, 237
    implicit, 237
    modeling of, 27
  penalty, 6
    convex, 83, 88

Costs, penalty: enumerated, 234
  estimating, 233-235
  marginal, 93
  modeling of, 26
  quadratic, 37
  resultant, 13
  separable, 72
  shortage (*see* penalty *above*)
  systems, 7
Critical inventory level, 116
Cumulative distribution function, 56, 90, 263
Cycle counting, 257
  event-based, 257
Cyclic models (*see* Time series)

Decision making, 28
Delivery lag (*see* Lead time)
Delphi method, 211
Demand forecasting, 179-220
  accuracy versus precision in, 188, 189
  and buffer stocks, 214
  characteristics of, 180
  cost of, 212
  errors in, 214, 216
  by exponential smoothing: first order, 191-194
    second order, 196-198
  extrinsic, 180, 208-210
  intrinsic, 180
  and inventory control, 213-217
  by linear regression, 194-196
    recursive, 195
  monitoring quality of, 188-190
  nonstatistical, 180
  precision versus accuracy, 188, 189
  statistical, 180
  (*See also* Time series)
Demand forecasts, aggregate, 217
Demand process, 3
Demand schedule, 71, 84
Demands:
  backlogged, 18, 71
    fractionally, 64
  correlated, 17

INDEX **269**

Demands:
  dependent (time series), 183
  deterministic, 15
  independent, 16
  internal, 142
  lost, 63, 94
  lumpy, 170, 171, 247
  modeling, 15-18
  probabilistic, 15-18
  stochastic, 15-18
  variable, 16
De Matteis, J. J., 173
Dynamic programming, 78-80
  (*See also* Algorithms)

Echelon, 143
  retail, 143
  wholesale, 143
Econometric model, 210
Economic lot size (*see* Economic order quantity)
Economic order quantity:
  classic, 32
  group (joint), 125
    stretched, 125
  group (multi-item), 133
  multiechelon, 165-173
    use of, 170
  Wilson, 32
Economic part-period ratio, 168
Economic production quantity, 130
EOQ (*see* Economic order quantity)
Expected costs, 93, 102
Explosion of requirements, 152
Exponential smoothing (*see* Demand forecasting)

FIFO (first in, first out), 223
First in, first out, 223
Flora, J. W., 233, 240
Flow, 76-78
Forecasting (*see* Demand forecasting)
Forrester, Jay W., 146, 173
Fortune, 210
Fourier series models (*see* Time series)

Functions:
  concave, 72
  convex, 73

General Electric Company, 210
Goyal, S. K., 115, 139
Gradient, 126
Groff, Gene K., 212, 218

Hadley, George, 65, 107
Hall, Thomas W., 240
Harris, F., 32, 37
Holding costs (*see* Costs, holding)

Indicators:
  business, 209
  economic, 209
  endogenous, 208
  exogenous, 208
  leading, 209
"Industrial Dynamics," 146
Interaction:
  cost, 111, 113-125
    material, 124-134
    ordering, 113
  demand, 112, 134-138
  among items, 111-176
  resource, 125-134
International Business Machines Corporation, 139, 262
Inventories:
  buffer, 5
  classes of, 4
  cost accounting for, 226-229
  functions of, 4, 5
  multiechelon, behavior of, 145-149
  pipeline, 3, 5
Inventory:
  defined, 3
  physical, 257
  status of, 69
  valuation of, 223-227
Inventory control, defined, 7

Inventory control system, 243-262
  data, 250-256
    effect of transactions on, 253
    fields, 251
    files, 251
    programs, 250
    records, 251
  integrity, 256-261
    data, 256
    procedural, 258
  interactive, 254
  procedures, 244-250
    computerization of, 249, 250
    execution, 247
    external reporting, 248
    planning, 244-247
    system maintenance, 247, 248
Inventory level:
  average, 25
  average residual, 57
  constrained, 125-129
  defined, 8
  residual, 57
Inventory-time plots, 18, 19, 72
Item master file, 251-253

Jenkins, Gwilym M., 218
Job order costing, 226
Johnson, R. E., 66

Kamat, Satish J., 137, 139
Keswani, A. K., 66

Lagrange multipliers, 126-129, 140
Lagrangian function, 127, 128
La Londe, B. J., 240
Lambert, Douglas M., 240
Last in, first out, 223
Lead time, 15, 56, 89
  cumulative, 157
  multiechelon, 146, 147
Least squares criterion, 190, 194
Life cycles, 216
LIFO (last in, first out), 223

Linear regression (*see* Demand forecasting)
Lost sales (*see* Demands, lost)
Lot sizing, multiechelon, 165-173
Love, Stephen F., 107, 173
Low-level coding, 154
Lower of cost or market, 223

Mack, Ruth P., 10
Magee, John F., 240
Markov chains, 103
Master production schedule, 151
  firm, 157
  tentative, 157, 163
Material costs (*see* Costs, material)
Material flow structure, 34
Material requirements planning, 150-173
  applicability of, 161-165
  net change, 159
  prerequisites to use, 161
  regenerative, 159
  use of simulation in, 163
Meal, H. C., 174
Miller, David W., 139
Modeling:
  demand behavior, 15-18
  supply behavior, 14, 15
Models (*see* Ordering decision models)
Module, 161
  common, 162
Montgomery, Douglas C., 66
MPS (*see* Master production schedule)
MRP (*see* Material requirements planning)
Mullick, S. K., 212, 218
Myers, John E., 66

National Lumber Manufacturers' Association, 210
Nelson, Charles R., 218
Netting, 152
Netting relationship, 152
Network:
  arborescence, 143

Network:
  coalescence, 143
  concave-cost, 76
  multiechelon: arborescence, 171
    coalescence, 171
    series, 172
  series, 143
  single-source, 73, 75
Network flow, extreme, 76, 77
  properties of, 78
Normal distribution (*see* Probability distributions, normal density)
Normal loss integral, 62, 97
  table of, 264

Open-order file, 254-256
Opportunity cost, 232
  (*See also* Costs)
Optimal policy curve, 129
Option combination, 162
Options, 134
  add-on, 134
  bidirectional, 135
  either-or, 134
Ordering costs (*see* Costs, ordering)
Ordering decision versus ordering policy, 20
Ordering decision models:
  classification of, 34-36
  continuous-review, 40-68
  deterministic, 15, 41-55, 71-89, 113-115
  formulating, summary, 28
  multiechelon, 142-176
  multiple-item, 111-141
  periodic review, 69-110, 135-138
    comparison of, 100-106
  quantity discount, 48-52
  single-period, 95
  stationary, 80-82, 93-100
  stochastic, 15, 56-65, 89-100, 115-125
Ordering frequencies:
  absolute, 113
  relative, 113

Ordering policies:
  base stock, 41, 58, 59
  can-order, 116
  continuous review, 21, 40, 41
  lot-size reorder-point, 41
  multiple item: coordinated replenishment, 112
    independent, 112, 120
    joint, 112, 117, 120
  optional replenishment, 70
  periodic review, 21, 70, 71, 81
  S, 41, 70
  s, Q, 41, 59-65
  s, Q, S, 70
  s, Q, S, T, 70
  s, S, 41, 70, 96-100
  s, S, T, 70
  single-item, 20, 21
  two-bin, 41
Ordering policy versus ordering decision, 20
Ordering schedule, 71, 75
Orders:
  firm planned, 159
  planned, 150
  special, 53
Orlicky, Joseph, 163, 173
Osborne, Harlow, 218

Pairwise perturbation, 87
Parent item, 159
Pareto, Vilfredo, 244, 262
Pareto effect, 244
Parker, George G. C., 218
Part-period, 168
Pattern, 132
Pattern cycle time, 132-134
Periodic method, 222
Perpetual method, 222
Planning horizon, 35, 41, 71, 150, 161, 166
  extension of, 87-89
  infinite, 81, 82, 89
  single-period, 95
Policies (*see* Ordering policies)
Predecessor, 143

Principle:
    of delayed timing, 150
    of internal control, 260
    of parsimony, 28, 185
Probability distributions:
    binomial, 155
    of demand, 16, 56, 90
    normal density, 62, 91
        table of, 263
Process costing, 226

Quantity discounts:
    all-units, 48, 124
    incremental, 51

Receipts:
    past due, 154
    scheduled, 156
Reject allowance, 155
Remnant stock, 117
Reorder point, 41
Requirements:
    backlogged, 144
    exploded, 152, 154
    gross, 144, 165
    net, 152
    pegged, 159
    planned, 150
Retail inventory method, 223
Revenue contribution, 26, 57, 92

Safety stock, 154
    (See also Buffer stock)
Saipe, Alan L., 134, 139
Scarf, Herbert, 107
Schedules:
    demand, 71, 84
    ordering, 71
Schleef, H. J., 66
Search, one-dimensional, 123
Segura, Edilberto L., 218
Series (see Time series)
Service level, 22, 117
Shared productive facilities, 129–134
Shortage, average, 57

Shortage costs (see Costs, penalty)
Silver, Edward A., 123, 139, 141, 174
Simons, Harry, 240
Simulation, 123, 141
    in material requirements planning, 163
Sinks, 73
SKU (stock-keeping unit), 69, 217
Smith, D. D., 212, 218
Smoothing constant, 192
    adaptive control of, 193
Standardized normal loss integral (see Normal loss integral)
Starr, Martin K., 139
Steady-state probabilities, 102
Stettler, Howard F., 261
Stock-keeping unit, 69, 217
Stockroom transactions, 247
Suboptimization in multiechelon lot sizing, 171
Substitution, 135–138
Successor, 143
Sum of squared errors (SSE), 187, 188
Supplier:
    external, 142
    internal, 142
Supply process, 3
Supply rate, finite, 15
Systems (see Inventory control system)
Systems costs, 7

Taylor, William, 139
Thompstone, Robert M., 139
Time between orders, 32
Time buckets, 150
Time-phased order point, 154
Time series, 181
    autocorrelation in, 184, 193, 204
    characteristics, 181–184
    cyclic, 186
    differencing, 186
    effects, 181
        cyclic, 198
        versus seasonal, 181, 182
    estimation of coefficients of, 187, 188

Time series:
  mean of, 183
  modeling, sequence of steps in, 181
  models: autoregressive, 186, 203-206
    base series, 198-200
    Box-Jenkins, 202-208, 212, 246
    cyclic, 198-202
    errors in, 184
    Fourier series, 200-202
    linear trend, 194-198
    moving average, 187, 188, 206-208
    recognizing autocorrelation, 202-208
    stationary, 190-194
  smoothed, 192
  sources of variation in, 181
  stationary, 182
    of order zero, 183
  variance of, 183
  (*See also* Demand forecasting)
Tracking signal, 189
Transaction recording, 250
Transition matrix, 103
Transportation algorithm, 85-88

Trial fitting, 157
Two-bin policy, 41

Unit vector, 83
University of Pennsylvania, 210
  Wharton School, 210

Value added, 226
Veinott, Arthur F., 107, 172, 174

Wagner, Harvey M., 66, 107, 174
Wagner-Whitin algorithm, 80
Wall Street Journal, 210
Weighted least-squares criterion, 191, 196
Whitin, Tom M., 65, 107, 174
Wight, Oliver W., 163, 174

Yule-Walker equations, 204, 205

Zangwill, Willard I., 107, 174
Zimmerman, Gary W., 262